A Concise History of the Christian World Mission

A PANORAMIC VIEW OF MISSIONS
FROM PENTECOST TO THE PRESENT

J. Herbert Kane

REVISED
EDITION

BAKER BOOK HOUSE
Grand Rapids, Michigan 49506

Copyright 1978, 1982 by Baker Books
a division of Baker Book House Company
P.O. Box 6287, Grand Rapids, MI 49516-6287

ISBN: 0-8010-5395-1

Tenth printing, December 1994

Printed in the United States of America

Excerpts from *A History of Christian Missions* by Stephen
Neill, © 1964, are used with permission of the author and
Penguin Books, Ltd. Quotations from *The Age of Faith*
and *Caesar and Christ* by Will Durant, © 1950 and 1944
respectively, are used with permission of Simon and
Schuster. Excerpts from *The First Five Centuries,* © 1937,
and *The Thousand Years of Uncertainty,* © 1938, by K. S.
Latourette, are used with permission of Harper and Row,
Publishers. Quotations from *The Triumph of Christendom
in the Roman Empire* by Edward Gibbon, © 1958, are
used with permission of Methuen and Company.

A Concise History
of the
Christian World Mission

Preface

This book has been prepared at the prompting of Dr. David M. Howard, Director of Urbana 76, who for many years has worked among university students and therefore has a sympathetic approach to their needs and problems.

It is Dr. Howard's opinion that all committed Christians should have a working knowledge of the Christian world mission. Since the books on this subject now in print are too long, too heavy, and too detailed for popular use, he suggested that I write a short survey of *modern* missions and add it to Part One of my *Global View of Christian Missions,* which is a panoramic view of missions from Pentecost to William Carey.

This paperback is the result of that suggestion. It is sent forth with the hope, not that it will supplant the larger volumes, but that it will whet the appetite for further and deeper study of the most significant enterprise in which the Christian church has ever engaged.

Deerfield, Illinois   J. Herbert Kane
January, 1978

Contents

PART ONE

Through the Ages

I

Christianity in the Roman Empire:
A.D. 30-500

The City of God was built at the confluence of three great civilizations, the Greek, the Roman and the Hebrew. Each contributed significantly to the progress and pattern of Christianity as it developed in the first three centuries of the Christian era.

The elements of Greek civilization are not hard to trace. They include art, architecture, literature, language, science and philosophy. We are still wondering how one small race could be so prolific in ideas, so dynamic in action, and so massive in achievement. The secret is to be sought not so much in the temper of the times as in the temperament of the Greek — his inquiring mind, his restless spirit and his zest for life.

Unlike the Egyptians, whose civilization was confined to the Nile valley, the Greeks, with their penchant for trade and travel, established colonies on the shores of the Mediterranean and the Black seas between the eighth and the sixth centuries B.C. Wherever they went they carried with them the benefits of their superior civilization.

In time the Greeks replaced the Phoenicians as the mercantile masters of the Mediterranean world. Although their voyages were not as long or lucrative as those of the Phoenicians, their influence on civilization was more powerful and certainly more permanent. The earliest ideas of scientific navigation and geography came from the Greeks. The Greek travelers, Strabo and Pausanias, are our most reliable informants when we study the topography of the Acts of the Apostles.

Seldom in history have the conquests of war contributed to the advance of civilization, but such was the case with the conquests of Alexander the Great. When the unmanageable pupil of Aristotle gave up the study of philosophy to mount the throne and ride the world, he embarked on a course of action destined to change the face of the Western world and prepare the way for the spread of the gospel.

> He took up the meshes of the net of Greek civilization, which were lying in disorder on the edges of the Asiatic shore, and spread them over all the countries which he traversed. The East and the West were suddenly brought together. Separated tribes were united under a common government. New cities were built as centers of political life. New lines of communication were opened as the channels of commercial activity. The new culture penetrated the mountain ranges of Pisidia and Lycaonia. The Tigris and Euphrates became Greek rivers. The language of Athens was heard among the Jewish colonies of Babylonia.[1]

Upon the untimely death of the great conqueror, Antioch and Alexandria became the capitals of the Greek kings of Syria and Egypt respectively. Both had had a large colony of Jews from the beginning. Both were residences of Roman governors. Both were centers of Christian activity and later became patriarchates of the Eastern Church.

The Greek language, regarded by some as the richest and most delicate the world has ever seen, became the language of culture and commerce from the Persian Gulf to the Gates of Hercules. It was the mother tongue not only of Plato and Aristotle in the West, but also of Ignatius and Eusebius in the East. It was used by Paul the Christian, Philo the Jew, and Cicero the Roman. Paul and his companions never had to learn a foreign language, nor had they any need for an interpreter. The Greek language was readily understood in all parts of the empire. As early as the third century B.C. the Old Testament was translated into this language, and the Septuagint was the Bible of Jesus and the apostles. Greek, the language of philosophy, became the language of theology as well.

> It was not an accident that the New Testament was written in Greek, the language which can best express the highest thoughts and worthiest feelings of the intellect and heart, and which is adapted to be the instrument of education for all nations; nor was it an accident that the composition of these books and the promulgation of the Gospel were delayed until the instruction of our Lord and the writings of His Apostles could be expressed in the dialect of Alexandria.[2]

The empire founded by Alexander and divided among his four generals did not last long. In politics integrity gave way to intrigue. Philosophy degenerated first into cynicism and later into skepticism. Social life became a round of worthless and frivolous amusements. Religion was powerless to halt the process of decay. Rome soon displaced Greece as the mistress of the Mediterranean world.

---

[1] Conybeare and Howson, *Life and Epistles of St. Paul* (London and New York: Longmans, Green and Co., 1901), p. 7.

[2] *Ibid.*, p. 9.

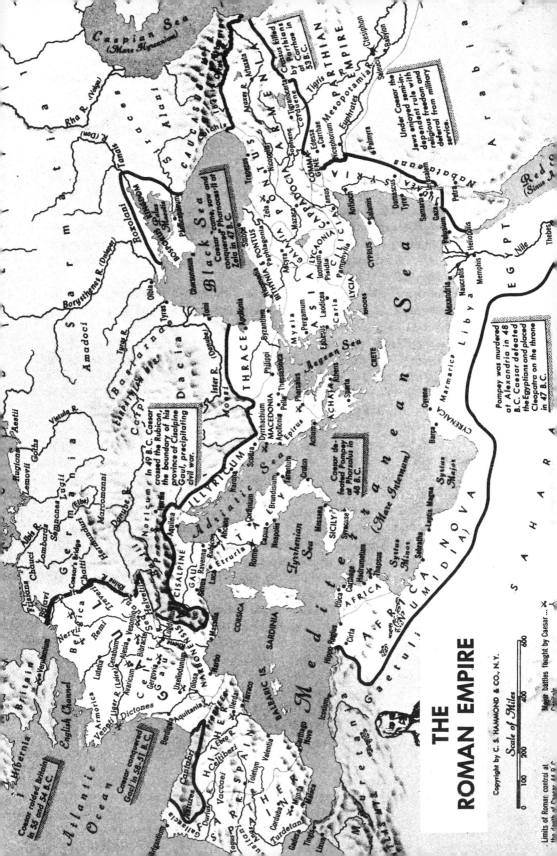

THE ROMAN EMPIRE

Copyright by C. S. HAMMOND & CO., N.Y.

Scale of Miles

0   100   200   300   400   500   600

Major battles fought by Caesar ... ⚔

Limits of Roman control at
death of Caesar, 44 B.C. ....

Caspian Sea
(Mare Hyrcanium)

Black Sea
Pharnaces came, saw and
Caesar conquered Pharnaces II at
Zela in 47 B.C.

Crassus killed
by Parthians
at Carrhae in
53 B.C.

PARTHIAN
EMPIRE

• Ctesiphon
• Seleucia • Babylon

Under Caesar, the
Jews enjoyed semi-in-
dependent rule with
religious freedom and
deferral service.

ARMENIA
• Artaxata

Pompey was murdered
at Alexandria in 48
B.C. Caesar defeated
the Egyptians and placed
Cleopatra on the throne
in 47 B.C.

Caesar de-
feated Pompey
at Pharsalus in
48 B.C.

In 49 B.C. Caesar
crossed the Rubicon,
the boundary of his
province of Cisalpine
Gaul, precipitating
civil war.

Caesar raided Britain
in 55 and 54 B.C.

Caesar conquered
Gaul in 58-51 B.C.

Mediterranean Sea
(Mare Internum)

EGYPT

Red Sea
(Sinus Arabicus)

SAHARA

At the height of its power Rome ruled an empire comprising more than one and a quarter million square miles, that stretched from Spain to the Euphrates, from the North Sea to the Sahara Desert. It had a population of a hundred million people—Italians, Greeks, Egyptians, Germans, Celts and others. Beginning with Augustus and lasting for approximately three hundred years, this vast empire enjoyed what Pliny the Elder termed "the immense majesty of the Roman peace." With peace came prosperity.

The Romans were men of action. They swept the pirates from the seas and on land they built the most enduring roads of antiquity, along which passed, with a minimum of danger and delay, not only the merchants and the legionnaires but also the messengers of the cross. Everywhere Roman legions kept the peace and Roman magistrates administered the law. The conquests of Rome prepared for and facilitated those of Christianity.

Rome ruled her empire with an iron hand. In matters pertaining to internal security she was exceedingly strict. She collected taxes from all the provinces and punished anyone who tried to evade the universal tribute. At the same time she gave the provinces as much autonomy as she could without jeopardizing the security of the empire. She was especially tolerant in the matter of religion. Judaism was accorded preferential treatment with the designation *religio licita*; and for a time the Christians were able to capitalize on their association with Judaism. Paul was a Roman citizen, and on more than one occasion he invoked his rights as a citizen to secure for the gospel the hearing it deserved. In the Acts of the Apostles Luke takes pains to point out that Christianity, in the first generation at least, consistently enjoyed the protection of the temporal power. "The cross followed the fasces, and the Roman eagles made straight the way for Christ."[3]

More closely connected with Christianity than either the Greek or Roman civilizations was the Hebrew civilization. The dispersion of the Jewish people was the greatest single factor in preparing the world for the coming of the Messiah and the preaching of the gospel. Scattered throughout the Roman Empire, the Jews were particularly numerous in Egypt, Syria and Babylonia. In A.D. 70 Strabo reported: "It is hard to find a single place on the habitable earth that has not admitted this tribe of men, and is not possessed by it."[4]

Wherever the Jews went they carried the knowledge and the worship of the one true God, the expectation of a coming Messiah and the Holy Scriptures in the universal Greek language. Wherever possible they organized synagogues, which became the religious and cultural centers of their communities. Attracted to the synagogues were many Gentiles — proselytes and other lesser adherents known as "God-fearing men."

[3] Will Durant, *Caesar and Christ* (New York: Simon and Schuster, 1944), p. 602.
[4] Josephus, *Antiquities of the Jews,* xiv, 7.

These factors were of immense help to the Christian missionaries as they traveled throughout the Roman world preaching the gospel and planting churches. Though designated "an apostle to the Gentiles," Paul's heart was always with his own people. In every city he made his way first to the synagogue, where he found Jews and proselytes. Only when the Jews refused his message did he turn to the Gentiles. The organization of the Christian church was patterned largely after that of the Jewish synagogue.

The Geographical Expansion

Christianity is the only truly universal religion in the world. Yet its Founder was born in a stable, lived in obscurity, and died on a wooden cross in a remote province of the Roman Empire about half-way between the time of Buddha and that of Mohammed. Although His untimely death at the age of thirty-three sent His disciples into confusion, His resurrection on the third day revived their Messianic hopes, rejuvenated their flagging spirits, and sent them out to win the world.

Their task was formidable; their chances of success almost nil. They had no central organization, no financial resources, no influential friends, no political machine. Arrayed against them was the ecclesiastical power of the Sanhedrin, the political and military might of the Roman Empire, and the religious fanaticism of the Jews. Moreover, their Leader, whose life and teachings were to constitute their message, was unknown outside His small circle of friends. He had written no books, erected no monuments, endowed no institutions. The task looked hopeless.

The Book of Acts opens with 120 timid disciples meeting secretly in an upper room in Jerusalem for fear of their enemies. A generation later, when the Book of Acts closes, the gospel had been preached as far west as Rome; and there was a thriving Christian church in almost every city of significance in the eastern part of the empire. What began as a Jewish sect in A.D. 30 had grown into a world religion by A.D. 60. The details, all too few, are found in the Acts of the Apostles.

Acts 1:8 gives us a clue to the projected expansion of the Christian faith. Beginning at Jerusalem, it was to extend by way of Judea and Samaria to the ends of the earth. Prior to the ascension Christ gave the apostles two commands: to go into all the world and preach the gospel; and to tarry in Jerusalem until they were endued with power from on high.

After a ten-day waiting period, spent in prayer and fasting, the promised Holy Spirit came. This historic event marked the beginning of the Christian church and the inauguration of the missionary movement, for in those days the church *was* mission.

There was no clean break with Judaism. Regarded as a reform movement by its friends and as a heretical sect by its enemies, Christianity remained an integral part of Judaism. It took many years to develop its own theology, chart its own course, and project its own image.

Though commanded to go into all the world and disciple all nations, the disciples showed a distinct preference for Jerusalem, where they continued their association with the temple, participating in its prayers and supporting its services. Much of their teaching was done there. Later they extended their ministry to over four hundred synagogues in Jerusalem. Their message was distinctly Jewish in flavor. It centered around a suffering Messiah, called for repentance, and promised forgiveness and restoration. The church that emerged was more Jewish than Christian. A generation after Pentecost its members were still frequenting the temple, keeping the Mosaic Law, taking vows and offering sacrifices (Acts 21:20-24). The church in Jerusalem never managed to throw off the swaddling clothes of Judaism. With the destruction of the city in A.D. 70 the church there ceased to exist. This was not an unmitigated tragedy, for had Jerusalem continued to be the center of Christian worship Christianity might never have become a world religion. With the destruction of Jerusalem the church was free to become what its Founder intended it to be — spiritual and not temporal, universal and not provincial. Otherwise, Jerusalem might have become the Mecca of the Christian world, and the Jordan River might have become to Christians what the Ganges River is to Hindus.

Peter was the dominant figure among the twelve apostles. Later other leaders emerged. Two of them, Stephen and Philip, stood out from the rest. Both had a very effective ministry, Stephen in the synagogues of Jerusalem and Philip in the city of Samaria. The first contact that Saul of Tarsus had with Christianity doubtless took place in the synagogue of the Cilicians, where he encountered the irresistible wisdom of Stephen (Acts 6:9).

The martyrdom of Stephen and the ensuing persecution was a blow to the infant church; but it became a blessing for it resulted in a further extension of the Christian gospel. Those who were scattered abroad went everywhere preaching the Word. Some traveled as far as Phoenicia, Cyprus and Antioch, where they preached the gospel to the Gentiles, for the first time.

Further impetus was given to the preaching of the gospel to the Gentiles by two events of great significance: the conversion of Saul of Tarsus, who became the apostle to the Gentiles; and Peter's experience in preaching the gospel to Cornelius. That Luke attached great importance to these two events is seen from the fact that the former is recorded three times and the latter twice in the Acts of the Apostles.

Under the teaching of Barnabas and Paul the church in Antioch increased in strength and numbers until it rivalled, and later replaced, Jerusalem as the mother church of Christendom.

From its founding by Seleucus I in 300 B.C. Antioch had been a cosmopolitan city whose sophisticated inhabitants included Macedonians, Greeks and local Syrians, and a large colony of Jews. By the time of Christ it had become one of the three most important cities of the empire. Strategically located on the main highway to the east, it was a natural meeting place of East and West. Greek culture and Roman administration combined to make Antioch an ideal center for the reception of the gospel. Protected by a degree of public order not possible in a fanatical city like Jerusalem, the church in Antioch grew rapidly in size and importance. In fact, Antioch was one of the few cities in the empire in which the preaching of the gospel did not precipitate a communal riot. It was there that the disciples were first called Christians.

Paul made Antioch his headquarters during the heydey of his missionary career. His three missionary journeys, which lasted less than fifteen years, took him into four populous provinces of the empire: Galatia and Asia in Asia, and Macedonia and Achaia in Europe. Following the great Roman roads, he planted churches in all the important cities along the way. By the end of his third journey he could report " . . . that from Jerusalem, and round about unto Illyricum, I have fully preached the gospel of Christ" (Rom. 15:19). "Having no more place in these parts," he set his sights on Spain. On his way he proposed to visit Rome to make that city his base for evangelizing the western half of the empire. He reached Rome in due time, but his missionary days were over.

Paul, of course, was not the only missionary of those days. There must have been scores of others, whose names have been lost to history. We know that Christian laymen, many of them displaced persons, carried the good news of the gospel wherever they went. Casual references are made to churches in Judea, Galilee, and Samaria (Acts 9:31), Syria and Cilicia (Acts 15:23), Pontus, Cappadocia, and Bithynia (I Pet. 1:1). When and by whom were they founded? It would be interesting to know. We learn from the second chapter of Acts that Jews and proselytes from fifteen different regions of the empire were present in Jerusalem at Pentecost and heard Peter and his colleagues preach the gospel. Doubtless many of them became converts to the Christian faith and returned home to preach Christ in the synagogues and establish Christian churches in their homes.

One thing is certain; the Acts of the Apostles does not tell the whole story. There are hints in Paul's epistles that the gospel had a much wider proclamation than that described by Luke. He states that the gospel had been "preached to every creature which is under heaven" (Col. 1:23); that the faith of the Roman church was "spoken of throughout the whole world" (Rom. 1:8); that the faith of the Thessalonian believers " . . . has gone forth everywhere . . . " (I Thess. 1:8, RSV).

Coming to the second and third centuries we find that information regarding the expansion of the Christian church is even more meager. We read of large and influential churches in Alexandria, Carthage and Edessa; but we do not know when or by whom they were established. Here again there are wide gaps in our knowledge. It would seem that Christianity continued to spread along the main roads and rivers of the empire: eastward by way of Damascus and Edessa into Mesopotamia; southward through Bostra and Petra into Arabia; westward through Alexandria and Carthage into North Africa; and northward through Antioch into Armenia, Pontus, and Bithynia. Later still it reached Spain, Gaul, and Britain before crossing the borders of the empire into more remote parts such as Ireland, Ethiopia, and China.

The silence of the New Testament regarding the entrance of the gospel into Egypt in the apostolic era is as puzzling as it is tantalizing. That the gospel went north from Jerusalem to Antioch without going south to Alexandria is unthinkable, especially when communications between the two cities were constant and convenient. The fact remains, however, that we know nothing of the origin of the church in Egypt except that tradition ascribes it to the work of John Mark.

We do know that Christians were reported in Alexandria in the reign of Hadrian (c. 125) and that by the end of the century there was a strong church there. Also in Alexandria there was a famous catechetical school, founded about 180 by Pantaenus, who later took the gospel to India. Pantaenus was followed by Clement, and Clement by the brilliant Origen. "These individuals can be credited with bringing Egyptian Christianity into the mainstream of the Christian tradition."[5]

West of Egypt was Cyrene, mentioned four times in the New Testament. If Cyrenians took the gospel to Antioch (Acts 11:19), it is safe to assume that they shared the good news with their own people; but of this we have no record. From Synesius we learn that by the end of the fourth century there were half a dozen bishoprics there.

Traveling west we come to Carthage, the center of Roman civilization in North Africa at that time. Christianity may have reached Carthage across the Mediterranean from Rome or Ephesus, or it may have entered from Egypt. In and around the city were vigorous Christian churches with an extensive Latin literature, including the first Latin translation of the New Testament. By the close of the second century the Christian community had grown so large that the doughty Tertullian could threaten the Roman magistrate with rebellion unless he desisted from persecuting the Christians. Animated by the zeal of Tertullian, directed by the abilities of Cyprian, and adorned by the eloquence of Lactantius, the Christian community could hardly fail to thrive. The outstanding feature of the North African church was the large number of bishops. Every town, almost every village, had one. Most famous of all was the towering figure

5 Walter Oetting, *The Church of the Catacombs* (Saint Louis, Mo.: Concordia Publishing House, 1964), p. 80.

of Augustine, Bishop of Hippo (354-430), whose writings gave form to Roman Catholic theology for a thousand years.

Did Paul realize his ambition to visit Spain? The New Testament is silent on this point. Clement of Rome states that he preached the gospel in the extreme west of the empire. If this is true, Paul was the founder of the church in Spain. All we know with certainty is that by the beginning of the third century Christianity was established in the south of Spain. Spanish Christianity, then as now, was not of the highest order. Idolatry, adultery, and even homicide marred its image.

The gospel made very slow progress in the cold climate of Gaul. It is thought that Christianity entered Gaul from the east. By the second century the church was fairly well established in the southern part around Lyons and Vienne. *Irenaeus,* Bishop of Lyons (175-200), preached to both Celtic- and Latin-speaking peoples. The response was not encouraging. As late as 250 scattered churches in half a dozen communities embraced only a small number of converts. A century later when *Martin of Tours* became bishop of that diocese the surrounding countryside was still largely pagan. An ex-soldier, Martin adopted military measures to ensure immediate results. He and his monks went about the countryside demolishing temples, destroying idols, preaching the gospel and baptizing converts.

We have no sure knowledge of how Christianity entered Britain. The first authentic information relates to three bishops from Britain who were present at the Council of Arles in the south of Gaul in 314. Evidently the gospel had reached Britain some time before, perhaps as early as the middle of the second century.

Early in the second century the Christians multiplied rapidly in Asia Minor, especially in Bithynia and Pontus. So much was this the case that Pliny, Governor of Pontus, wrote to the Emperor Trajan for instructions on how to deal with a situation that threatened to get out of hand. During the third century a mass movement took place in Pontus under the leadership of *Gregory Thaumaturgus.* It was said that when he became bishop of his native city about 240 there were only seventeen Christians, but when he died thirty years later there were only seventeen non-Christians. The transition from paganism to Christianity was facilitated by the widespread use of miracles and the fact that Gregory Thaumaturgus allowed the Christians to substitute Christian festivals for pagan feasts.

Sometime during the third century Christianity spread beyond the borders of the Roman empire. In time it became established in Parthia, Ethiopia, Ireland, India, and even China.

The gospel traveled eastward from Antioch along the main trade route via Duro-Europos to Ctesiphon and Seleucia, twin cities on the Tigris River. The first Christians may have been Jews, "dwellers in Mesopotamia," who heard Peter at Pentecost (Acts 2:9). By A.D. 225, churches were found throughout the Tigris-Euphrates valley from the Caspian Sea to the Persian Gulf. Edessa became a center of strong Christian influence and missionary outreach. By the end of the second century Christianity had become the state religion. Syriac, the language of the church there, was the first language into which the New Testament was translated. By the beginning of the fourth century Edessa may have been predominantly Christian.

The gospel entered Armenia from Cappadocia probably towards the close of the third century. As a result of a mass movement led by the great missionary, *Gregory the Illuminator,* and sparked by the conversion of King Tiridates, Armenia became a Christian kingdom. The New Testament first appeared in the Armenian language in 410. The Armenian church has weathered many a storm and is today one of the oldest churches in Christendom.

Tradition says that it was the apostle *Bartholomew* who first took the gospel to Arabia. Cretes and Arabians were in Jerusalem on the day of Pentecost (Acts 2:11) and may have taken the new faith home with them. We know that by the end of the fourth century there was a Christian settlement in Hirah. It seems fairly certain that by 525 Christianity was firmly established there.

How and when did the gospel penetrate the vast subcontinent of India? Eusebius states, and the Mar Thoma Christians firmly believe, that their church was established in the first century by the apostle *Thomas.* *Pantaenus* is reported to have lèft the catechetical school in Alexandria to take the gospel to India about 180. Certainly Christianity has been in India since the third century, making the Mar Thoma Church the oldest Christian church east of the Khyber Pass. Other Syrian churches in India are very old.

Did the Ethiopian eunuch baptized by *Philip* (Acts 8:26-39) take the gospel back to Ethiopia? If so, his efforts were not very successful, for we have no evidence of a Christian church in that land until about the middle of the fourth century. The story is a fascinating one. Two young Christians, shipwrecked in the Red Sea, were taken as slaves to Ethiopia, where they served in the royal court at Axum. There they preached the gospel with great effect and made many converts. When the work got beyond their time and strength, one of them, *Frumentius,* returned to Egypt to appeal for help. Athanasius, Patriarch of Alexandria, made Frumentius a bishop and sent him back to Ethiopia, where he served as head of the Ethiopian (Coptic) Church until his death.

The Goths were the first of the Teutonic peoples north of the Danube to adopt Christianity in large numbers. Their earliest knowledge of the gospel was received from Christian prisoners taken during their many incursions into the empire during the third century. The systematic evangelization of the Goths, however, was the work of *Ulfilas* (c.311-c.380), whose father was a Cappadocian and his mother a Goth. After spending ten years in Constantinople, where he became a Christian, he returned home to evangelize his own people. His outstanding work was the translation of the Bible into the Gothic language. To do this he had to reduce the language to writing. He was the first of a long line of illustrious missionaries who have made significant contributions to linguistics and to literature as well as to the dissemination of the Scriptures.

Latourette states that the conversion of the Franks towards the close of the fifth century "was the single most important stage in the spread of the faith among the non-Roman peoples in the northwestern part of the continent of Europe."[6] The Franks had been in touch with the Roman Empire for many years and some of them had become Christians; but the breakthrough came when their king, Clovis, with three thousand of his warriors, embraced the Christian faith and was baptized on Christmas Day, 496. His decision to become a Christian sprang from mixed motives, one of which was an obligation to keep a vow he made at the height of the battle to embrace the Christian faith if the Christian God would grant him victory. He got the victory and honored his vow to become a Christian. Though not obliged to do so, most of his subjects followed his example.

The last area to be evangelized in this period was Ireland, the most westerly part of the then known world. The apostle to Ireland was *Patrick,* who, contrary to common belief, was not an Irishman at all. Born of Christian parents in Roman Britain about 389, and with only a smattering of education, he became the greatest missionary of his time.

At the age of twelve he was carried captive to Ireland, where he was put to work herding sheep. During his exile a spiritual experience changed his whole life and made real to him the nominal faith of his childhood. After six years of lonely servitude he escaped to France, where for several years he served as a monk in the Abbey of Lerins. Finally he returned to England to receive a warm welcome from his family.

But his heart was still with the benighted people of Ireland and he could not rest. In a dream he heard voices calling him: "We beseech thee, holy youth, to come and walk again amongst us as before." This he took to be God's call to return to the land of his captivity. Ignoring the pleas of parents and friends, he returned to Ireland, where he spent the rest of his life.

A man of deep personal piety and warm evangelical fervor, Patrick gave himself without reserve for thirty-five years to the evangelization of Ireland. Exposed to many kinds of danger from Druid chieftains, armed soldiers and robber bands, he baptized thousands of converts, planted hundreds of churches and ordained many to the clergy.

Patrick's influence continued long after his own time and extended far beyond the borders of his own country. The monasteries which became an integral part of Celtic Christianity were not only centers of Christian culture but also of missionary zeal. As such they played an important role in the evangelization of northern Europe in the following centuries.

---

6 K. S. Latourette, *The First Five Centuries* (New York: Harper and Brothers, 1937), p. 208.

By the end of the fifth century Christianity had, with varying degrees of success, become established in all parts of the empire and even beyond, from the Sahara Desert in the south to Hadrian's Wall in the north, and from India in the east to Spain in the west.

Mention should be made here of the earliest contact with the great land of China. At an early date Christianity was established in Mesopotamia and Persia. From there it spread into India, Central Asia, and China. This was the Nestorian form of Christianity, which took its name from Nestorius, Patriarch of Constantinople, who was condemned at the Council of Ephesus (A.D. 431) as a heretic and banished beyond the frontiers of the Roman Empire. In subsequent centuries the Nestorian Church became one of the greatest missionary churches of all time.

Nestorian Christianity entered China by way of Central Asia in A.D. 635, at the beginning of the T'ang dynasty, during which Chinese culture reached its zenith. Under Emperior T'ai Tsung China was probably the wealthiest and most civilized empire in the world. Changan (modern Sian), its capital, was the largest and most prosperous city on earth at that time.

Our principal and most authentic source of information regarding the Nestorian mission is the Nestorian Stone, carved at Sian in the eighth century and discovered in 1625. The inscription on this monument tells in some detail the story of the origin and spread of Christianity in China. According to this record the first Christian missionary, *Alopen,* arrived in China in A.D. 635. He was warmly welcomed by Emperor T'ai Tsung, who himself studied the religion, approved it, and gave orders for its dissemination. Alopen had taken with him a copy of the Scriptures, which he and his fellow monks translated into Chinese. In the capital he built a monastery for twenty-one monks. The new religion spread through "ten provinces" and monasteries were reported in a "hundred cities."

It would appear that Christianity was for a period of two hundred years confined largely to these monasteries, where the monks gave themselves to the study of the language and the translation of Christian books into Chinese. In spite of imperial favor Christianity met with opposition, chiefly from the Buddhists.

In A.D. 845 Emperor Wu Tsung, an ardent Taoist and opposed to all forms of monastic life, issued a decree dissolving all monasteries and ordering the monks to return to private life. The Buddhists, who had some two hundred thousand monasteries, were hardest hit. The Nestorians, with their monastic form of Christianity, likewise suffered a major setback.

They were not, however, completely wiped out. Under the Mongols in the thirteenth century they were so important that a government bureau was established to supervise their monasteries, which had been restored to them. We read of Nestorian churches in such famous eastern cities as Chinkiang, Hangchow, and Yangchow. One source gives the number of Nestorians in China as thirty-thousand.

When the Franciscans under *John of Monte Corvino* arrived in Peking in 1294 they found the Nestorian mission strongly established but bitterly opposed to the newcomers. They spread false rumors about the Franciscans and tried to bring them into disrepute with the emperor. That they were to some extent successful is suggested by a statement attributed to John of Cora. Speaking of Nestorians, he said:

> They have very handsome and devoutly ordered churches, with crosses and images in honor of God and the saints. They hold sundry offices under the said Emperor, and have great privileges from him; so that it is believed that if they would agree and be at one with the Minor Friars and the other good Christians who dwell in that country, they would convert the whole country and the Emperor likewise to the true faith.[7]

Numerical Strength

Jesus was not enamored of numbers. He was more interested in the caliber of His disciples than in the number of His converts. He chose twelve apostles and gave most of His time and thought to them. The multitudes came and went; many of them were interested only in the "loaves and fishes." Jesus did not commit Himself to them, for He knew their fickleness (John 2:25). In days of popularity He refused to be exalted to the place of kingship (John 6:15). When reverses came and the crowds dwindled He refused to be dejected (Matt. 15:12, 13). He referred to his band of followers as a "little flock" (Luke 12:32). On occasion He went out of His way to make entrance into the kingdom as difficult as possible (Luke 9:57-62). The gate He described as "straight" and the way as "narrow." He acknowledged that those who find the one or favor the other are "few" (Matt. 7:13, 14).

Nevertheless, numbers are not to be despised altogether, for quantity as well as quality is a measure of success. He did tell His apostles to "go . . . into *all* the world" (Mark 16:15) and "make disciples of *all* nations" (Matt. 28:19, RSV). How many followers did He leave behind? It is difficult to say. One hundred and twenty were found in the upper room prior to Pentecost (Acts 1:15). Paul refers to five hundred brethren who saw the Lord after the resurrection (I Cor. 15:6). Doubtless there were more.

During the early days of the Christian mission three thousand are mentioned as being baptized in one day (Acts 2:41). Later the figure increased to five thousand (Acts 4:4). As time went on the Word of God "increased" (Acts 6:7). Conversions were a daily occurrence (Acts 2:47). Believers were "the more added to the Lord" (Acts 5:14). Multitudes

---

[7] Henry Yule, *Cathay and the Way Thither* (London: The Hakluyt Society, 1925), Vol. I, pp. 189-190.

were healed of various diseases (Acts 5:16). The number of disciples in Jerusalem "multiplied greatly" among them a "great company" of priests (Acts 6:7); so much so that the Sanhedrin accused Peter and John of filling Jerusalem with their doctrine (Acts 5:28).

When Philip carried the gospel to Samaria the people "with one accord gave heed," and there was "great joy in that city" (Acts 8:6-8). In Antioch the hand of the Lord was with the first messengers and a "great number" believed (Acts 11:21). Later, under the preaching of Barnabas, "much people" were added to the Lord (Acts 11:24). In Antioch of Pisidia "almost the whole city" came together to hear Paul (Acts 13:44). In Thessalonica a "great multitude" believed (Acts 17:4). "Many" of the Corinthians believed (Acts 18:8). During Paul's three-year stay in Ephesus "all they which dwelt in Asia heard the word, . . . both Jews and Greeks" (Acts 19:10). Some idea of the number of believers can be gained from the value of the magic spells and charms—"Ephesian letters" as they were called—that were burned. Fifty thousand pieces of silver would be equivalent to $10,000 if the silver *drachma* were the unit of money used.

Luke's account of Paul's labors leaves us with the impression that the churches founded by him were numerically large as well as spiritually prosperous. Athens, where only a few responded, was the exception (Acts 17:34). When we leave the Acts of the Apostles we are on less sure ground. We have very few statistics, and we cannot be sure that those we have are accurate. Figures given for primitive Christians are often exaggerated, sometimes out of piety, sometimes out of fear.

During the second century Christianity continued to make steady gains, especially in the East. Christians were especially numerous in Asia Minor. In the second decade of the second century Pliny, the governor of Bithynia, complained that the temples were almost deserted and that the new superstition had invaded not only the cities but the countryside as well. A little later Justin Martyr wrote: "There is no people, Greek or Barbarian, or any other race . . . among whom prayers and thanksgiving are not offered in the name of the crucified Jesus to the Father and creator of all things." About the year 200 Tertullian boasted: "We are only of yesterday, but already we fill the world."

Such statements, however, must not be taken too literally. They should be interpreted in the light of Origen's statement that the proportion of the faithful was "very inconsiderable when compared with the multitude of the unbelieving world."[8]

Harnack informs us that Christians were by no means numerous until after the middle of the second century. Gibbon has difficulty in accepting Justin Martyr's description, calling it a "splendid exaggeration . . . of a devout but careless writer."[9]

---

[8] Origen, *Contra Celsum,* 1, viii, p. 424.

[9] Edward Gibbon, *The Triumph of Christendom in the Roman Empire* (New York: Harper and Brothers, 1958), p. 68.

It was not until the third century, when the empire began to break up, that large numbers of people turned to Christianity. "In the chaos and terror of the third century men fled from the weakened state to the consolations of religion, and found them more abundantly in Christianity than in its rivals."[10] At the beginning of this century Christianity was already dominant in the cities of Phrygia; and throughout Asia Minor the Christians formed a large minority of the population. In North Africa conversions were so numerous as to approximate a mass movement.

A forty-year period of peace, from 260 to 300, gave the church an opportunity to extend its influence without the handicaps and hardships which accompany persecution. These four decades, just before the Diocletian persecution, were a time of unprecedented growth for the Christian church. Converts by the thousands flocked into the churches, bringing their patrimony, and in some cases their paganism, with them. The church became the richest religious organization in the empire. "In almost every city the ancient churches were found insufficient to contain the increasing multitude of proselytes; and in their place more stately and capacious edifices were erected for the public worship of the faith."[11] By the close of the third century the two greatest numerical strongholds of the faith were Asia Minor and North Africa. Edessa was well on the way to becoming the first state to make Christianity the official religion.

So far as statistics go, we have only two cities which afford anything like an accurate estimate of the strength of the church—Rome and Antioch.

We know that in A.D. 250 the church in Rome supported one hundred clergy and fifteen hundred poor persons. Assuming the population to be not less than one million, Gibbon estimates the number of Christians at fifty thousand. Harnack, working with the same figure, estimates thirty thousand. Fifty years later, according to a third opinion, the Christian community numbered one hundred thousand.

Antioch was the oldest and most illustrious church in the East. According to Chrysostom, towards the end of the fourth century Christians accounted for half of the population of five hundred thousand. Gibbon, however, considers this figure too high and suggests 20 percent rather than 50.

Exactly how many Christians were there at the close of the third century? Frankly, we do not know. We have no reliable figures for the empire, much less the church; but this has not deterred scholars from hazarding a guess. Will Durant estimates the population at one hundred million, while Stephen Neill would settle for half that figure. Estimates of the numerical strength of the church also vary. Ten per cent of the population would be a generous estimate. By far the larger portion of

---

10 Will Durant, *op. cit.*, p. 650.

11 Edward Gibbon, *op. cit.*, p. 125

these was found in the East. Durant believes that the Christians represented a fourth of the population in the East and only a twentieth in the West.

Following the conversion of Constantine Christianity entered a period of expansion. Enjoying royal patronage and supported by state funds, the church grew rapidly in the fourth century. "It seems likely that the number of Christians in the empire at least quadrupled itself in the century that followed the Edict of Milan."[12] The church in Rome reported twelve thousand men and a proportionate number of women and children baptized in one year. Barbarians, who held back when Christianity was a proscribed religion, rushed to embrace the new faith of their conquerors. In North Africa, where the native populations had remained unresponsive to the Christian message, great changes took place. In no time at all "the cities of Egypt were filled with bishops, and the deserts of Theais swarmed with hermits."[13] By the fourth century the majority of the inhabitants of Edessa had embraced Christianity.

Not content with supporting Christianity, Rome came in time to discriminate against the native religions. Gratian (367-383) withdrew state aid to the pagan cults and confiscated temple properties. Theodosius (379-395) went a step further; he closed the temples and punished those who attempted to sacrifice in secret. Emboldened by such edicts, the Christians, often led by monks, took it upon themselves to destroy pagan temples. Apostates from Christianity were deprived of civil as well as ecclesiastical rights. Anyone wanting to practice religion was virtually shut up to Christianity. Little wonder that the church quadrupled its membership in the fourth century.

The success, however, was by no means complete. In all parts of the empire pockets of resistance remained. Strangely enough, the Jews proved to be most impervious to the Christian message. They were wooed for a time, but never won. After the destruction of Jerusalem the break between the Jews and the Christians widened. Very few converts were made after the first century. The Christians grew impatient with their recalcitrant spirit and came first to hate, and then to persecute, them. "Such an injustice as that done by the Gentile church to Judaism is almost unprecedented in the annals of history . . . The daughter first robbed her mother, and then repudiated her."[14] Consequently Christianity never took root in Jewish, or even in Semitic, soil. Like Buddhism, it died out in the land of its birth and came to bloom in foreign lands.

Nor did Judaism survive in Palestine beyond 135, when the fanatical Jews under Bar Cocheba made their last desperate attempt to regain their

---

[12] Stephen Neill, *A History of Christian Missions* (Baltimore: Penguin Books, 1964), p. 46.

[13] Edward Gibbon, *op. cit.*, p. 64.

[14] Adolf Harnack, *The Mission and Expansion of Christianity* (New York: Harper and Brothers, 1962), p. 69.

freedom. After three flaming years and more than a million casualties the Jews were crushed, not to rise again until modern times.

> From this moment they entered their Middle Ages . . . No other people has ever known so long an exile, or so hard a fate. Scattered into every province and beyond, condemned to poverty and humiliation, unbefriended even by philosophers and saints, they retired from public affairs into private study and worship . . . Judaism hid in fear and obscurity while its offspring, Christianity, went out to conquer the world.[15]

Christianity became strongly entrenched among the Latin-speaking people in and around Carthage; but it met with considerably less success among the Punic people and left the Berbers almost untouched. In Persia, where the new faith had to compete with Zoroastrianism, it does not appear to have made much headway. In Egypt the Christian faith was for a long time confined to the city of Alexandria, which, in a sense, was a foreign colony whose culture was quite distinct from that of the surrounding areas. As late as Origen's time it was a rare thing to meet an Egyptian who was a Christian. Paganism persisted in the cities of Gaul, Italy and Spain well into the first century, and in Phoenicia and Palestine into the sixth century. Until the academies were closed by imperial decree in A.D. 529 Athens remained a stronghold of pre-Christian philosophy, while the hinterland of Greece seems hardly to have been penetrated by the gospel.

Who were the early Christians and from what classes did they come? Judged by their enemies, they were the dregs of humanity. Celsus describes them as "worthless, contemptible people, idiots, slaves, poor women and children."[16]

Paul intimates that even in the Corinthian church there were not many wise, mighty, or noble" (I Cor. 1:26). This should occasion no great surprise. Gibbon observed: "Such is the constitution of civil society that, whilst a few persons are distinguished by riches, by honor, and by knowledge, the body of the people is condemned to obscurity, ignorance and poverty. The Christian religion, which addressed itself to the whole human race, must consequently collect a far greater number of proselytes from the lower than the superior ranks of life."[17]

As time went on and the fortunes of the church improved, the upper classes were attracted in larger numbers. In the early part of the second century Pliny reported that a great number of persons of every order of men had deserted the religion of their ancestors. About A.D. 200 Tertullian claimed that "every age, condition and rank is coming over to us." Later on, when Christianity became the religion of the state, a general

---

15 Will Durant, *op. cit.,* p. 549.

16 Origen, *Contra Celsum,* iii, 49-55.

17 Edward Gibbon, *op. cit.,* pp. 69, 70

stampede brought an increasingly large number of persons of high rank into the church.

It is noteworthy that during all this time there was no organized missionary endeavor such as characterized later periods. The gospel was preached by laymen. "Nearly every convert, with the ardor of a revolutionary, made himself an office of propaganda."[18] With no weapon but truth and no banner but love, these single-minded, warm-hearted followers of Jesus traveled by land and sea to all parts of the empire, and wherever they went they gladly shared their new-found faith with friends, neighbors and strangers. As slaves, traders and, later on, soldiers, they used their secular calling to advance the cause of Christ. Even as exiles they carried the contagion of their faith to distant shores and inhospitable regions.

Cultural Penetration

Jesus was more interested in the salvation of the individual than in the reformation of society. He spoke frequently about the former, rarely about the latter. This is not to say that He was unmindful of, or indifferent to, the needs of society. He summed up the whole duty of man when He said: "Thou shalt love the Lord thy God with all thy heart, and thy neighbor as thyself." The order is important. The gospel is first personal, then social.

In the parable of the leaven (Matt. 13:33) and again in the parable of the salt and the light (Matt. 5:13-16) we are made aware of the way in which the Christian presence is to affect its environment. As salt, the Christians were to penetrate and permeate pagan society, arresting its decay, rejuvenating its institutions, and giving it new force and flavor. As light, the Christians were to illuminate the darkness of paganism by dispelling its ignorance and superstition by the truth of the gospel. Light is beneficial only if it is set on a high place where it can be seen. Salt is effective only on contact. It preserves only when it penetrates.

Jesus chose twelve men, entrusted them with His truth, imbued them with His spirit, invested them with His power, and sent them forth into the world. Everywhere and at all times they were to be as salt and light. They were to be different from other men, in character and conduct, in manners and morals, in motives and ideals; only so could they save the sinner, or reform society.

The early Christians resided for the most part in the cities, where they lived their lives, reared their children, and plied their trade side by side with their pagan neighbors. Little by little, without fuss or fanfare, these simple, wholesome, joyous Christians made their presence felt and their secret known. The light was shining. The salt was penetrating. The

---

[18] Will Durant, *op. cit.*, p. 602

leaven was working its way through the fabric of society. By the year 200 Christian influence had become so pervasive that Tertullian could write:

> We are a new group but have already penetrated all areas of imperial life—cities, islands, villages, towns, market-places, even the camp, tribes, palace, senate, the law-court. There is nothing left for you but your temples.[19]

Nor did they live in isolation, for Tertullian went on to say:

> We are no Brahmins. . . . dwelling in woods and exiled from life. . . . We live with you in the world, making use of the forum. . . . the bath. . . . the workshop. . . . the weekly market, and all other places of commerce. We sail with you, till the soil with you and traffic with you.[20]

Yet all the time they were considered by themselves and others as a separate and distinct people. Peter had called them a "chosen generation, a royal priesthood, an holy nation, a peculiar people" (I Pet. 2:9). They never forgot their divine calling or their heavenly destiny. They confessed that they were "strangers and pilgrims." They were ex-patriots—a colony of heaven—and they eagerly anticipated the return of Jesus Christ to inaugurate His reign of righteousness. So different were they that they came to be called "the third race"—the Romans being the first, the Jews the second.

Their attitude toward politics was narrow and negative. They believed that the world system of which Satan was both god (II Cor. 4:4) and prince (Eph. 2:2) was alienated from (Eph. 4:18), hostile to (Rom. 8:7), and under the judgment of, God (II Thess. 1:7, 8). While they were "in" the world and could not escape from it, they were not "of" it. The insistent call was: " . . . come out from among them, and be ye separate . . . " (II Cor. 6:17).

Nevertheless they had a wholesome view of the role of government. Taking their stand with Paul (Rom. 13), they were law-abiding citizens. They believed government to be a divinely established institution and were prepared to support it loyally. They paid taxes willingly, if not joyfully, remembering the words of Christ: "Render therefore to Caesar the things that are Caesar's" (Matt. 22:21, RSV).

On the other hand, they were not wholly satisfied with the political structure, local or imperial, because it was part of the world system they believed to be essentially evil. At best, it was a necessary evil—better than anarchy. At worst it was tyrannical and demonic.

Emperor worship was universally regarded by the Christians as outright idolatry and resisted to the death. At the same time, they resolutely repudiated the charge of treason, and tried to make their point by reminding their enemies that from the earliest times they had prayed for

---

[19] Tertullian, *Apology* 37.
[20] Tertullian, *Apology* 42.

the well-being of the emperor, and had promoted the peace and prosperity of the empire.

For the first two hundred years the Christians refused to participate in any form of government service—civil or military. Gradually this attitude changed. They began by making exception of those who had been in government employ before they became Christians. By the end of the third century Christians were found in all walks of life—the court, the civil service, and the military.

By their family solidarity, their honest toil, their submission to authority, their passion for righteousness, their love of human kind, and many other virtues, Christians constituted one of the most stable elements in the social structure. Melito in his *Apology* to Marcus Aurelius was quick to point out that Christianity was helping to undergird the state, and that ever since the advent of the new religion the empire had continued to flourish.[21]

The early Christians attached little importance to worldly wisdom. Among the twelve apostles there was not one man of letters. Jesus Himself remarked that the mysteries of the gospel were hid from the wise and prudent and revealed unto babes (Matt. 11:25). Paul deplored the fact that the world "by wisdom knew not God" (I Cor. 1:21), and conceded that even in the Corinthian church there were "not many wise" (I Cor. 1:26). Though himself a man of wide learning and brilliant mind, Paul in his proclamation of the gospel purposely avoided "excellency of speech or wisdom" (I Cor. 2:1), and warned his readers of the dangers of speculative philosophy (Col. 2:8).

It is not surprising that the early Christians regarded Christianity primarily as a way of salvation, not a system of philosophy. They were content to preach "Jesus Christ and Him crucified" in terms as simple as they were direct. It was not until the second century when a more sophisticated group, among them some philosophers, entered the fold that they felt obliged to wrestle with Greek thought. "The Church now won to its support some of the finest minds in the empire. Ignatius, bishop of Antioch, began the powerful dynasty of post-apostolic fathers, who gave a philosophy to Christianity, and overwhelmed its enemies with argument."[22]

Justin Martyr considered philosophy a good thing and coupled it with piety. Clement of Alexandria declared boldly that it was a gift of God to the Greeks, conducive of piety and a schoolmaster to bring the Hellenic mind to Christ. Others went still further and found in Socrates a forerunner of the truth, and in Seneca a kindred spirit. Realizing that if Christianity were to hold its own in a sophisticated society, it must

---

[21] Eusebius, *Ecclesiastical History,* IV, 26.
[22] Will Durant, *op. cit.,* p. 611.

ultimately win the intelligentsia, these Christian apologists attempted to express Christian truth in philosophical terms.

The new venture was not without its dangers and detractors. Tatian and Tertullian denounced all philosophy, good as well as bad. Tatian went to incredible lengths and was guilty of gross injustice. Tertullian asserted that the gospel appealed to faith, not reason; and that Christianity was credible precisely because it was absurd. The two feared that the simplicity of the gospel would be corrupted by the refinements of human reason. Perhaps they were not altogether wrong, for knowledge was as often the parent of heresy as of piety.

In time Christian teachers came to regard Christianity itself as a philosophy. After all, did it not deal with the problem of being in nature, God and man? Was it not concerned with the origin of the world, the meaning of life and the destiny of man? Christians were convinced that their doctrine was really the truth, and therefore the true philosophy. Indeed, it was more, it was the wisdom of God—the highest form of philosophy. All truth, wherever found, comes from God and is therefore "Christian." Some went even further and suggested that the best in Greek philosophy had been borrowed from Christianity.

The most influential of the apologists was the brilliant Origen, who at eighteen years of age succeeded Clement as head of the Catechetical School in Alexandria. He is reputed to have written six thousand "books" and corresponded with emperors. His most famous defense of Christianity, *Contra Celsum*, which appeared in 248, "impressed pagan thinkers as no apology had done before him. With him Christianity ceased to be only a comforting faith; it became a full-fledged philosophy, buttressed with Scripture but proudly resting on reason."[23]

But the real conflict between Christian and pagan philosophy was a matter of power, not polemics. The pagan philosophers, including Socrates, had more questions than answers. The Christian philosophers did not have all the answers; but they had more and better answers. Above all, they had the answer to the greatest of all questions—How can man be *good* as well as wise? The pagan philosophers spent their time *explaining* the world. The Christian philosophers quietly went about the task of *changing* the world.

It is a mistake to suppose that any "slave question" troubled the early church. Both Jesus and the apostles accepted the institution of slavery as an integral part of the economic and political system. Slaves were admonished by Paul to "remain in the state in which" they were "called" (I Cor. 7:20, RSV). It never occurred to the early Christians to abolish slavery even among themselves. Instead they depended on Christian love to ameliorate the conditions under which the slaves lived. Masters were to be kind and considerate, and were to give to their slaves that which was just

---

23 Will Durant, *op. cit.*, p. 615.

and equal because they themselves were accountable to a Master in heaven (Eph. 6:9). Slaves, on their part, were expected to be honest, industrious, faithful, and loyal (Titus 2:9, 10), and not to take advantage of the fact that they were regarded as brethren in the Lord.

If the slave were afforded an opportunity to secure his freedom, he was to accept it; otherwise he was to be content with the spiritual freedom he enjoyed in Christ (I Cor. 7:21, 22). Masters were encouraged to set their slaves free. Congregations often allocated funds for the emancipation of slaves. In some communities, churches held special ceremonies of manu-mission. Instead of attacking the power structure head-on, the church was content to allow the leaven of the gospel to permeate pagan society, hoping that by precept and practice they would convince their friends and neighbors of the dignity of man and the worth of the individual.

The Character of the Early Church

The two outstanding virtues of the early church were charity and chastity. Both come to focus in James' definition of genuine religion. "Pure religion and undefiled before God and the Father is this, To visit the fatherless and widows in their affliction, and to keep himself unspotted from the world" (James 1:27).

It was said of the early Christians that they recognized one another by means of secret marks and signs, and loved one another almost before they got acquainted.

The love that became the hallmark of the Christian religion may be traced to three powerful influences: the noble example of perfect love seen in the Master (John 13:34, 35), the lofty teachings of the Savior contained in the Gospels (Matt. 5:43-48), and the dynamic afforded by the ministry of the Holy Spirit (Rom. 5:5).

Probably no parable made a greater impression on the early church than the parable of the sheep and the goats in Matthew 25. Certainly the works of charity listed there were to an amazing degree incorporated into the program of the early church.

In the early part of Acts we find the disciples practising a form of Christian communism which permitted them to have all things in common (Acts 2:44; 4:32). The church in Antioch sent relief funds to the poor saints in Jerusalem (Acts 11:27-30). Later on the Gentile churches in Macedonia and Achaia sent similar gifts to Jerusalem (II Cor. 9). Certainly Paul was concerned for the social implications of the gospel and instructed the rich to help the poor (II Cor. 8:14) and the strong to support the weak (Rom. 15:1). Converts were urged to bear one another's burdens and thus fulfill the law of Christ (Gal. 6:2). They were told to "do good to all men, and especially to those who are of the household of faith" (Gal. 6:10, RSV).

John teaches that divine love inevitably expresses itself in human compassion (I John 3:17, 18). James says the same about faith (James 2:14-16). Both love and faith express themselves in works of charity.

The early Christians began where Jesus told them to begin—by loving one another. Moreover, they followed His example and teaching, and expressed their love in deeds, not words. Harnack lists ten different areas in which early Christian philanthropy manifested itself: alms in general, support of teachers and officials, support of widows and orphans, support of the sick and infirm, the care of prisoners and convicts in the mines, the care of poor people needing burial, the care of slaves, providing disaster relief, furnishing employment and, finally, extending hospitality.[24]

All of this was, of course, in stark contrast to the pagan practices of the day. Plato suggested that allowing the poor to die shortened their misery. Cicero advised charity only for those who would use it wisely. Roman society cared nothing for orphans, allowing them to be reared for prostitution. Slaves were regarded as goods and chattels and were bought and sold as such. Christian compassion was not restricted to Christian circles. It was offered indiscriminately to all classes and conditions of men. Referring to the great plague during the reign of Maximius Daza, Eusebius reports:

> Then did they show themselves to the heathen in the clearest light. For the Christians were the only people who amid such terrible ills showed their fellow-feeling and humanity in their actions. Day by day some would busy themselves with attending to the dead and burying them; others gathered in one spot all who were afflicted by hunger throughout the whole city, and gave bread to them all.[25]

Considering the paucity of their numbers and the meagerness of their resources, the primitive Christians did more for the amelioration of human suffering than any succeeding generation of believers.

> The works of charity that Christians accomplished in the Roman Empire continue to be one of the greatest stars in the church's crown. Even the pagans noticed this. Lucian, who is known more for his satire than his appreciation, wrote: "It is incredible to see the ardor with which the people of that religion help each other in their wants. They spare nothing. Their first legislator (Jesus) has put into their heads that they are all brethren."[26]

The second great virtue of the early Christians was purity. Here again the disciples took their cue from Jesus, both His example and His teaching. The sinless character of Jesus Christ was a unique phenomenon in the world of men. Born without sin, He lived without sin. The only time He knew sin was when he "bore our sins in his body on the tree" (I Pet. 2:24, RSV). He fraternized with publicans and sinners but always with a

---

24 Adolf Harnack, *op. cit.*, p. 153.

25 Eusebius, *Ecclesiastical History*, IX, 8.

26 Walter Oetting, *op. cit.*, p. 80.

view to winning them to a life of purity. He forgave sinners but always with the proviso: "Go and sin no more." Constantly He warned men of the devastating effects of sin—sins of the spirit as well as sins of the flesh. He lived a life of holiness and tried to inculcate the same in His followers. He pronounced a special blessing on the pure in heart. The essence of His ethic was summed up in the command: "Be ye therefore perfect, even as your Father which is in heaven is perfect" (Matt. 5:48).

The early church found itself in a hostile environment every aspect of which was inimical to the pursuit of holiness. Roman life in those times was characterized by two great sins—idolatry and immorality. Her religious life was dominated by the first, her social life by the second. To live in such a world and yet keep themselves "unspotted from the world" was a perennial problem for the early Christians.

The first problem was idolatry. Apostolic preaching concerning idolatry is clearly spelled out in the New Testament. " . . . you turned to God from idols, to serve a living and true God, and to wait for his Son from heaven, . . . who delivers us from the wrath to come" (I Thess. 1:9, 10, RSV). The God and Father of our Lord Jesus Christ is the living and true God, maker of heaven and earth, and sustainer of all things (Acts 14:15). In Him we live and move and have our being (Acts 17:28). To know Him is life eternal (John 17:3). Jesus Christ came from heaven to invade Satan's kingdom (Matt. 12:29), destroy his works (I John 3:8), and deliver men from his tyranny (Heb. 2:15). Christians have been delivered from the kingdom of darkness and translated into the kingdom of light (Col. 1:13). Since this is so, there can be no communion between light and darkness, no concord between Christ and Belial, no agreement between the temple of God and idols (II Cor. 6:14-16).

> The duty of keeping oneself free from all contamination with polytheism ranked as the *supreme* duty of the Christian. It took precedence over all others. It was regarded as the negative side of *the duty of confessing one's faith*, and the "sin of idolatry" was more strictly dealt with in the Christian church than any other sin whatsoever.[27]

The war against idolatry continued during the second and third centuries when the Christian apologists intensified their polemic against the pagan gods. Their method of attack was twofold: To demonstrate the folly of pagan teaching about idols, and to rouse moral indignation against the gods by exposing their abominable vices. They were careful, however, not to encourage iconoclasm. If a Christian smashed an idol and was slain in the act, he was not reckoned among the martyrs. Idol making was declared an illegal occupation and had to be given up even if no other means of livelihood were available. Christians were not allowed to practise as astrologers or magicians.

---

27 Adolf Harnack, *op. cit.*, p. 202.

But more subtle and dangerous than idol worship was emperor worship for it carried with it the stigma of treason. It was at this point that the Christians found themselves most sorely pressed. A pinch of incense tossed on the altar would have satisfied the demands of the imperial cultus; but this the Christians refused to do, for they regarded it as an act of worship—and therefore idolatrous. At the same time, they repudiated the charge of treason by pointing to their submission to the laws of the state and their prayers for the well-being of the emperor. They would acknowledge his authority when living and revere his memory when dead; but they adamantly refused to worship his person.

> By embracing the faith of the gospel, the Christians incurred the supposed guilt of an unnatural and unpardonable offense. . . . They dissolved the sacred ties of custom and education, violated the religious institutions of their country, and presumptuously despised whatever their fathers had believed as true or had revered as sacred. The whole body of Christians unanimously refused to hold any kind of communion with the gods of Rome, of the empire, and of mankind.[28]

Naturally this kind of conduct excited the suspicion and hostility of the Romans. Lucian regarded them as half-crazy fanatics. Tacitus called them haters of the human race. Porphyry considered them barbarians. A few gave them grudging praise; but the vast majority of writers and thinkers regarded them as an "utter abomination."

The most puzzling aspect of Christianity was its mode of worship. The philosophers could understand and even approve of monotheism; but their "secret worship" was unnatural, monstrous and repugnant. Caecilius spoke of them as a people who skulk and shun the light of day, silent in public but talkative in holes and corners, and went on to ask:

> Why have they no altars, no temples, no recognized images. . . . unless what they worship and conceal deserves punishment or is something to be ashamed of?. . . . The lonely and wretched Jews worshipped one God by themselves, but they did it openly, with temples, altars, victims and ceremonies. . . . But the Christians! What marvels, what monsters, do they feign![29]

Immorality was rampant in all parts of the empire, especially in the urban centers where most of the Christians lived. Such cities as Ephesus, Corinth and Rome were cesspools of iniquity, in which, according to Tacitus, "vice had charms for all orders of men." In contrast to all this was the wholesome life of the Christians whose business practices, domestic arrangements, civic responsibilities and social relationships reflected the new life in Christ.

Aristides, defending the Christians against the charge of immorality, wrote: "They do not commit adultery nor fornication, nor bear false witness, nor embezzle what is held in pledge, nor covet what is not

---

[28] Edward Gibbon, *op. cit.*, p. 80.
[29] Caeculius, *Minut. Felix*, VIII, f.

theirs. . . . And their women, O Emperor, are pure as virgins, and their daughters are modest; and their men keep themselves from every unlawful union and from all uncleanness."[30]

In private life new converts were taught to live "soberly, righteously and godly in this present world" (Titus 2:12). In civic life they were exhorted to "Honour all men. Love the brotherhood. Fear God. Honour the king" (I Pet. 2:17). Not only the grosser sins of the flesh but the more refined sins of the spirit—the evil eye, the impure thought, the quick temper, the sharp tongue, and the idle word—all were to be eschewed. Anger, wrath, malice, gossip, and jealousy belonged to the old life, and were to be put away (Col. 3:8).

Once baptized, the Christian was expected to avoid all sinful practices. If he sinned, he was required to confess. If the sin were grave, he was expected to demonstrate his sorrow by becoming a public penitent. Those who persisted in sin were excommunicated.

Nowhere was the principle of separation from the world more scrupulously carried out than in the matter of entertainment. The arena, the circus, and the theater were scrupulously avoided. No church member was permitted to be an actor or a gladiator, or to teach acting. The passion for public games was almost irresistible. It required much self-discipline for the Christians to refrain from something so universally popular.

The church frowned on the theater because of the immorality of the gods and men portrayed there. The gladiatorial shows were condemned on two counts: First, they were dedicated to the gods and, therefore, smacked of idolatry. Secondly, the church took the stand that watching a person being put to death was tantamount to doing the deed oneself.

The Christians, of course, were powerless to stop the shows, but their protest paid off, because by the time Constantine came to power public opinion had developed to the point where the state was able to curtail the sadistic spectacles.

Marriage was regarded as an honorable estate, but celibacy was recommended as ideal. Christians were permitted to marry only within their own circle. Divorce, so common in Roman society, was permitted only if the unbelieving partner demanded it. The remarriage of widows and widowers was frowned upon. Homosexuality was condemned with an earnestness rare in antiquity. Children were a gift from God and were to be reared in His fear. Abortion and infanticide, which were decimating the pagan population, were equated with murder and, therefore, prohibited. Women, though emancipated by the power of the gospel, were nevertheless expected to be examples of humility and modesty especially in places of public worship. They were to adorn themselves not with cosmetics and jewels but with a "meek and quiet spirit" (I Pet. 3:4). Ornamental clothes and elaborate hair-dos were unseemly in women professing godliness.

---

[30] Aristides, *Apology* 15

With standards so high, it was easy to fall short. No church was perfect and some of them, like Corinth, were plagued with many irregularities, both ethical and theological. But on the whole it is correct to say that the Christians, for all their imperfections, represented a new breed of men whose character and conduct excited the reluctant admiration of the pagan world. Pliny the Younger reported that the Christians led peaceful and exemplary lives. Galen remarked on their self-discipline and said that in their pursuit of moral excellence they were in no way inferior to true philosophers.

Every institution, however, deteriorates with time, and the Christian church was no exception. Decline set in about the beginning of the third century and greatly accelerated during the forty years of peace from 260 to 300. Peace brought prosperity and prosperity proved more harmful than persecution. New wealth made possible the acquisition of property and the building of stately edifices. Converts flocked into the churches in large numbers.

> In the interval between the Decian and the Diocletian persecution the Church had become the richest religious organization in the empire, and had moderated its attacks upon wealth. Cyprian complained that his parishioners were mad about money, that Christian women painted their faces, that bishops held lucrative offices of state, made fortunes, lent money at usurious interest, and denied their faith at the first sign of danger. Eusebius mourned that priests quarreled violently in their competition for ecclesiastical preferment. While Christianity converted the world, the world converted Christianity.[31]

The Persecution of the Church

Jesus was extremely frank with His disciples. He told them exactly the kind of treatment they could expect from a hostile world. "In the world ye shall have tribulation. . . . Ye shall be hated of all men for My sake. . . . If they have persecuted Me, they will persecute you also." He even went so far as to warn them that "he that killeth you will think that he doeth God service."

The history of the early church verifies these words. Stephen was stoned. James was beheaded. On one occasion Peter's life was spared at the eleventh hour only by angelic interference. Paul's testimony was "I die daily." He expected his converts to live dangerously and taught that they must " . . . through much tribulation enter into the kingdom of God" (Acts 14:22). To Timothy he wrote: " . . . all who desire to live a godly life in Christ Jesus shall suffer persecution" (II Tim. 3:12, RSV). Peter warned the Christians, "Think it not strange concerning the fiery trial which is to try you" (I Pet. 4:12).

---

[31] Will Durant, *op. cit.,* p. 657.

During the first generation—the period covered by the Acts of the Apostles—the persecution originated with the synagogue, not the senate. Throughout the Acts of the Apostles Luke is at pains to point out that not only did Rome look with leniency on the new sect, but actually afforded protection to its chief proponents. More than once Paul and his companions owed their lives to the timely intervention of local Roman officials.

It is difficult to ascertain exactly the reason, nature, and extent of the persecution suffered by the early church at the hands of the Romans. The situation is clouded by charges and countercharges the veracity of which it is sometimes difficult to evaluate. Historical documents are tantalizingly scarce, and those we do possess leave much to be desired when it comes to objectivity. Doubtless the Christian apologists, in the heat of public debate, exaggerated the virtues of the Christians. On the other hand, their enemies patently trifled with the truth when they referred to the Christians as "imbeciles" (Lucian), "god-forsaken fools" (Celsus), and "haters of the human race" (Tacitus).

As long as Christianity was regarded as a Jewish sect, it enjoyed the privileges of *religio licita* granted to Judaism. But as time went on the rift between Christianity and Judaism widened. By A.D. 50 the followers of Jesus had acquired an image of their own and were known as Christians (Acts 11:26). Following the burning of Rome by Nero in 64 the profession of Christianity seems to have become a capital offense. In order to clear himself, Nero looked for a scapegoat and found it in the Christians, whom he subjected to the most fiendish kind of treatment. Tacitus describes the persecution in these words:

> They were put to death with exquisite cruelty, and to their sufferings Nero added mockery and derision. Some were covered with skins of wild beasts, and left to be devoured by dogs; others were nailed to crosses; numbers of them were burned to death; many, covered with inflammable matter, were set on fire to serve as torches during the night.[32]

Particularly provocative was the adamant refusal of the Christians to worship the emperor. "The rejection of the imperial cultus was a crime which came under the head of sacrilege as well as of high treason, and it was here that the repressive measures taken by the state against Christianity almost invariably started."[33]

The law regarding emperor worship was not uniformly applied. Local magistrates were often men of culture and tolerance. Many emperors enforced the ordinance with deliberate negligence. Hadrian instructed his appointees to give the Christians the benefit of the doubt. Trajan forbade Pliny, governor of the troublesome province of Bithynia, to "search" for

---

[32] Tacitus, *Annals*, XV, 44.
[33] Adolf Harnack, *op. cit.*, p. 296.

the Christians or to take action against them unless their accusers were willing to be identified by name.

The second period of persecution coincided with the reign of Domitian (81-96), during which the Apostle John was banished to the Isle of Patmos. Several years later, Ignatius, bishop of Antioch, and Polycarp, bishop of Smyrna, died martyrs. When natural calamities plagued the empire during the reign of Marcus Aurelius (161-180), the Christians were again singled out for special attention. In Vienne and Lyons the infuriated populace stoned all Christians who ventured on to the streets. Under Commodus (180-192) the situation improved but worsened again during the latter years of Septimius Severus (192-211) when baptism became a crime. In A.D. 203 many Christians suffered martyrdom in Carthage.

It is important to note that there were no empirewide, centrally directed persecutions until the third century. "No church was subjected to relentless and continuous persecution over a long period of time, and the number of martyrs was much smaller than the piety of later ages has imagined it to be."[34] In the early period, before the Church became a force in the empire, individuals who confessed Christ were simply executed. Such persons were known as "martyrs" or "witnesses." In the third century, when they could not be destroyed summarily without decimating the population, they were tortured until they recanted. Those who refused to recant were called "confessors."

During the first two centuries persecution was local and intermittent. In duration and severity it varied in time and place, depending as much on the temper of the people and the disposition of the local magistrates as on the intentions of the emperors. Government officials acted against the Christians when encouraged by an outraged populace, whose superstitious fury was sometimes provoked and sometimes assuaged by the zeal of the Christians.

The Christians were generally despised, often hated, by the people among whom they lived. They were accused of being atheists, immoral, and unpatriotic. It was also generally believed that Christians incorporated into their secret worship such hideous practices as eating human flesh and drinking human blood, and of indulging in nocturnal orgies of all kinds. That the charges were false made little difference, especially during periods when the fortunes of the empire were low and the tempers of the people were high.

Such persecutions were not wholly harmful to the Christian cause.

> These transient persecutions served only to revive the zeal and to restore the discipline, of the faithful; and the moments of extraordinary rigour were compensated by much longer intervals of peace and security. The indifference of some princes and the indulgence of others permitted the Christians to

[34] Stephen Neill, *op. cit.*, p. 43.

enjoy, though not perhaps a legal, yet an actual and public, toleration of their religion.[35]

The first half of the third century was marked by sporadic persecutions under Severus, Maximinius, and Decius. Then followed a forty-year period of unprecedented peace which began in 261 with the proclamation by Gallienus of the first edict of toleration. The peace was abruptly broken in 303 by the edict of persecution issued by Diocletian. Designed as a general law for the whole empire, it ushered in the last and most severe of the persecutions. The edict decreed the destruction of Christian churches, the dissolution of Christian congregations, the burning of Christian books, and the exclusion of Christians from public office. Christians who persisted in meeting in secret were marked for death.

The persecution, inaugurated with the burning of the cathedral in Nicomedia, lasted for ten years. In Italy and the East the edict was carried out with military dispatch. Martyrs were found in all parts of the empire except Gaul and Britain where only a few churches were burned. Fifteen hundred martyrs died and countless Christians lost their possessions. Thousands of believers, including the bishop of Rome, recanted.

Lasting peace came when Constantine in 313 issued the Edict of Milan, confirming religious toleration and restoring to the church the properties confiscated during the previous decade.

The patient endurance of the Christians under persecution and the triumphant faith of the martyrs facing death constitute one of the most glorious pages in church history. To a remarkable degree they followed the teachings of the Master: "Love your enemies, bless them that curse you, do good to them that hate you, and pray for them which despitefully use you, and persecute you" (Matt. 5:44).

During the first two centuries every kind of torture was used to extract the confession, "Caesar is Lord," but to little avail. Every known method of execution was employed, but few recanted. They went cheerfully to prison, to the mines, and into exile. Far from shunning death, they seemed, on occasion, to actually seek it. Condemned to be devoured in Rome by wild beasts, Justin Martyr implored both friend and foe not to intervene. Tertullian informs us that the Christians gave thanks even when condemned to die. So importunate for death were some of them that their attitude provoked the anger and disgust of the proconsul Antoninus, who exclaimed, "Unhappy men! unhappy men! if you are thus weary of your lives, is it so difficult for you to find ropes and precipices?"[36]

Far from destroying Christianity persecution only served to strengthen it. The blood of the martyrs proved to be the seed of the church. For every person who died a martyr's death, scores forsook their pagan gods and embraced the Christian faith.

---

[35] Edward Gibbon, *op. cit.*, p. 115.
[36] Edward Gibbon, *op. cit.*, p. 112.

There is no greater drama in human record than the sight of a few Christians, scorned or oppressed by a succession of emperors, bearing all trials with a fierce tenacity, multiplying quietly, building order while the enemies generated chaos, fighting the sword with the word, brutality with hope, and at last defeating the strongest state that history has known. Caesar and Christ had met in the arena, and Christ had won.[37]

The Conversion of Constantine

The Diocletian persecution, the greatest test and triumph of the church, was followed by a period of unprecedented peace. The epochal event that marked the turning point was the conversion of Emperor Constantine. About to engage in bloody battle with Maxentius for the throne, Constantine is reported by Eusebius to have seen in the sky a flaming cross and the words, "In this sign conquer!" Adopting the sign of the cross, Constantine inflicted a crushing blow on Maxentius and entered Rome as the undisputed ruler of the West.

Early in 313 Constantine issued his famous Edict of Milan, in which he granted complete freedom to all religions in the empire and ordered the restoration of church property confiscated by Diocletian. Ten years later, after defeating Licinius in the East and becoming the sole emperor, Constantine declared himself a Christian and invited his subjects to do the same.

Two events in Constantine's reign are of great significance to the Christian Church. One was the Council of Nicea, convened by the emperor in 325; the other was the completion of Eusebius's *Ecclesiastical History* in the same year.

Eusebius, the most erudite cleric of his day and a favorite of Constantine's court, placed the church forever in his debt when he produced his monumental *Ecclesiastical History,* which traced the development of Christianity from its beginnings to the Council of Nicea. The objectivity usually associated with historians is lacking in Eusebius; nevertheless, it is safe to say that he approached his sources critically and his statements are as accurate as those in any ancient work of history. It is the most comprehensive and authoritative work we have on the history of the church in the first three centuries. Without it we should be greatly impoverished.

The Council of Nicea was summoned by Constantine, whose motives were not less political than religious. The church was gravely divided; the emperor wished to unite the church as a steppingstone to uniting the empire. This first ecumenical council was attended by 318 bishops and many clergy of lower rank. It met in the imperial palace, Constantine presiding and taking part in the debate. The controversy between Athana-

---

37 Will Durant, *op. cit.,* p. 652.

sius and Arius was most bitter. The former won the day. The council drew up a statement in which it declared that Jesus Christ was "begotten, not made, being of one essence with the Father."

Following the conversion of Constantine, Christianity suddenly became popular and people flocked in great numbers to its banner. New and finer churches were erected, sometimes with state funds, sometimes with treasures confiscated from heathen temples. The alliance between the church and the state brought a measure of prosperity and prestige, but it hardly enhanced the spiritual stature or strengthened the moral fiber of the Christian community. With thousands embracing the faith there seemed little need for missionary effort. Individual conversion and personal commitment were no longer matters of great concern. Converts entering the church brought with them their paganism as well as their patrimony. From Constantine to the present time the Christian church in the West, Protestant as well as Roman Catholic, has at different times and in varying degrees been identified with and supported by the state. Ecclesiastical power has been wedded to political power to the detriment of spiritual power.

Was the conversion of Constantine genuine? Was his espousal of the Christian religion politically motivated? Would Christianity have conquered the Roman Empire without his endorsement? There can be no final and authoritative answers to these questions. Maybe it is unfair to expect the Christian emperor of a predominantly pagan state to be absolutely genuine in the expression of his religion, or to be completely pure in his motives. Leaders in public life have always found it difficult to resist expediency. Compromise and concession form the warp and woof of political life. Even an absolute monarch cannot with impunity ignore the social, political and economic currents of his time.

Certainly there were sound reasons, some personal and some political, why Constantine should encourage the spread of the Christian religion. To begin with, Christianity was not new to him. His mother, Helena, had been a Christian and doubtless she had told him something of the new faith. His knowledge of Roman history would have impressed him with Christianity's powers of survival—ten separate periods of persecution had failed to destroy it. Under the banner of the cross his armies had achieved great victories. His support of the church was worth a dozen legions in his wars against Maxentius and Licinius. Moreover, the Christians were a stable element in society, providing a good foundation on which to build a solid empire. As a group they were hard-working and law-abiding. They made good neighbors, good citizens and good soldiers. Unlike their cousins, the Jews, they seldom revolted. Their Scriptures taught them to honor all men, to love the brotherhood, to fear God, to honor the king. What more could an emperor ask? If anybody could help him consolidate his hold on the empire, surely these strange people, members of "the third race," could.

On the other hand, it was necessary for Constantine to proceed with caution. After all, the Christians represented not more than 10 percent of the total population. While currying favor with them he could not afford to alienate the pagan element in the empire. For a time he played both sides off against the middle. Consequently there was no clean break with paganism. He built Christian churches at the same time that he restored pagan temples. At the dedication of Constantinople he employed pagan as well as Christian rites. He used magic formulas to protect crops and heal disease. To the end he continued to function as *pontifex maximus* of the traditional cult.

With the consolidation of power he took a stronger stand for the Christian faith. Pagan effigies were removed from his coins. Bishops were invested with juridical as well as ecclesiastical power. Church property was exempted from taxation. Sunday was declared to be the Christian day of worship. Large sums of money were given for church buildings and Christian philanthropy. For reasons known only to himself, however, he postponed baptism until he was on his deathbed.

Durant describes him as a "masterly general, a remarkable administrator, a superlative statesman."[38] Be that as it may, he was extravagant, capricious, ruthless, and unscrupulous. He was passionately ambitious and susceptible to flattery. As an absolute monarch he was not averse to the use of force, actually killing his own wife, his son, and his nephew.

---

38 Will Durant, *op. cit.,* p. 664

II

Christianization of Europe:
A.D. 500-1200

During the Dark Ages Ireland stood out as a beacon in the gathering gloom. From the sixth to the eighth centuries it was the most advanced country in western Europe. Free from the disastrous invasions of the barbarians, the church there kept the lamp of learning burning when the lights all over Europe were going out. Attracting scholars from England and the Continent, she received them all with boundless hospitality, sharing with them the highest education available in that day. Had it not been for the great monastic schools of Ireland, learning would almost certainly have perished from western Europe.

Equally important, if not more so, was the missionary zeal which was the outstanding characteristic of the Irish church. From the time of Patrick the church had been thoroughly evangelical and evangelistic. During the sixth and seventh centuries it became one of the greatest missionary churches of all time. With an extensive knowledge of the Scriptures and a personal experience of the power of the Holy Spirit, its missionaries flung themselves with fiery zeal into the battle against heathenism, which threatened to engulf Christian Europe. With holy enthusiasm they gave themselves to the evangelization of foreign peoples: the fierce Picts of Scotland, the savage Angles and Saxons of England, and the Frisians of the Low Countries. In the face of hardship, persecution, and even martyrdom, they pressed on through Gaul, Holland, Germany, Switzerland, and into northern Italy. Wherever they went they founded monasteries, which became centers of Christian culture and missionary activity. From these monasteries they went out to evangelize the masses, and to them they returned for rest and renewal.

What is the debt the world owes to primitive Celtic Christianity? The answer is that it produced the greatest missionary effort the world has ever seen; that when Europe was overrun by the barbarian hordes, these wandering Irish saints pushed their settlements right into the heart of European heathendom, and that from the North Sea to the Lombardic plains, from beyond the Rhine to the borders of Brittany, Ireland kept the lamp of learning alight in those dark days, and not only made possible the Christianization of barbarian Europe, but educated and supplied the greatest teachers down to the time of Charlemagne.[1]

Britain. The origin of Christianity in Britain is wrapped in obscurity. We do not know exactly when or by whom the gospel was first introduced into that country. That Christian churches existed there in the third century seems fairly certain. The first authentic information relates to the presence of three bishops from London, York, and Lincoln who were present at the Council of Arles in southern France in 314. When the Angles and the Saxons invaded Britain in the fifth century, much of this early form of Christianity was swept away, leaving only isolated remnants in the inaccessible regions of the west. It was not until the sixth century that Christianity took permanent root in Britain. This was effected by a twofold invasion, in the north from Ireland in 563 and in the south from Rome in 596.

It was fitting that Ireland, which earlier had been evangelized from Britain, should in turn give to Scotland her greatest apostle. He was the famous *Columba,* a man of royal birth, liberal gifts, and vast learning. A native of Donegal, he gave the first half of his life to the gospel ministry in his homeland, where he founded many churches and monasteries. The most famous were those at Derry and Darrow. Described by his biographer as "angelic in appearance, graceful in speech, holy in work, with talents of the highest order and consummate prudence," Columba in his forty-second year crossed the Irish Channel with twelve companions and established on Iona, an island off the west coast of Scotland, a monastery destined to become one of the most famous centers of missionary activity of all time. The membership of the monastery was divided into three categories: Seniors, devoted to spiritual concerns, especially the copying of the Scriptures; Working Brethren, employed in manual labor; and Juniors, who were neophytes under instruction.

All were monks with cowl, white tunic, and leathern sandals. There was manual labor and hard service to be performed in field and kitchen, as well as study and worship in cell or chapel, and all was done to the end of bringing the gospel to those among whom Christ had not been named.[2]

Columba and his companions traveled extensively throughout Scotland and the offshore islands, evangelizing peasants and fisherfolk, teaching

---

[1] Gough Meisser, "The Mission and Expansion of Celtic Christianity" in W. A. Philips, *History of the Church of Ireland* (London: Oxford University Press, 1933), p. 49.

[2] V. Raymond Edman, *The Light in Dark Ages* (Wheaton, Ill.; Van Kampen Press, 1949), p. 149.

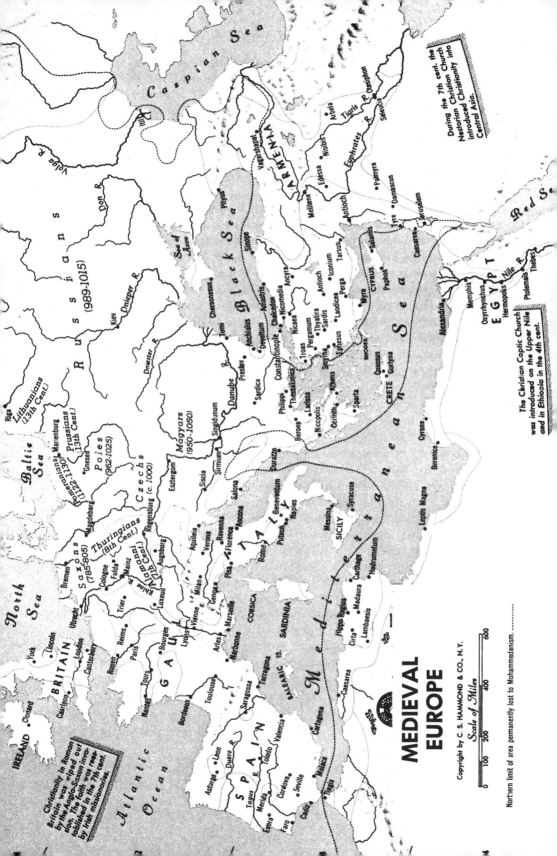

MEDIEVAL EUROPE

Copyright by C. S. HAMMOND & CO., N.Y.

Scale of Miles

0   100   200   400   600

Northern limit of area permanently lost to Mohammedanism. ---------

During the 7th cent. the Christian Church sent Nestorian Christianity into introduced Christianity into Central Asia.

The Christian Coptic Church was introduced on the Upper Nile and in Ethiopia in the 4th cent.

Christianity in Roman Britain was wiped out by the Anglo-Saxon invasion. The faith was reestablished in the 7th cent. by Irish missionaries.

Caspian Sea

Black Sea

Mediterranean Sea

Red Sea

Baltic Sea

North Sea

Atlantic Ocean

Sea of Azov

Volga R.
Don R.
Dnieper R.
Dniester R.
Danube
Rhine R.
Tigris R.
Euphrates R.
Nile R.

ARMENIA
RUSSIANS (989-1015)
Lithuanians (13th Cent.)
Prussians (13th Cent.)
Pomeranians (1122-1130)
Poles (962-1025)
Czechs
Magyars (950-1050)
Thuringians (8th Cent.)
Saxons (785-805)
Alamanni (7th Cent.)
GAUL
BRITAIN
IRELAND
SPAIN
ITALY
SICILY
SARDINIA
CORSICA
CRETE
CYPRUS
EGYPT
BALEARIC IS.

Riga
Kiev
Vagharshapat
Arbela
Nisibis
Edessa
Melitene
Antioch
Palmyra
Damascus
Tyre
Jerusalem
Caesarea
Salamis
Paphos
Pityus
Sinope
Chersonesus
Amastris
Tomi
Preslav
Sardica
Singidunum
Sirmium
Siscia
Salona
Durazzo
Constantinople
Chalcedon
Nicomedia
Nicaea
Ancyra
Iconium
Tarsus
Laodicea
Perga
Myra
Antioch
Pergamum
Thyatira
Sardis
Ephesus
Smyrna
Nicopolis
Troas
Philippi
Thessalonica
Beroea
Larissa
Athens
Corinth
Sparta
Gortyna
Cnossus
Alexandria
Memphis
Oxyrhynchus
Hermopolis
Ptolemais
Thebes
Cyrene
Berenice
Leptis Magna
Hadrumetum
Carthage
Madaura
Lambaesis
Cirta
Hippo Regius
Caesarea
Tingis
Cadiz
Seville
Cordova
Malaga
Valencia
Cartagena
Toledo
Merida
Ebora
Faro
Astorga
Leon
Saragossa
Tarragona
Toulouse
Bordeaux
Nantes
Tours
Narbonne
Arles
Marseille
Vienne
Lyons
Bourges
Paris
Rouen
Reims
Trier
London
Canterbury
York
Lincoln
Caerleon
Clonard
Utrecht
Bremen
Cologne
Mainz
Fulda
Trier
Luxeuil
Augsburg
Regensburg
Magdeburg
Marienburg
Gnesen
Esztergom
Aquileia
Verona
Milan
Genoa
Pisa
Florence
Ravenna
Ancona
Rome
Naples
Puteoli
Beneventum
Messina
Syracuse
Carthage
Hadrumetum

Tagus R.
Duero R.
Rhone R.
Tiber R.

converts, building churches, and establishing monasteries, all of them under the central control of Iona. A man of rare zeal and piety, Columba left his stamp not only on Iona but on the whole of Scotland. He died in 596; but the monastery at Iona continued for two hundred years to send missionaries to all parts of the British Isles and Europe.

Not content with the evangelization of Scotland, the Irish missionaries, with considerable courage and at great cost, carried the gospel to the savage Angles and Saxons of Northumbria, whose cruelties had incurred the hate and fear of the Britons. *Aidan,* the most illustrious of the successors of Columba, established a monastery at Lindisfarne, an island off the east coast of England, from which he launched his crusade into the heart of Northumbria in 635. For seventeen years Aidan, assisted by many fellow monks, preached the gospel of peace to the fierce Angles and Saxons with great effect. Oswald, the king of Northumbria, who was converted to the Christian faith in the heat of battle, actively supported the Christian mission by endowing monasteries. Churches sprang up everywhere and multitudes pressed into the Kingdom of God. Aidan was followed by *Cuthbert,* who by his godly life and arduous labors completed the evangelization of the Angles.

In the meantime a second Christian invasion of England had taken place. The year before Columba died (596), Pope Gregory the Great dispatched *Augustine* with forty Benedictine monks to England. Hearing terrifying tales of the savagery of the Anglo-Saxons, Augustine turned back in Gaul; but the pope ordered him to continue on his way. Landing in Kent, Augustine and his companions, now reduced to seven, were well received by King Ethelbert, who already had some knowledge of the gospel through his Frankish wife, Bertha, herself a Christian. Ethelbert listened attentively to Augustine, but remained unconvinced. Nevertheless, he gave him liberty to preach the new religion and provided food and lodging for him and his monks in Canterbury. Within a year, in response to the persuasion of his wife, Ethelbert embraced Christianity. Shortly thereafter, in accord with the custom of the times, his parliament adopted the new faith and in a single day ten thousand persons were baptized, Canterbury Cathedral was founded, and Augustine became the first of a long line of distinguished archbishops of Canterbury.

For a time the Celtic and Roman forms of Christianity were in conflict. Under the leadership of *Wilfrid,* Bishop of York (634-709), however, the Roman form prevailed. It remained for Theodore of Tarsus to organize England into a regular ecclesiastical province of Rome, with the authority of the Archbishop of Canterbury extending over the entire country. With the evangelization of the Saxons in Sussex by Wilfrid towards the close of the seventh century, the conversion of England is said to have been completed.

England, in receiving the gospel from the Irish church, imbibed its missionary spirit, and during the next two centuries sent a steady stream of missionaries, many of them outstanding personalities, to evangelize the pagan parts of Europe.

Gaul. Gaul had been evangelized on several previous occasions, but after each effort paganism reasserted itself; so the work had to be undertaken again in the sixth century. *Columban* led the way. He was distinguished for his unusual piety and his knowledge of the Scriptures. After training at the famous monastery of Bangor under Congall, greatest of its masters, he set out at the age of forty with twelve companions for Germany. Stopping short of his ultimate destination, he settled down in Burgundy and established a monastery at Luxeuil. After twenty years of arduous toil, like John the Baptist he incurred the wrath of the court by his outspoken denunciation of immorality in high places. Expelled from Luxeuil, he and his Celtic monks crossed the Rhine and preached the gospel to the wild ancestors of the modern Swiss. Like Martin of Tours, he waged war against paganism with fiery zeal, smashing idols and burning temples, establishing monasteries in their place. Caused to flee a second time, he repaired to northern Italy, where he established his last monastery at Bobbio. It was said of Columban that he was "always learning, always teaching, always wandering, always preaching."

Holland. The first English missionary contact with the people of the Low Countries, known as Frisians, occurred when Bishop Wilfrid stopped off in Frisia on one of his many trips to Rome. He preached with great power and baptized many of the leading men and thousands of the masses.

In 692 the Northumbrian monk, *Willibrord,* who had trained under Wilfrid in Ripon and Egbert in Ireland, and eleven companions crossed the North Sea to become the first missionaries to the Frisians. Supported by the patronage of Pepin, mayor of the palace, and suspected by the weaker Frisians and their king, Radbod, Willibrord labored through forty years of vicissitudes, setting up monasteries at Utrecht, Antwerp, Echternach, and Susteren. During those years his greatest difficulty was not persecution but politics. Not unnaturally, the missionaries were identified by the Frisians with the power-hungry Pepin and his Franks; and Willibrord found himself caught up in the political tensions existing between the two peoples. Nevertheless, on the whole the mission was successful and a strong church was established among the Frisians.

Germany. Christianity came to Germany as the gift of the Irish and English monks. Regarded by many as the greatest missionary of the Dark Ages, *Boniface* (680-754), an English noble and Benedictine monk, went to Germany in middle life. A brilliant missionary career stretching over forty years earned for him the title of the Apostle to Germany. In 722 he was consecrated by Pope Gregory II as bishop of the German frontier without a fixed see. A turning point in his ministry occurred when in a dramatic gesture he dealt a crushing blow to idolatry. Deciding that the time had come for a showdown between the pagan gods and Jehovah, he seized an axe and in the presence of thousands of enraged heathen and terrified half-Christians chopped down the sacred oak of Thor at Geismar in Hesse. When the huge tree crashed to the ground and Boniface was left unscathed, the pagans recognized the superior power of the Christian God and came in droves to be baptized.

A brilliant scholar, a great organizer, and an ardent evangelist, Boniface laid the foundation of the church in Germany. Great monasteries were established at Reichenau (724), Fulda (744), and Lorsch (763). In 741 he was called on to reform the Frankish Church, which had fallen on evil days, harboring in its hierarchy drunkards, adulterers, and even murderers. In this he was only partially successful. In 741 he was made Archbishop of Mainz. Ten years later he presided at the coronation of Pepin when he became king of the Franks.

In his old age the spirit of the pioneer reasserted itself. Leaving Germany, he repaired to a region of Holland where the Frisians were still pagan. Preaching again with great power he won many converts. As so often happens, the non-believers stirred up trouble which led to violence; and on June 5, 755, Boniface and fifty of his companions were killed.

The Saxons. The conversion of the Saxons coincided with the reign of Charlemagne (771-814). It was effected by military conquest rather than moral or religious persuasion. The unholy alliance between the church and the state, which culminated in 800 in the formation of the Holy Roman Empire, prompted the church to employ carnal means to achieve spiritual ends. Nowhere was this policy more disastrous than in the work of Christian missions, especially among the Saxons. This is one of the pages we should gladly remove from church history if we could.

Charlemagne, the first ruler of the Holy Roman Empire which was to endure for a thousand years, was one of the greatest emperors in history. Like many emperors, he was bent on conquest; but in his case he mixed religion with politics, and offered to the barbarian tribes whom he subjugated the comforts of religion as well as the benefits of civilization. "Once· a German tribe had been conquered, its conversion was included in the terms of peace, as the price to be paid for enjoying the protection of the emperor and the good government that his arms ensured."[3]

Alas, the savage Saxons wanted neither Christianity nor civilization. Both had to be imposed by force of arms, and in the process atrocities were committed. On one occasion forty-five hundred Saxon men, women, and children were killed in one day by order of Charlemagne. Villages were burned, crops were destroyed, whole communities were wiped out—all in an effort to impose Christian civilization on a pagan people. Little wonder

---

[3] Stephen Neill, *A History of Christian Missions* (Baltimore: Penguin Books, 1964), p. 79.

that the missionaries won few converts. The Saxons, of course, fought back, using their own brand of cruelty. Quite frequently the missionaries were made the object of attack and not a few were killed; but always there were others who came forward to fill their ranks. Gradually, by patience, pains, and prayer, the missionaries won their way, and the gospel finally prevailed. By the death of Charlemagne the "conversion" of the Saxons was complete.

Scandinavia. The Vikings of Scandinavia were the scourge of England and the Continent during the ninth century. So devastating were their raids on the monasteries and churches that for a time they threatened to terminate the missionary outreach of the English Church. The tide turned only when Alfred the Great won a decisive victory in 878 and forced some thirty leading Vikings to accept Christianity.

About this time intrepid missionaries began invading Denmark, Norway, and Sweden on preaching missions, but with little success. The Scandinavians much preferred their own way of life, including their pagan gods. Consequently the response was small. It took several hundred years for a people's movement to develop; but when it did, it occurred simultaneously in all three countries. For the most part the transition was peaceful; only in Norway was force employed.

Emperor Louis the Pious took an active interest in the spread of the Christian religion into the northern regions. In 823 he dispatched Ebo, Archbishop of Rheims, to Denmark. Without the backing of an army, Ebo achieved little by way of immediate results. Later on, following the conversion of Denmark's King Harald, the emperor sent a second mission, this time under the leadership of the greatest missionary of that period, *Anskar* (801-865), a French monk trained in the famous monastery in Corbie founded by Columba. Owing to the sullen hostility of the people, the results of this mission were limited. Later Anskar, again at the behest of Louis, made two visits to Sweden, one of them at the invitation of King Olaf. On his first journey the ship was seized by pirates and Anskar lost all his possessions. Undaunted, he finally reached Sweden, where he spent eighteen months and led many nobles into the faith. He also built the first church in that land.

On his return King Louis arranged with Pope Gregory IV to make *Anskar* the legate to all the Swedes, Danes, and Slavs of northern Europe. About 832 he was consecrated Archbishop of Hamburg. Immediately Anskar set about making his see the center of a vast network of missionary activity. He summoned monks from his old monastery at Corbie to assist in the training of missionaries to be sent into all parts of Scandinavia. With great perseverance and tact he was able to gain the confidence of King Horic of Denmark, a bitter foe of Christianity, who gave permission for the building of two churches in his realm.

It was Anskar's fate to live in an age when the political fortunes were not conducive to the rapid spread of a new faith. Consequently he did not enjoy anything like the enormous success of Boniface in Germany. Nevertheless, in spite of many handicaps and occasional reverses, including the sack of Hamburg, he managed by patience and perseverance to prepare the way for the ultimate conversion of Scandinavia, where to this day he is venerated as the Apostle of the North.

Denmark.   As we have noticed, Denmark was the first of the Scandinavian countries to receive the gospel. Earliest Christian contacts were with the Hamburg See just over the German border. *Rimbert,* disciple of Anskar, carried on his work in Denmark and Sweden; but the political instability of the times and the weak state of the church rendered missionary work exceedingly difficult. Early in the tenth century King Gorm, a staunch opponent of Christianity, took steps to banish it from Denmark. Churches were destroyed and priests were killed. The tide turned when Henry the Fowler, King of Germany, in 934 subjugated the Danes and compelled one of their rulers to embrace Christianity. Archbishop Unni of Hamburg saw in this event an opportunity to renew the work laid down by Anskar seventy years before. The fortunes of the church in Denmark varied from reign to reign. Under Harald Bluetooth, successor of Gorm, Christianity flourished; under Harald's son, Sweyn, it languished. Christianity was finally established in Denmark under the world famous Canute, Christian king of Denmark and England from 1018 to 1035. Toward the end of the century twelve missionary monks from England went to Denmark at the invitation of the king and there founded monasteries. The missionary phase of Denmark's Christianization came to an end with the establishment of an archbishopric in 1104.

Norway.   The gospel went to Norway not from Denmark but from England. Its introduction was attended by a good deal of violence. The leading agents were not missionaries but kings. King Haakon, who was reared in England, where he became a Christian, was the first to introduce Christianity to Norway. Meeting with rather strong opposition by people and leaders, he proceeded cautiously lest he precipitate a rebellion. He died in 961 without achieving his purpose.

Christianity took root in Norway during the reign and with the active support of Olaf Tryggvason (963-1000). Like his predecessor, Haakon, he spent some time in England and accepted Christianity there. A one-time Viking, "handsome, huge of stature, daring, and fearless," Olaf succeeded where Haakon failed. By an ingenious policy which combined force and favor, he did much to bring Norway closer to Christianity. It remained, however, for his successor, Olaf Haraldson, to administer the *coup de grâce* to paganism and make Christianity the religion of Norway shortly after the turn of the eleventh century.

Sweden. On the occasion of Anskar's second visit to Sweden in 853 the council in Gothenland declared itself in favor of the new religion; but the few missionaries who followed Anskar in Sweden failed to press forward with the vision and vigor necessary to get the new and strange religion established in a hostile environment.

As in the case of Norway, it was from England, and to a lesser degree from Denmark, that the initial thrust of the gospel reached Sweden. By the tenth century there were many English missionaries in the country. Olaf Scotkonung (993-1024) was the first monarch to profess and promote the Christian faith. Unlike the kings of Norway, Olaf eschewed the use of force to make converts. During the long reign of Olaf's son, King Anund Jacob (1024-1066), Christianity spread to all parts of Sweden. With the establishment of the first bishopric at Uppsala in 1164, Sweden became a nominally Christian country.

Eastern European Countries. As we move into this part of the world we are reminded of the fact that Christianity for many centuries had been flowing in two great streams, one emanating from Rome and the other from Constantinople. We are familiar with the former; we need to take a closer look at the latter.

> It flows mainly from Constantinople, not from Rome. Its mother language in its Bible, and in its worship services is Greek, not Latin. It is more interested in abstract theology and less in its practical application than the western arm of the church; it can claim fewer missionary conquests. The heads of the eastern church, called patriarchs, were generally controlled by the emperor in Constantinople, the emperor being the head of the eastern church, as the pope was the head of the western branch. The civilization that grew up in connection with the eastern church was called Byzantine, because Byzantium was the earlier name of the city that the emperor Constantine later named Constantinople after himself.[4]

From the time of Mohammed to the fall of Constantinople (1453) the great Byzantine Empire was a bulwark against the inroads of Islam in eastern Europe. Byzantine influence ebbed and flowed, as the influence of all empires does; but "even in its worst days, Constantinople was by far the greatest and most civilized city of the Christian world."[5]

Moravia. During the tenth century, when the Byzantine Empire underwent a renaissance, the Eastern Church began to take an interest in the non-Christians to the north. The first people to attract attention were the Slavs, and the first missionaries to go were *Constantine* and *Methodius*. These two brothers, one a philosopher and the other an artist, were sent to Moravia (now part of Czechoslovakia) at the request of Ratislav, a prince of Moravia, by the patriarch of Constantinople. The request, though

---

[4] Basil Mathews, *Forward Through the Ages* (New York: Friendship Press, 1960), p. 50.

[5] Stephen Neill, *op. cit.*, p. 83.

politically inspired, provided an opportunity to extend the Christian faith into virgin territory. Constantine, a teacher by training, laid the foundation of Slavic culture by reducing the language to writing and translating the Gospels and the liturgy. The use of the vernacular in worship, a practice encouraged by Constantinople but condemned by Rome, was a new departure and established a precedent which came to full bloom in the modern missionary enterprise of the nineteenth and twentieth centuries.

The pope in Rome tried to bring their work under his jurisdiction. Several visits to Rome took place; and Constantine died there in 869. Returning north by himself, Methodius completed the translation of the entire Bible into Slavic. During these years he kept in touch with the pope, who alternately condemned and condoned the use of the vernacular.

To add to his troubles the German clergy, who regarded him as an intruder into what they considered to be their ecclesiastical domain, were relentless in their opposition to the Byzantine missionary and his Slavic literature. On one occasion they imprisoned him for three years in a monastery in Swabia. After his death in 885 the Christian communities in Moravia fell on evil days. Driven out of Moravia, his disciples carried the gospel to Bulgaria, where the prevailing climate was more conducive to the development of an indigenous Christian culture.

The Bulgars.   The conversion of the Bulgars was greatly accelerated by the baptism of King Boris in 865. Shortly thereafter he established a monastery, which became a radiating center of Slavic Christian culture. He sent his son Simeon to Constantinople to be educated as a monk. Later, he dispatched a famous missionary, *Clement,* to Macedonia, where he founded a missionary training college. By the time of his death (907) the Bulgars had become the Christian leaders of the Slavic world. His son, King Simeon, made history when he persuaded his bishops to declare the Bulgarian church self-governing and to elect a patriarch as its head. From Bulgaria the Christian faith spread to what is now Yugoslavia and Russia.

Though much of their work was swept away, Constantine and Methodius "can be regarded without question as the first authors of the great Slavonic Christian culture which still persists in the world today."[6] K. S. Latourette states that they "deserve to be ranked among the greatest of Christian missionaries."[7]

Russia.   Two attempts were made to introduce Christianity into Russia. Both were abortive. The first occurred about the middle of the ninth century when Patriarch Photius sent an unsuccessful mission to the court of Kiev. A century later Princess Olga, after being baptized with

6 *Ibid.,* p. 88.

7 K. S. Latourette, *The Thousand Years of Uncertainty* (New York: Harper and Brothers, 1938), p. 166.

great pomp in Constantinople, tried to introduce Christianity into her realm; but she met with stubborn opposition from her nobles. It was under her grandson, Vladimir (980-1015), that Christianity took permanent hold in Russia. Before making up his mind Vladimir examined various religions. At one point he was deeply interested in Islam; but he finally decided in favor of Christianity. His marriage to the sister of the Greek emperor served to confirm his confession of the new faith. At the same time it provided legal grounds for Russia's claim to be the successor of the Byzantine Empire.

Poland. It is not known exactly when Christianity first reached Poland. The early agents were Slavs and Germans. The establishment of Christianity in Poland paralleled the development of the monarchy in the tenth and eleventh centuries. It began with the conversion of Duke Mieszka, whose baptism in 966 may have been prompted by the persuasion of his Christian wife, Dobrawa, sister of the king of Bohemia.

During the reign of his son, Boleslaw (992-1025), Poland became the largest kingdom in eastern Europe. Owing to Boleslaw's active support of the Christian cause, the fortunes of the church prospered along with those of the state. During his reign Christianity experienced rapid growth; but following his death both the political and the ecclesiastical power structures fell apart. A period of severe persecution ensued, during which churches and monasteries were destroyed and the clergy driven out. Under Boleslaw III (1102-1139) a measure of political stability and ecclesiastical order was restored to Poland. Missionary work was resumed and a large number of Pomeranians embraced the faith.

Space forbids any treatment of the conversion of such peoples as the Magyars, Wends, Prussians, and others. Suffice it to say that by 1200 almost the whole of Europe was nominally Christian. Bishop Stephen Neill succinctly describes the conditions under which Christianity won its way in Europe during this seven hundred-year period.

> The record in place after place tends to be much the same. The first bishop is martyred by the savage tribes; his blood then appropriately forms the seed of the Church. Initial successes are followed by pagan reactions; but the Church comes in again under the aegis of deeply converted rulers, with whom one or more outstanding bishops are able to work in harmony. The initial Christianity is inevitably very superficial; but this is in each case followed by a long period of building, in which the faith becomes part of the inheritance of the people. Political alliances, frequently cemented by marriages, form a large part of the picture; and as in the cases of Clovis and of Ethelbert of Kent, the influence of Christian queens seems to have played a notable part in the work of conversion.[8]

---

[8] Stephen Neill, *op. cit.*, p. 90.

III

Encounter with Islam:
A.D. 600-1200

"The explosion of the Arabian peninsula into the conquest and conversion of half the Mediterranean world is the most extraordinary phenomenon in medieval history."[1] So says Will Durant. Certainly, the greatest threat ever faced by the Christian church came from the sudden rise and rapid spread of Islam in the seventh century. A militant, missionary religion, Islam remains to this day Christianity's most dangerous rival.

The founder of Islam, Mohammed, was born in 570 in Mecca, an important caravan town strategically located on the main trade route between India and Egypt. He was an illiterate member of the Quraish, the ruling tribe in Mecca. At the age of forty he saw a vision that was to change the face of the world and make him the most important figure in medieval history. The angel Gabriel is said to have appeared to him and summoned him to his life's work with the words: "O Mohammed! thou art the messenger of Allah, and I am Gabriel." Thereupon Mohammed began preaching to the people of Mecca and to the pilgrims who gathered there, calling them to a new morality and a monotheistic faith. Persecution broke out and Mohammed fled from Mecca to Medina in 622. Known as the *Hejira,* this event marks the beginning of the Muslim calendar.

After his death in 632 his followers conquered and unified the warring tribes of Arabia, and in the flush of easy and rapid victory went out on their mission of conquest and conversion.

With lightning speed they conquered Damascus (635), Antioch (636), Jerusalem (638), Caesarea (640), and Alexandria (642). By 650 the Persian

---

[1] Will Durant, *The Age of Faith* (New York: Simon and Schuster, 1950), p. 155.

Empire had been destroyed. Across North Africa they swept, meeting little or no resistance. The Christian stronghold of Carthage fell in 697. By 715 the greater part of Spain was in Muslim hands. Crossing the Pyrenees and penetrating into France, they were stopped by Charles Martel in 732 at the Battle of Tours—one of the most decisive battles of history. About the same time the Arabs entered the Punjab in India and advanced far into Central Asia.

Following the eighth century there was a five hundred-year period of stalemate. During this time the Seljuk Turks, earlier evangelized by the Nestorians, became Muslims and occupied large areas of Asia Minor. It was against these intruders that the Crusades were launched. Certain areas in Syria and the Holy Land were regained, but on the whole the Crusades were a failure.

A second tide of Muslim conquest occurred in the thirteenth and fourteenth centuries. The Ottoman Turks and the Mongols of Central Asia became fierce and fanatical followers of the prophet and went on the rampage, pillaging and destroying everything in their path. By the fifteenth century the Ottoman Turks had invaded Greece and the Balkans. Constantinople fell in 1453. At this time the Moors were retreating in Spain, giving up Alhambra, their last stronghold, in 1492.

To consolidate their power, the Arabs established the Umayyad Caliphate in Damascus (661-750) and the Abbaside Caliphate in Baghdad (750-1058). It should be noted that while Europe was in the darkest period of the Dark Ages, Arab civilization was at its height. When the lights were going out all over "Christian" Europe, it could be said of Damascus that "if a man were to sojourn here a hundred years, and pondered each day on what he saw, he would see something new every day."[2] Baghdad boasted twenty-six public libraries and countless private ones. "Princes like Sahib ibn Abbas in the tenth century might own as many books as could then be found in all the libraries of Europe combined."[3]

It is generally believed that the Muslims in their conquests gave their victims a choice between the Koran and the sword. This is not correct. Christians and Jews were regarded by Mohammed as "the people of the book" and were accorded a special status—dhimmis, or "protected people." They were allowed to continue the practice of their religion, under certain restrictions, provided they rendered to the new Caesar the things that belonged to him, particularly a heavier form of taxation. Even in Baghdad, right under the nose of the Caliphate, there was a large Christian community with churches, monasteries, and schools.

In Egypt and Syria non-Catholic Christians fared better than they had under the Byzantine rulers, who were not averse to using pressure to

---

[2] *Ibid.*, p. 231.
[3] *Ibid.*, p. 237.

propagate the Catholic form of the faith. Likewise, the Nestorians in Persia were better off under the Arabs than they had been under the Zoroastrian rulers. The Arab conquerors, recognizing the administrative skill of the Christians, used some of them in political office. The Christians in turn shared the Greek civilization with their new rulers, translating into Arabic the classical writings of Greece.

They did, of course, suffer various forms of discrimination, which reduced them to second-class citizenship. They were required to wear a colored patch on their clothing as a mark of inferiority, much like the Jews in Nazi Germany. Intermarriage with Muslims was outlawed. In the political life of the country they could rise only so high; beyond that they could not go. They were allowed to continue the practice of their religion, but with certain well-defined restrictions. They could not build new churches; nor could they ring church bells. They could perform their worship within the quiet precincts of their own buildings, but they could not propagate their faith in the community. Conversion was a one-way street; one could convert from Judaism or Christianity to Islam, but not from Islam to Christianity. To do so was to become an apostate from the faith and a traitor to the cause. To be an Arab was to be a Muslim. To become a Christian was to cease to be both. Moreover, the Law of Apostasy, still in force in Islam, permitted the community to kill any member who defected from the faith. The Law is not always followed, but it is there and it acts as a strong deterrent. To initiate a Muslim into the Christian faith by baptism is almost certain to precipitate a communal riot in most Muslim countries. The Muslims of Iran belong to the Shi-ites and are, therefore, more tolerant than the Sunnis. Indonesia, where the government insists on a genuine form of religious freedom, is the one Muslim country in the world where Muslims in large numbers have embraced the Christian faith. In recent years a mass movement toward Christianity has taken place, involving some several million persons, many of them Muslims.

The only major faith younger than Christianity, Islam has become a world religion, second only to Christianity in its missionary zeal and worldwide outreach. Indeed, in some parts of Africa it is making converts faster than is Christianity.

It was in North Africa in the seventh century that the Christian church suffered its greatest losses. Besides being strong in numbers, the church of North Africa produced three of the greatest leaders and theologians of the early church: *Tertullian,* the brilliant defender of the faith, in the second century; *Cyprian,* the energetic builder of the church, in the third century; and *Augustine,* the greatest theologian since Paul, in the fourth century. Under this great intellectual and spiritual giant the church in North Africa, comprising some five hundred dioceses (one-fourth of all Christendom), had a better educated clergy and exercised greater ecclesiastical power than did the churches of Alexandria or Rome.

How shall we account for the demise of such a church? Doubtless there were many contributing factors of a social or political nature. Some of the Christians, not wishing to live under alien rule, emigrated to Europe. Such an exodus naturally weakened the church. Among those who remained were many who, deciding that discretion was the better part of valor, threw in their lot with the new rulers, embracing their faith and supporting their rule. Others saw in the swift and devastating military victories of the Muslims the hand of God in human affairs and decided not to fight against Him. Some undoubtedly were impressed with the claims of Islam as a later and therefore higher revelation of God. Still others preferred the protection and prestige that come from identification with the paramount power. But all of these factors combined hardly account for the disappearance of so strong a church in so short a time.

The real reason for the disappearance of the church in North Africa must be sought elsewhere. Actually, the church was not so strong as it appeared. Numerically it was large, but spiritually it was weak. To begin with, it had never become truly indigenous. It was too closely identified with Latin culture and Roman power. The congregations were composed mostly of Latin-speaking people in and around Carthage. Few of the Punic people ever embraced the Christian faith, and the Berbers were left untouched. Because of this the church never took root in the native soil. A second reason was the failure to give the Scriptures to the people in their own tongue. They were available in Latin, but no translations were ever made into the language of the Punic people or the Berbers.

Moreover, theological controversies had sapped the energies of the church. Before the time of Augustine the church had been racked by the Donatist controversy. Theologians, instead of closing their ranks and presenting a united front to the common enemy, were preoccupied with fratricidal warfare. They were more interested in defending the purity of the gospel than in demonstrating its power.

Another factor was the loss of evangelical faith and fervor among the Christians. With the passing of time the Christian gospel was gradually smothered under a growing sacramental system accompanied by sacerdotal control. Church members had long since left their first love and were Christians in name rather than fact. Consequently when the Muslim hordes swept across North Africa, the Christian church had neither the will nor the power to resist. In a few short decades it disappeared, leaving hardly a trace of its former glory.

The Crusades

The second major encounter between Christianity and Islam came with the Crusades in the twelfth and thirteenth centuries. There are two black pages in the history of the church and its relations with other peoples: one, the long-standing, almost universal, persecution of the Jews; the other, the Crusades against the Muslims.

There were seven Crusades in all, occurring at intervals between 1095 and 1272. Organized and abetted by different leaders, among them Peter the Hermit, Bernard of Clairvaux, and Richard the Lion-Hearted of England, they had the sanction and support of the Roman Catholic Church, at least in the early stages.

As usual in any great undertaking involving many diverse peoples, the motives were mixed. There were economic, political, and even personal factors. The strongest motives, however, were religious; and it is with these that we are chiefly concerned.

First there was the almost universal desire on the part of the Western church to wrest from the Seljuk Turks the sacred places in Palestine, especially the Holy City of Jerusalem. The Arabs had been in control of Palestine since the seventh century. Their continued presence there not only affronted the Christian church; it also rendered difficult, if not dangerous, Christian pilgrimages to the Holy Land.

Then there was the eagerness of the Roman Catholic Church to assist the Byzantine Empire, centered on Constantinople, to resist the inroads of the Turks. In the eleventh century the Byzantine Empire fell on evil days. The decline began in 1025 with the death of Emperor Basil II and worsened in 1056 when the Macedonian dynasty came to an end. Internal dissensions and foreign aggression threatened the existence of the state. The greatest threat came from the Seljuk Turks. Originally from Central Asia, and converts to Islam, in the eleventh century they built an empire which included Persia, Mesopotamia, Syria, Egypt, and Palestine. They fought their way into Asia Minor and in 1071 inflicted a stunning defeat on the Byzantine army at Lake Van in Armenia. Under such conditions it was only natural that the Byzantine emperors should look for help to their Christian brethren in the West; and the popes in Rome were happy to lend assistance.

In the third place, there was an admirable desire on the part of the Roman See to heal the breach between the Eastern and Western branches of the church and thus restore Christian unity. During the tenth and eleventh centuries relations between Rome and Constantinople had deteriorated. In 1054 the Patriarch of Constantinople was excommunicated by Pope Leo IX. The Crusades afforded an excellent opportunity to heal the rift.

So far as the primary objectives were concerned, the Crusades were a failure. The holy places, liberated at such cost in blood and treasure, were held for only one hundred fifty years, after which they reverted to Muslim control. Not only were the Crusaders ejected; but Islam, under the Ottoman Turks, was carried across the Balkans in the fourteenth and fifteenth centuries and to the gates of Vienna in the sixteenth century.

Instead of strengthening the Byzantine Empire against the onslaughts of Islam, the Crusades served only to weaken it. In fact, Constantinople suffered greater damage at the hands of the Crusaders than it did when it fell to the Turks in 1453.

As for healing the breach between the Eastern and Western branches of the church, the Crusades succeeded only in widening it still further.

There were, however, some lasting benefits. Through the Crusades Europe was introduced to the more advanced civilization of the East. While Europe was in the eclipse of the Dark Ages, Arab civilization, based on Baghdad, shed its light and luster over the entire Middle East. During the Crusades Arab civilization proved itself superior to Christian civilization in the arts, education, and war. Hundreds of Arab terms found their way into the languages of Europe. Printing, gunpowder, and the compass all came from the East in the wake of the Crusades. The arts, sciences, and inventions of both Greek and Saracen were introduced to Europe by the Crusaders.

The Crusades also acted as a stimulus to travel by land and sea and to the expansion of maritime trade. The knights lost the Holy Land, but the merchants gained control of the Mediterranean. European cities came to life and commerce flourished. Items which had been luxuries now became articles of common trade: spices, sugar, textiles, fruits, scents, gems, and others. "The Crusades had begun with an agricultural feudalism inspired by German barbarism crossed with religious sentiment; they ended with the rise of industry and the expansion of commerce, in an economic revolution that heralded and financed the Renaissance."[4]

The Effects of the Crusades on Christianity

The most calamitous result of the Crusades was the alienation of the entire Muslim world. The fact that the Christian church would resort to war to regain the holy places of Palestine was itself a denial of its own religion. Once the victim of Muslim aggression, it now became an aggressor. Such a course of action was a denial of the teaching of Christ and contrary to the practice of the early church.

Moreover, the atrocities committed by the Crusaders in the name of Christ left an indelible scar on the Muslim mind. When Jerusalem was liberated in 1099 the Crusaders, not content with wiping out the one thousand-man garrison, proceeded to massacre some seventy thousand Muslims. The surviving Jews were herded into a synagogue and burned alive. The Crusaders then repaired to the Church of the Holy Sepulchre, where they publicly gave thanks to Almighty God for a resounding victory.

---

[4] *Ibid.,* p. 613.

In Christendom the Crusades have largely been forgotten, but their sordid memory festers to this day in the minds of the Muslims of the Middle East. The hate engendered at that time has not been dissipated even after nine hundred years. Christianity's reputation for cruelty and revenge is a millstone around the neck of the Christian missionary in the Middle East.

IV

Roman Catholic Missions:
A.D. 1300-1700

The Roman Catholic Church is by far the oldest, largest, and most influential organization in the world. Its half billion members are to be found in practically every country of the globe. Throughout its long history it has known periods of expansion and recession. At the zenith of its power, during the Holy Roman Empire, it completely dominated the political, cultural, economic, and religious life of Europe. Its greatest losses occurred at the time of the Protestant Reformation, when large sections of Europe broke away from the Roman Catholic Church. What the Church of Rome lost in Europe, however, she regained through her missionary endeavors in Asia, Africa, and the New World during the next few centuries. While the Protestant churches of Europe were consolidating their gains in that continent, the Roman Catholic Church went out to conquer the non-Christian portions of the world.

The development of Roman Catholic missions coincided with the expansion of the overseas empires of Portugal and Spain. Franciscan missionaries accompanied the Portuguese expeditions to Madeira (1420), the Azores (1431), and the Cape Verde Islands (1450). Trinitarian missionaries sailed with Vasco da Gama to India in 1498. Franciscans arrived in Brazil with Cabral in 1500. Iberian kings, no less than the Roman popes, were zealous for the conversion of the heathen. In 1537 Pope Paul III ordered that the Indians of the New World be brought to Christ "by the preaching of the divine word, and with the example of the good life." Ferdinand and Isabella issued a royal order stating: "Nothing do we desire more than the publication and the amplification of the Evangelic Law, and the conversion of the Indians to our Holy Catholic Faith."

As early as 1454 Pope Nicholas V granted to Portugal exclusive patronage privileges in Africa and the East Indies. With Spain's incursion into the New World, Portugal's monopoly on world exploration was broken. To avoid rivalry between the two Iberian powers, Pope Alexander VI in 1493 issued a Demarcation Bull which divided the world into two spheres of influence. Portugal was to retain all the patronage privileges in Africa and the East Indies, while Spain was to enjoy similar privileges in the New World. (The following year Brazil, discovered by Cabral, was transferred to Portugal.) In return for these extensive privileges, the kings of Portugal and Spain were to be responsible for the spread of the faith and the conversion of the heathen in their overseas dominions. Ecclesiastical appointments were to be made by the civil authorities. All expenses were to be borne by the state. This system, known as the *Patronato*, meant that the missionaries had as big a stake in the explorations as the merchants.

As time went on and Catholic missions extended to all parts of the world, it became apparent that the patronage system was not altogether satisfactory. To correct its weaknesses, Pope Gregory XV in 1622 founded the Sacred Congregation for the Propagation of the Faith. Through it the Holy See was able to direct more closely the conversion of the heathen overseas and to effect the restoration of the heretics at home. In 1628 a central seminary in Rome, the College of Propaganda, was established to train native clergy from all parts of the mission world.

On the whole the civil authorities of Portugal and Spain took their Christian responsibilities seriously.

> Beginning with Columbus and Vasco da Gama, all the Spanish and Portuguese explorers regarded their expeditions as likewise crusades and missionary voyages, for the purpose of seeking Christians (as well as spices) and of opposing the unbelievers with fire and sword if they rejected the Christian law which the missionaries first preached with the spiritual sword.[1]

The Roman Catholic Church was fortunate in having at its command scores of religious orders whose dedicated members were trained and ready for any kind of service. Their vows of obedience and celibacy provided the two most desirable qualities for pioneer missionary work, servility and mobility. Their communal life, characterized by austerity, was an ideal preparation for the rigors of the missionary vocation. When, therefore, the church decided to carry its message to the heathen world, it had no need to call for volunteers. By royal decree or papal command it could, with the greatest of ease, deploy its army of servants to any part of the habitable globe.

Four orders in particular were called upon to share the burden and the glory of the missionary enterprise: the Franciscans, founded by Francis of

---

[1] Joseph Schmidlin, *Catholic Mission History* (Techny, Ill.: Divine Word Mission Press, 1933), p. 264.

Assisi (1182-1226); the Dominicans, founded by a Spanish priest, Dominic (1170-1221); the Augustinians, organized by Pope Alexander IV in 1256; and the Jesuits, founded in 1540 by a Spanish nobleman, Ignatius Loyola.

Additional missionary orders were founded during the eighteenth and nineteenth centuries, among them the Passionists (1720), the Redemptorists (1732), the Holy Ghost Fathers (1841), the White Fathers (1866), and the Divine Word Fathers (1875). The famous Maryknoll Fathers, an American mission, was established in 1911 and sent its first missionaries to South China in 1918.

Naturally, the Catholic countries of Europe supplied the greatest number of missionaries. In the early decades they came largely from Portugal and Spain, the two great colonizing powers of that period. Italy and France contributed their quota, as did Germany and Ireland. Until recent years comparatively few Catholic missionaries came from the United States.

In the long course of history Roman Catholic missions have encountered their full share of opposition and persecution. Sometimes the losses were inflicted by Protestant powers, as when the Dutch seized Ceylon (1658) and the British annexed Canada (1793). The American occupation of the Philippines in 1898 ended the Roman Catholic monopoly, but did not greatly interfere with Roman Catholic missions, in that country. At other times they were driven out by non-Christian rulers, who feared that the new religion would either undermine the local regime or destroy the indigenous culture, as was the case in China (1368), Japan (1614), and Korea (1864). In other countries Roman Catholic missions suffered at the hands of Catholic civil authorities, as in South America, where many Franciscan missions were closed during the wars of independence in 1811 and 1812.

Of all the religious orders, none has had a more turbulent history than the Society of Jesus. Wherever the Jesuits went they seemed to stir up trouble. So intolerable were their actions that they were persecuted even in Catholic countries. About the middle of the eighteenth century they were expelled from most of the countries of South America and the Philippines. So strong was the opposition that the Society was dissolved by Clement XIV in 1773. Even after its restoration forty years later, the Jesuits were expelled again from various Catholic countries of Europe.

With such a vast network of religious orders in all parts of the world, it was necessary for the Roman Catholic Church to work out some system of comity to avoid duplication, to say nothing of competition. Consequently, certain orders were assigned to certain countries. In the East the Paris Foreign Missions Society was responsible for Siam, Tibet, and Burma; the Dominicans for Formosa; and the Missioners of the Sacred Heart for Melanesia. In the larger countries, such as India, China, and Japan, most of the major and many of the minor orders were to be found. There prudence dictated that the various orders be assigned to different parts of the country. For example, in China the Dominicans worked in Fukien and the Divine Word Missioners concentrated on Shantung.

China

Roman Catholic missions outside of Europe may be said to have begun about 1294 with the arrival in China of the Franciscan friar, *John of Monte Corvino.* Friar John had labored with marked success in Persia before being sent by the pope on his historic mission to the oldest and greatest empire of the East.

Strangely enough, opposition came not from the Chinese but from the few remaining Nestorians, survivors of the Nestorian Church that flourished in China for two hundred years during the T'ang dynasty. By spreading vicious tales about the Roman Catholics, they hoped to stir up animosity against the newcomers. Nevertheless, John won the confidence of the Chinese emperor, built a church in Peking, and baptized thousands of converts. For eleven years he labored alone, devoting special care to the training of 150 Chinese seminarians. Later he was appointed first archbishop of Peking by Pope Clement V.

The Roman Catholic faith spread down the coast until it reached Fukien, some 800 miles south of Peking. When John died in 1330 there were about one hundred thousand converts in China. All this took place under the patronage and protection of the Mongol rulers of China. When in 1368 the Chinese again became masters in their own house, the Ming rulers expelled the missionaries and Christianity died out.

Two hundred years later a second attempt was made to plant Roman Catholicism in China. The leader this time was *Matteo Ricci* (1552-1610) of the Society of Jesus. Using the Portuguese colony of Macao as a jumping-off place, Ricci reached Peking after a long and arduous overland trek stretching over twenty years.

To win the favor of the Chinese, Ricci adopted their culture and appeared in the guise of a Confucian scholar. By presenting European time-pieces to local officials he gained permission to travel northward, founding mission stations in Kwangtung, Nanchang, and Nanking. Because of the Western gifts sent by Ricci to Emperor Wan Li, he was allowed to enter the capital in 1601. There Ricci and his companions acted as the emperor's official clock-winders. Intellectuals flocked to converse with the great scholar from the West. Many of them became converts. Through Ricci's influence in Peking, other Jesuits were permitted to travel and reside in various parts of the vast empire. By 1650 there were a quarter of a million converts.

Later missionaries, Franciscans and Dominicans, quarreled with the Jesuits, accusing them of compromising with heathen practices in the concessions they made to Confucianism. Particularly vexatious was the controversy regarding the term for God. The Jesuits favored *T'ien* (Heaven, or Providence), used by Confucius. The matter was referred to Rome and the pope decided on *T'ien Chu* (Heavenly Lord). The emperor took offense, and shortly after 1700 he declared that all missionaries must follow the lines laid down by Ricci and the Jesuits or leave the country. Many missionaries, including four bishops, complied. All others were expelled. In 1724, and again in 1736, edicts of persecution were issued against the Christian church. Once more Christianity suffered a major setback in China.

Japan

Regarded by many as the greatest Roman Catholic missionary of all time, *Francis Xavier* in 1540 launched the missionary work of the Society of Jesus, which was destined to become the largest and most effective missionary agency of the church. On May 6, 1542, he landed at Goa, then a Portuguese colony on the west coast of India. After three busy years in South India, during which he won thousands of converts, he made his way to the Malay Peninsula and the adjoining islands, where he spent another three years. Consumed with a holy passion "for the greater glory of God," his restless spirit would not allow him to remain long in one place. In 1549, with two other Jesuits, and a Japanese convert as interpreter, he set out for the Land of the Rising Sun, whose people, he said, were "the delight of his soul." During his two years in Japan he traveled widely, teaching, preaching, and administering the sacraments. Other Jesuits followed him and continued the work.

The chaotic political conditions prevailing at the time, together with a decadent Shintoism and a degenerate Buddhism, created a favorable climate for the Christian faith, which bore rapid and abundant fruit. By 1581 there were 200 churches and 150,000 professing Christians. They came from all classes: Buddhist monks, Shinto priests, scholars, samurai, and the common people. Two daimyos embraced Christianity and ordered their subjects to do the same or go into exile. Nobunaga, the Minister of the Mikado, gave moral support to the new religion, albeit from ulterior motives. By the turn of the century Christian converts numbered half a million.

With the assassination of Nobunaga, the Christian mission fell on evil days. The new leaders, Hideyoshi and Iyeyasu, were suspicious of the political intentions of the Jesuits and turned against the Catholic faith. Nor was the cause of Christ helped by the quarreling between the Jesuits on the one hand and the Franciscans and Dominicans on the other. Following the anti-Christian edicts of 1606 and 1614, all foreign missioners were expelled and the Japanese Christians were called upon to recant or face death. The persecutions which followed were as barbaric as any in the history of the Christian mission. Finally, in 1638, some thirty-seven thousand Christians made a last desperate stand in the old castle of Shimabara. After four months of heroic but futile resistance they surrendered, only to become the victims of wholesale slaughter. For 230 years Japan remained a hermit nation, effectively sealed off from contact with the rest of the world.

The Philippines

The Philippine Islands were discovered by Magellan on his fateful voyage around the world in 1521. Systematic missionary work began with *Father Legaspi* and the Augustinians in 1564. They were followed by the Franciscans (1577), the Dominicans (1587), and the Jesuits (1591), all of whom taught the semi-savage islanders Christianity and the arts of civilization. The women were raised from practical slavery to virtual emancipation by the introduction of the Christian concept of the family. Today almost 85 percent of the Filipinos are professing Christians. Some of the credit for this amazing achievement goes to Philip II of Spain, who made the spread of the faith the chief aim of the colonization of the distant islands named after him.

With a full complement of missionary teachers, preachers, and doctors, the Catholic mission was able to make a significant impact in the islands. Churches, hospitals, and schools soon came into being. A college for girls was established as early as 1593. In Manila the Jesuit College of San Jose, founded in 1601, was a national center of learning. The Dominican College of Santo Tomas, opened ten years later, became a pontifical university. Within a century of the discovery of the Philippine Islands the missionaries had baptized some two million persons. An indigenous clergy was gradually developed and by 1800 Filipinos had been raised to the episcopate.

To the Roman Catholic Church must go the credit for stopping the spread of Islam from Indonesia through the archipelago. The Muslims advanced from the south; the Roman Catholics from the north. They met on the island of Mindanao, where today there are 1.5 million Muslims, known as Moros.

The Roman Catholic faith achieved one of its greatest successes in the Philippines. There are several reasons for this. The Jesuits established a good educational system throughout the islands. They allowed the converts to retain many of their religious beliefs and practices. The Spanish intermarried with the local people, thus eliminating the color bar and producing a composite culture. Added to this is the fact that Spain was able to maintain political and economic control of the islands for an unbroken period of almost four centuries. During this time the church was unhindered in carrying out the progressive Christianization of the islands.

Indochina

The pioneer missionary in this part of Southeast Asia was a French Jesuit Father, *Alexander de Rhodes* (1591-1660). He mastered the Annamese language and introduced Christianity to the educated and influential classes. Among his early converts were two hundred Buddhist priests, a number of whom entered his catechetical school. Besides theology, Father Rhodes taught the catechists how to care for the sick so that they might have ready access to the homes of the people. Success attended his methods. In a comparatively short time 300,000 converts were made. On his return to France he was instrumental in establishing the Paris Foreign Missions Society in 1658. Later on, when France annexed Indochina, her colonial administrators found it advantageous to have French priests and the Catholic Church on hand to help them. Until 1911, when the Christian and Missionary Alliance was permitted to enter the country, the Roman Catholics were the only missionaries admitted to the French colony. After the Philippines, Vietnam is the most Christian country in Asia. In South Vietnam there are four million Roman Catholics, eight hundred thousand of whom are refugees from North Vietnam.

India

A new era began when Vasco da Gama rounded the Cape of Good Hope and discovered a sea route to India in 1498. The Franciscan priests who accompanied him launched the missionary program of the Catholic Church in that part of Asia.

The Muslim Moguls and the Portuguese explorers arrived in India about the same time. Several factors combined to give the Muslims the advantage over the Catholics in the winning of converts. The Portuguese, interested primarily in trade, were content with several small colonies on the west coast; whereas the Moguls, bent on political conquest, overran the greater part of the subcontinent. The profligate lives of the Portuguese merchants scandalized the Indian population and brought Christianity into disrepute. The rigid caste system of Hinduism constituted an almost insuperable obstacle to the acceptance of the new religion. Portugal's sensitive defense of her right of patronage seriously hampered the work of all non-Portuguese missionaries. Under these circumstances it is not surprising that Islam won many more converts than Christianity.

While all the great religious orders were represented in India, it was the Jesuits who made the greatest impact. As already noted, *Francis Xavier,* the first Jesuit missionary, spent three years in India in the 1540's. A generation later, Christianity excited the intellectual curiosity of Emperor Akbar, the most illustrious of the Mogul rulers of northern India. In

1579 he invited missionaries to the splendid court of the Peacock Throne. *Father Rudolf Acquaviva* (1550-1583) was chosen to head the mission band. Akbar was strongly attracted to the Jesuit leader and frequently engaged him in religious discussion. When, however, he refused to become a Christian, the Jesuits were recalled to Goa. Soon afterward Acquaviva was murdered by fanatical Hindus. When Akbar heard of the death of his friend, he wept bitterly. In the 1590's the Jesuits returned to the Mogul court and were warmly received by the emperor, who issued a decree permitting his subjects to embrace Christianity. For a time the Jesuit mission received subsidies from the court. A Christian church was erected at Lahore, but the number of converts was never very large.

The most famous of all Roman Catholic missionaries to India was *Father Robert de Nobili,* an Italian Jesuit of noble birth who reached Goa in 1605. The following year he took up residence at Madura in the south, where hitherto very few converts had been won. De Nobili discovered that the cultural barrier between East and West was a stumbling block. The Indians despised the Europeans because they ate meat and drank wine. Posing as a Roman Brahmin, he adopted the Indian way of life, including food and dress. He gave himself to the study of the Hindu Scriptures and acquired a reputation as a European holy man. Soon the Hindus were flocking to his door. For forty-two years he labored among the upper classes, making thousands of converts. After his death his colleagues carried on in the tradition set by de Nobili. By the close of the seventeenth century there were 150,000 Christians in the Madura mission.

The New World

The discovery of America had religious as well as economic and political motivation. Ferdinand and Isabella were both genuinely concerned for the Christianization of the natives. It is not surprising, therefore, that Columbus, known as "Christbearer" as well as "Colonizer," should have raised crosses wherever he went in the New World. On his second voyage he included in his company a group of priests as well as a doctor and a surgeon.

The first missionaries to the New World were Franciscans and Dominicans. The former arrived in Brazil with Cabral in 1500, in Haiti two years later, and in Mexico in 1523. The Dominicans began their missionary work in Haiti in 1510, in Cuba in 1512, in Colombia in 1531 and in Peru in 1532. They were joined by the Augustinians at an early date. In 1549 the Jesuits began to arrive in Brazil. By 1555, in the wake of the explorers and conquistadors, Roman Catholic missionaries had taken Christianity to the West Indies, Mexico, Central America, Colombia, Venezuela, Ecuador, Peru, Chile, and Brazil.

The treatment meted out to the red man by the Spaniards was so cruel that the native population in the West Indies disappeared completely and Negro slaves from Africa were brought in to take their place. The only voice raised against this form of genocide was that of the friars. Most famous of these was *Father Bartholomew de Las Casas* (1474-1566), a Dominican missioner, who made seven voyages to Spain to plead the cause of the oppressed Indians.

Strangely enough, the Spanish kings, who were so solicitous for the red man, were not disturbed by the gigantic slave trade between Africa and the New World. During the seventeenth century one thousand slaves landed each month at Cartagena for distribution among the Spanish-American colonies. For three centuries the evil traffic continued unabated, during which time, it is estimated, Brazil alone received between six and eight million slaves for the sugar plantations.

Conditions aboard the slave ships were incredibly bad. Half the human cargo died at sea. Jesuit missionaries ministered to the survivors on their arrival at Cartagena, feeding them, cleaning their sores, telling them of Christ, and baptizing those near death. The most outstanding of these was *St. Peter Claver* (1581-1654), who labored among the slaves for forty-four years. He instructed and baptized 300,000 black people. Pope Leo XIII made him the patron of all missionary work among Negroes throughout the world.

The Spanish conquest of the New World fell into three stages. During the first stage the padres with the armies checked and rebuked the excesses of the rough soldiers in their treatment of the Indians. In the second, or frontier, stage the priests founded mission settlements, known as reductions, to facilitate the Christianization of the Indians. These reductions were under the control of the religious orders. They varied in size from a few dozen to several thousand persons. In these reductions the Indians were considered wards of the crown. The Spanish kings forbade officials or settlers to interfere with the missionaries in their efforts to convert the Indians to the Christian faith and the Spanish culture. Traveling Spaniards might not remain in the reductions more than two or three days. The average reduction lasted from ten to twenty years. Then the Indians were turned over to the care of the secular clergy. In the third and final stage frontier conditions gave way to orderly, civilized municipalities. Within a century the Spaniards in Latin America filled a vast stretch of territory with churches, schools, libraries, courts of justice, aqueducts, and roads. The universities of Lima and Mexico City were nearly one hundred years old when Harvard College was founded in 1625. By 1575 books in twelve Indian languages had been printed in Mexico City.

Roman Catholic missions in colonial times were divided into eight principal regions.

Dominican and Franciscan priests arrived in 1514 in the Cumana missions of northeastern Venezuela. Cacao, coffee, and sugar plantations were established by the padres. The Indians were trained in stock raising. The decline of the Cumana missions began in the eighteenth century, when many of the reductions were prematurely handed over to the parish clergy and the civil authorities.

Between 1658 and 1758 a hundred missions were founded by the Capuchins in the llanos of Caracas, the vast Venezuelan plains, where the great cattle ranches of today are located. These reductions were ruined during the wars of independence.

Missions on the Orinoco River were established by the Jesuits in 1670. These extended over the border into the northern part of Brazil. Frequent attacks by the Carib Indians rendered settled work difficult. The Capuchins and Franciscans joined the Jesuits on the upper Orinoco in 1734 and took over the entire mission when the Jesuits were expelled some thirty years later.

The Jesuits pioneered in the eastern part of Colombia, reaching the region as early as 1629. The Indian converts risked their lives trying to persuade the more savage jungle Indians to enter the reductions. When the Jesuits were expelled in 1767 the work languished.

It was 1724 before a mission was established in Guiana through the endeavors of the Capuchins and the Franciscans. A hundred years later the mission came to a temporary end when the revolutionists attacked the missionaries. Fourteen of them died of neglect in prison and twenty others were massacred.

The pioneer in the Maynas missions of Ecuador, Peru, and western Brazil was a Jesuit who arrived in 1560. Franciscans also labored in this field. The area was quite productive; the Jesuits alone are reported to have baptized half a million Indians. Outstanding among the missionaries was Jesuit *Father Samuel Fritz* (1654-1724). Known as the apostle to the Amazon Indians, he spent forty years of his life exploring the Amazon country and persuading the jungle Indians to accept the amenities of village life. Here, as elsewhere, the missions declined upon the departure of the Jesuits.

The missions of the Chaco frontier, in the eastern part of present-day Bolivia, were founded by the Jesuits and the Franciscans. Work in this inhospitable region was difficult. The Chaco Indians were particularly intractable. Some of the early missionaries were murdered by members of their own flock.

The last, and from some points of view the most successful, mission was that of the reductions administered by the Jesuits in Paraguay. Actually, the region embraced sections of Brazil, Argentina, and Bolivia. Religion was the mainspring of life in these reductions. The day began and ended with prayer; and the great feasts of the church were celebrated with much splendor, albeit not always without residual pagan practices. Each reduction was a little town, laid out in a fixed pattern around the plaza of an impressive stone church. The Indian houses were all alike, to avoid jealousy. Various crops were successfully cultivated and cattle raising was developed on a considerable scale. Artistic work in wood, stone, silver, and gold was produced by the Indians. In the one hundred reductions founded by the Jesuits before they were expelled in 1767 almost one million Indians were baptized. Voltaire, no friend of the church, was obliged to acknowledge that the Jesuit reductions were a "triumph in humanity."

Roman Catholic missions in South America suffered two catastrophic setbacks: the expulsion of the Jesuits about the middle of the eighteenth century, and the losses incurred during the wars of independence in the second decade of the nineteenth century.

Three thousand Jesuits were expelled from various countries of South America, beginning with the Portuguese colony of Brazil in 1759. Members of the other orders did what they could to fill the gap; but they had their own missions to man and could ill afford to accept additional commitments. Nor were there any indigenous clergy to step into the void. Because of the rights of patronage granted to Spain and Portugal, the policies of the Sacred Congregation of Propaganda could not be applied in Latin America. The highest posts were given to Spanish-born clergy, who looked down on the Creole priests. As for the Indians, no adequate effort was made to train them for the priesthood. Consequently, the vacuum left by the departure of the Jesuits could not possibly be filled. When the Jesuits returned some sixty to seventy years later, it was to find their former work swept away. To this day the shortage of well-trained native-born clergy is one of the greatest weaknesses of Roman Catholicism in that part of the world.

Almost as disastrous were the wars of independence in the early years of the nineteenth century. Up to that time church and state were one. Moreover, the vast majority of the administrators, civil and ecclesiastical, were from Spain—or, in the case of Brazil, from Portugal. Under such a system the Roman Catholic Church possessed immense authority and enjoyed vast prestige. When the revolutionists went on the rampage, however, their hatred of colonialism was not confined to the civil authorities; it spilled over to the religious hierarchy. With the fall of the Spanish empire in South America, Catholic missions were deprived of the moral and economic support of the Spanish sovereigns. Moreover, the new governments were anticlerical, some of them violently so. The Roman Catholic missioners were nearly all Spanish; naturally, their allegiance was to the crown. Not a few of them returned to Spain, including some bishops; and their departure had disastrous results for their abandoned flocks. Many of the mission reductions, already declining because of the expulsion of the Jesuits in the previous century, were forcibly turned over to the jurisdiction of the secular clergy and the civil authorities before the Indians had been sufficiently Christianized. Under these conditions the patronage system broke down; and the Vatican, in an attempt to salvage what it could of its former ecclesiastical empire, was obliged to come to terms with the new regimes on an individual basis. These agreements, known as concordats, differed from country to country. Some countries called for complete freedom of religion; one, Uruguay, became a secular state; others made certain concessions to Rome. In a few instances the new governments were anticlerical to the point of interference and even persecution.

The missionary endeavors of the Roman Catholic Church were not confined to Latin America. For many years extensive missions were carried on in what is now the United States and Canada. The Franciscans entered Florida in 1526. By 1542 they had reached New Mexico. Two years later they began work in Texas. Before the end of the century they had established a mission in Lower California. By 1655 Spanish missionaries, Dominicans and Franciscans, had founded thirty-five missions in Florida and Georgia. They were later wiped out, however, by the British in 1704. Jesuit beginnings in Virginia and South Carolina were likewise shortlived. In 1612 two Jesuits founded a mission for the Abnakis in Maine. In 1626 a Franciscan, *Father Joseph de la Roche,* explored the territory of New York State, then occupied by the fierce Iroquois.

In 1632 *Father Andrew White* (1579-1656) and two other Jesuits sailed into Chesapeake Bay with Lord Baltimore in search of a land with religious liberty. Father White set about the task of converting the Indians after he learned their language. For this purpose he prepared a catechism. Ten years later, white marauders from Virginia plundered the Jesuit mission in Maryland. Father White was sent in chains to England, where he was condemned to death. The sentence, however, was never carried out.

In New France (Canada) the conversion of the Indians was a major concern of the early French explorers. Samuel de Champlain, founder of Quebec, declared, "The salvation of a single soul is worth more than the conquest of an empire." When the first explorer, Jacques Cartier, went to Canada in 1534 he took a party of priests with him; but it was not until eighty years later that organized missionary work got under way. It began with Champlain, who took the first Franciscans to Quebec in 1611. One of them began missionary work among the Hurons. Two Jesuits began work among the Micmac Indians of Nova Scotia in 1611. The Recollects arrived in 1615 and the Capuchins fifteen years later. A vicariate apostolic for Canada was established in 1658. The first diocese (Quebec) was organized in 1674. The missionaries in Canada were French and of a much higher caliber than the Spanish priests in Latin America. Missionary work in this part of the world was exceedingly difficult owing to the sparse population scattered over an immense area, the rigors of the Canadian winters, and the warlike propensities of the Indians, especially the Iroquois.

The pioneer Jesuit among the Hurons was *John de Brebeuf* (1593-1649), a Norman of noble lineage. For three years he labored alone on the banks of Lake Huron until reinforcements arrived. Several of his colleagues were murdered by the Mohawks. When the Iroquois finally destroyed the Hurons, Father Brebeuf and other Jesuits were massacred in a most barbarous fashion. The wars between the French and the British administered a further blow to Roman Catholic missions in Canada.

Judged by their passion for souls, their courage in the face of danger, their willingness to endure hardship, and their undying love for their persecutors, these missionaries must be regarded as among the greatest in the history of the church.

Africa

By virtue of the patronage system, first introduced by Pope Nicholas in 1454, Portugal was saddled with the responsibility of Christianizing Africa. In 1483 Diogo Cao, a Portuguese explorer, reached the Congo. Four years later Bartholomew Diaz discovered the Cape of Good Hope. Missions were established in Congo and Angola on the west coast and in Mozambique, Rhodesia, and Madagascar on the east coast.

Much effort was spent in an attempt to bring Christianity to the Congo. The first Christians were hostages carried away by Diogo to Portugal, where they were given Christian instruction and baptized. The first five mssionaries arrived in 1491 and received a warm welcome from the king.

The king, his wife, and one son all embraced Christianity and were baptized. The king's conversion proved to be superficial, however, for later on, under pressure, he returned to his former vices. His son, christened Alphonse, remained steadfast in the face of opposition from his brother and others. He lived a consistent Christian life and supported the mission, building churches and asking for more missionaries. Reinforcements arrived in 1509, in 1512, and again in 1521. A royal legation was sent from the Congo to Pope Julius in Rome, and a group of native princes was sent to Lisbon to be trained for the priesthood. One of the latter was Henry, the crown prince, who on his return was consecrated the first bishop of San Salvador, the national capital.

The first contingent of Jesuits, four in number, arrived in 1548 and was solemnly received by the king at the gates of San Salvador. They are reported to have baptized over five thousand converts within three months. They had grandiose plans for a special college for the nobility; but this fell through when a conflict with the king compelled them to return to Portugal.

The Congo mission received a boost when Queen Zinga of Matamba, after a serious lapse, experienced a genuine conversion in 1655 and thereafter gave moral and material support to the mission. During her reign the Capuchins arrived and threw themselves into the work of extirpating paganism. The fortunes of the Congo mission rose and fell depending on the attitudes of the various kings and queens. Some were ardent Christians and did much to strengthen Christianity among their own people. Others, after a superficial conversion, lapsed back into pagan ways and brought the Christian faith into disrepute. Still others preferred the old religion to the new and opposed, sometimes persecuted, the missionaries and their converts. By the middle of the seventeenth century Christianity in Congo gradually died out for lack of priests.

Angola was opened up to trade by the Portuguese in 1520 on condition that the king and his people become Christians. The first missionary was a priest from Congo, who succeeded in converting the king; but he later reverted to paganism. The king of Portugal sent several priests from San Thome to Angola. Their mission was unsuccessful and they returned. In 1560, after the decline of the Congo mission, four Jesuits accompanied the Portuguese ambassador to Angola to convert King Dambi; but the king would have nothing to do with the strange religion and put its emissaries in prison. Later on the tide turned with the conversion of a new king and one thousand of his subjects. By the close of the century there were twenty thousand Christians in Loando and Massagan. About the middle of the seventeenth century the Jesuits returned to Loando and four monasteries were established in connection with the bishopric of Saint Paul.

In Guinea, missions were established in Benin as early as the fourteenth century, but they were permitted to lapse. At the beginning of the seventeenth century, when the Jesuits returned to resume the work, they found several kings desirous of instruction. Some of them were baptized, along with many of their subjects. Later the mission was augmented by the arrival of the Carmelites in Upper Guinea and the Capuchins in Lower Guinea. In mid-century the mission expanded into Gambia and Sierra Leone.

Catholic missions were no more successful on the east coast of Africa. The Franciscan missioners, with Cabral in 1500 and Francis Xavier in 1541, stopped off in east Africa on their way to India to preach to the Muslims and the pagans. Neither would give them a hearing. Strangely enough, the first missionaries to Mozambique were dispatched from Goa. They proceeded up river to Tongue, where they baptized King Gamba of Inhambane and four hundred of his subjects. *Father Goncalo,* leader of the expedition, traveled up the Zambesi past Sena and Mabate, whose people he also baptized, into the kingdom of Monomotapa, whose emperor professed conversion as the result of a dream involving the Madonna which had been presented to him by the missionary. When he and his court were baptized it looked as if the Christian faith was well on its way to being firmly established in east Africa. Alas, a sudden turn of events, engineered by a Muslim conspiracy linking the missionary with the political ambitions of Portugal, resulted in the murder of Goncalo. Persecution followed and the mission was called off. A punitive expedition sent by Portugal to avenge the death of Goncalo served only to further alienate the rulers of east Africa.

In 1577 the Dominicans entered Mozambique and penetrated inland, burning Muslim mosques as they went. The Jesuit converts of another day had reverted to paganism, which did not help the cause at all. In 1607 the Jesuits made a second attempt to establish a beachhead in the hinterland of Mozambique. This time they were more successful. By 1624 they could report two dozen missionaries, twelve of them in the Mozambique college. About the same time the Dominicans had thirteen stations and twenty-five missionaries. Farther to the north, around Mombasa, the Augustinians had been at work since the turn of the century. One of their prize converts was King Jussuf, who gave great promise but relapsed into Islam and proceeded to murder all the Christians in the area. From 1630 on the Zambesi mission languished.

Madagascar proved to be one of the most difficult of all the African fields. First on the scene, in 1648, were the Vincentians, sent out by the Congregation of Propaganda. The two pioneer missionaries died within a few months of their arrival at Fort Dauphin. A second team of three missionaries met the same fate several years later. A third attempt was made, but it likewise came to nothing with the untimely death of the three members of the team. Finally, in 1674, the Madagascar mission collapsed, after only twenty-five years of abortive effort.

By the middle of the eighteenth century there was hardly a trace of Roman Catholic missions in Africa. How are we to account for failure on such a grand scale? Several factors might be mentioned: the fearfully high mortality rate among the missionaries due to the enervating climate and the lack of modern medicine; the unholy alliance between the Portuguese and the slave trade, which put the Christian religion in a very bad light since all the missionaries were from Portugal; the failure of the church to promote educational work and to train qualified leaders for the indigenous church; and the unstable political conditions in the many kingdoms of Africa, their intertribal warfare and their penchant for murder and plunder. More pertinent, and perhaps more potent, than the above were the superficial missionary methods, which resulted in hasty "conversions" and mass baptisms.

V

Origin of Protestant Missions in Europe: A.D. 1600-1800

One would naturally expect that the spiritual forces released by the Reformation would have prompted the Protestant churches of Europe to take the gospel to the ends of the earth during the period of world exploration and colonization which began about 1500. But such was not the case. The Roman Catholic Church between 1500 and 1700 won more converts in the pagan world than it lost to Protestantism in Europe. Why did the Protestant churches take so long to inaugurate their missionary program? What were some of the contributing factors?

The first, and perhaps the most potent, factor was the theology of the reformers. They taught that the Great Commission pertained only to the original apostles; that the apostles fulfilled the Great Commission by taking the gospel to the ends of the then known world; that if later generations were without the gospel, it was their own fault—a judgment of God on their unbelief; that the apostolate, with its immediate call, peculiar functions, and miraculous powers, having ceased, the church in later ages had neither the authority nor the responsibility to send missionaries to the ends of the earth.

There were, of course, exceptions to this point of view. *Hadrian Saravia* (1531-1613) and *Justinian von Weltz* (1664) wrote treatises urging the church to assume its responsibility for the evangelization of the world. But they, and others like them, were "voices crying in the wilderness." Frequently they were ignored; more often they were refuted, even ridiculed. Strangely enough, it was Erasmus who called most earnestly for the evangelization of the whole world.

That this negative view of world missions became orthodox Lutheranism is evident from the official document of the theological faculty of Wittenberg published in 1651 when it was asked by Count Truchsess for an interpretation of the Great Commission.

Moreover, there were the Predestinarians, whose preoccupation with the sovereignty of God all but precluded the responsibility of man. If God wills the conversion of the heathen, they will be saved without human instrumentality. If God does not will the salvation of the heathen, it is both foolish and futile for man to intervene. Calvin wrote: "We are taught that the kingdom of Christ is neither to be advanced nor maintained by the industry of men, but this is the work of God alone."

Added to this was the apocalypticism which anticipated, with some dismay, the rapidly approaching end of the age. Luther particularly took a dim view of the future. In his *Table Talks* he wrote: "Another hundred years and all will be over. God's Word will disappear for want of any to preach it."

A second factor is found in the sad plight of the Protestant churches of the sixteenth and seventeenth centuries. Compared with the Roman Catholic Church they were extremely small in both strength and numbers. Moreover, the Catholic Church launched the Counter Reformation and thereby regained much of the territory lost to the Reformation. The war against Rome was long and bitter and the outcome was by no means certain. The Thirty Years' War reduced Germany to economic and social chaos. The Protestant churches, preoccupied as they were with the problem of survival, may be excused for having neither the vision nor the vigor necessary for world evangelization.

Equally, if not more, enervating was the internecine warfare carried on between the Lutheran and Reformed churches themselves. If they had joined forces to present a united front to the common enemy, they might have done a better job with evangelism at home and missions overseas; but as it was they were torn asunder by ecclesiastical strife. They were united in only one thing—their hatred for the "papists." They no sooner broke with Rome than they fell to fighting one another.

In Saxony the popular saying was, "sooner papist than Calvinist." The exclusive Lutherans denied that the Calvinists were even Christians. Anathemas were hurled back and forth between the contending parties. In the middle of the sixteenth century the churches of the Augsburg Confession split in bitter controversy over the Eucharist. "Controversy over 'pure doctrine' played a larger role here perhaps than in any other period of church history, and the stage was filled with a fanatical race of scribes and pharisees abusing each other over mint, anise, and cummin."[1]

A third factor was the isolation of Protestant Europe from the mission lands of Asia, Africa, and the New World. Spain and Portugal,

---

[1] James H. Nichols, *History of Christianity, 1650-1950* (New York: Ronald Press, 1956), p. 43.

both Roman Catholic countries, were the great exploring and colonizing powers of the post-Reformation period. For more than a century they enjoyed complete mastery of the seas and a monopoly on world trade. Wherever their ships went they carried both merchants and missionaries. The kings of Portugal and Spain were deeply committed to the Christianization of their overseas colonies. Later on the Dutch and then the British got in on the act; only they were interested primarily in commerce, not colonization. The Dutch East India Company, founded in 1602, stated that one of its objectives was to plant the Reformed Faith in its territories overseas, but seldom did they work at it. The British East India Company entertained no such ambitions. While providing chaplains for its own personnel, it was adamantly opposed to missionary work among the indigenous population. Time and again it refused to transport missionaries on its ships, and forbade missionaries to reside in its territories.

A fourth factor was the absence in the Protestant churches of the religious orders which played such a prominent role in the spread of the Catholic faith throughout the world. Referring to the worldwide missionary program of the Roman Catholic Church one of its historians says:

> As papal missionary agencies, even apart from the curia, the various Religious Orders engaged ever more energetically in the missions, and vied with one another in spreading the Gospel. In the first place, the older missionary Orders renewed their activities—the Franciscans and Dominicans, and also the Augustinians and Carmelites after their internal reform. . . . The new Orders included (besides the Capuchins) one which apart from its general fitness as a regular Order, was also adapted and impelled by its deepest nature and its most intimate aims to attain the summit, to speak relatively, in missionary achievement—the Society of Jesus. The qualities which fitted it for this work were especially its cosmopolitan character, its faculty of accommodation and mobility, its military organization and centralization, its absolute obedience and the complete submerging of the individual in the common cause.[2]

When the Protestant churches, two centuries later, launched their missionary enterprise they had nothing to compare with the religious orders of the Roman Catholic Church. The largest group were the Moravians—one of the so-called sects. With few exceptions, their missionaries were unlettered men with more zeal than knowledge, artisans and farmers, married men, with ground to till, houses to build, and families to support. Fettered thus with family ties and domestic duties, the Protestant missionaries were no match for their Catholic counterparts. Certainly they had nothing comparable to the military discipline of the Society of Jesus.

Beginnings on the Continent

Several abortive attempts were made before the modern missionary enterprise got under way in Europe. The earliest attempt was made in

---

[2] Joseph Schmidlin, *Catholic Mission History* (Techny, Ill.: Divine Word Mission Press, 1933), p. 259.

Brazil, when Calvin in 1555 sent four clergymen and a group of French Huguenots to found a colony for persecuted Protestants on the Bay of Rio de Janeiro. Desultory attempts were made to Christianize the Indians, but without success. Later their leader, Villegagnon, turned traitor and abandoned the colony to the tender mercies of the Portuguese, who proceeded to destroy it. The few survivors were later killed by the Jesuits.

At the instigation of the Dutch East India Company, a seminary was established at the university of Leyden in 1622 for training chaplains and missionaries for service in the East Indies. But the venture was short-lived. It lasted only twelve years, during which time a dozen missionaries were sent forth. The majority of them returned after five years without having learned the vernacular of the people among whom they labored.

In 1661 *George Fox,* founder of the Society of Friends, sent three of his followers as missionaries to China; but they never reached their destination.

The first Lutheran to attempt missionary work was an Austrian, *Baron Justinian von Weltz,* who about 1664 issued a clarion call to the church to assume its missionary responsibilities. In three pamphlets, he set forth the missionary obligation of the church; called for the organization of a missionary society or association to get the job done; and advocated the opening of a training school for missionary candidates. But the times were not propitious. The churches, though orthodox in doctrine, were lacking in spiritual life and missionary vision. Not content with remaining indifferent, his colleagues, almost to a man, rose in indignation against him, calling him a dreamer, a fanatic, and a heretic. "The holy things of God," they said, "are not to be cast before such dogs and swine."

Undeterred by opposition and ridicule the disconcerted baron proceeded to Holland, where he abandoned his baronial title. Following ordination as an "apostle to the Gentiles," he sailed for Dutch Guiana (Surinam), where he died an early death before he could reap a harvest. Another missionary adventure had failed. Before the Protestant churches could launch a continuing missionary endeavor they must be inwardly renewed.

Pietism in Germany

The modern missionary enterprise was the direct outcome of the Pietist movement which began in Germany following the Thirty Years' War, which ended with the Peace of Westphalia in 1648. As the Protestant Reformation was a revolt against the false doctrines and corrupt morals of the Church of Rome, so the Pietist movement was a revolt against the barren orthodoxy and dead formalism of the state churches of Protestant Europe.

The father of Pietism was *Philip Spener* (1635-1705). As a Lutheran pastor, first in Strasbourg and later in Frankfort, Spener tried to raise the spiritual tone of his flock by the systematic cultivation of the spiritual life. Cottage meetings for prayer and Bible study supplemented the Sunday sermon and brought the members together in an atmosphere of fellowship hitherto unknown. Pietistic theology can be summed up in a few sentences. There can be no missionary vision without evangelistic zeal; there can be no evangelistic zeal without personal piety; there can be no personal piety without a genuine conversion experience. True religion for the Pietist is a matter of the heart, not the head; hence the emphasis on the cultivation of the spiritual life.

Like many reformers before him, Spener incurred the wrath of the hierarchy. Civil and ecclesiastical authorities denounced the man and his movement. But in spite of opposition and even persecution, Pietism proved contagious and won adherents in the Lutheran churches. When the universities of Saxony closed their doors to the new sect, the Pietists opened their own university at Halle in 1694. For ten years Spener built up the school. Following his death in 1705 the most influential leader was *August Francke* (1663-1727), who had been dismissed from Leipzig University because, following a deep religious experience which changed his whole life, he conferred with Spener and wholeheartedly embraced Pietism. Largely through his influence, Halle became the educational center of Pietism and the fountainhead of the missionary enterprise of the eighteenth century.

> The university was surrounded with other institutions; a pauper school, a boys boarding school, an orphanage, a Latin school, and some 6,000 pietist clergy were trained in the Halle theological faculty, which was the largest divinity school in Germany. Bogatzky was one of the most influential of the devotional writers of Halle, and Freylinghausen the chief hymn writer. Even the Reformed pietists in the Lower Rhine contributed regularly to Halle. Colonial Lutheranism in America was largely evangelized from Halle.[3]

The Danish-Halle Mission

Out of Halle University grew the first Protestant mission—the Danish-Halle Mission. The men, and much of the support, were furnished by Halle; the initial impetus originated in Denmark. Hence the name—Danish-Halle Mission.

In 1620 Denmark established its first trading colony at Tranquebar on the east coast of India. From the beginning chaplains were sent out to minister to the spiritual needs of the colonists; but it was almost one hundred years before missionary work was initiated among the indigenous population. In 1705 Dr. Franz Lutkens, court chaplain at Copenhagen,

---

[3] James H. Nichols, *op. cit.*, p. 84

was commissioned by Frederick IV to recruit missionaries for the East Indies. Failing to find suitable men in Denmark, Lutkens conferred with Spener and Francke in Germany, hoping that the Pietist center at Halle could furnish volunteers. Two names were suggested: *Bartholomew Ziegenbalg* and *Heinrich Plütschau,* both of whom had studied at Halle under Francke.

From its inception the mission encountered opposition both in Europe and in India. The Lutheran churches in Germany failed to support it. Instead, support, moral and material, came from Halle and interested individuals. Indeed, Warneck goes so far as to say that "but for Francke the Danish mission would soon have gone to sleep."[4] Owing to their Pietist convictions, the two missionaries had difficulty in getting the Danish hierarchy to ordain them. Belatedly and somewhat reluctantly they were ordained, and sailed for Tranquebar on November 29, 1705. Their departure raised a storm of protest in Lutheran circles in Germany. Some leaders, such as V. E. Loscher, were comparatively mild in their criticism and were content to sound a "cursory warning" against supporting the mission. Most of the critics were much more violent in their denunciation of the young mission. The faculty of theology at Wittenberg called the missionaries "false prophets" because their "orderly vocation was not ascertained."

On landing at Tranquebar on July 9, 1706, they were greeted with undisguised hostility by the Danish governor even though they carried credentials from King Frederick IV. Moreover, their Pietism did nothing to ingratiate them with the chaplains belonging to the East India Company, who regarded them as intruders and treated them accordingly. The Danish governor, uncertain as to his course of action, alternately persecuted and protected them. On one occasion he sent Ziegenbalg to prison.

Plütschau's term of service was short, lasting only five years. Ziegenbalg, never very robust, was able to give a total of fifteen years to India. On his furlough (1715) he traveled widely in Europe and aroused much interest in the Tranquebar mission. He was received by the kings of Denmark and England. He spent some time at Halle, where he met and greatly influenced young Zinzendorf, who later became the father of the Moravian missionary movement. By the time of his death in 1719 the mission had friends in Denmark, Germany, Great Britain, and even New England.

Moravian Missions

The origin of the Moravian Church goes back to 1467, when the persecuted followers of John Huss, with certain Waldensians and Mora-

---

[4] Gustav Warneck, *History of Protestant Missions* (New York: Revell, 1904), p. 44.

vians, banded together to form the *Unitas Fratrum* (United Brethren). After being almost wiped out by the Counter Reformation, the remnant, under the leadership of Christian David, migrated in 1722 to Saxony, where they were given refuge by Count Zinzendorf on one of his estates near Dresden. Known as *Herrnhut* (The Lord's Watch), this colony became the source and center of a missionary movement destined to circle the globe.

Nicolaus Ludwig Zinzendorf (1700-1760), godson to Spener and student at Francke's grammar school in Halle, decided as a young man to devote all his time and treasure to the cause of Christ. An ardent Pietist by parentage and profession, he declared: "I have one passion; it is He and He alone." He soon became the recognized leader of the colony and set about to organize its religious life. He became bishop of the Moravian Church in 1737. For thirty years he inspired and guided its worldwide missionary activities. He and Francke were, by all odds, the greatest missionary leaders of the eighteenth century.

The missionary impulse came about in a strange way. Zinzendorf, on a visit to Copenhagen in 1730, met a Negro from the West Indies and two Eskimos from Greenland, each of whom pleaded for missionaries. He was deeply moved by the appeal and decided to do something about it. On his return to *Herrnhut* he placed the challenge before the group. The response was immediate and enthusiastic.

Their first mission (1732) was to the Negro slaves on the Danish island of St. Thomas in the Virgin Islands. Greenland was next, in 1733, and St. Croix, also in the Virgin Islands, in 1734. Ten of this last group died in the first year; but it was not difficult to get recruits to fill up the depleted ranks. Other mission fields were opened: Surinam (1735), the Gold Coast and South Africa (1737), the North American Indians (1740), Jamaica (1754), and Antigua (1756). Between 1732 and 1760, 226 Moravians entered ten foreign countries.

> Within twenty years of the commencement of their missionary work the Moravian Brethren had started more missions than Anglicans and Protestants had started during the two preceding centuries. Their marvelous success was largely due to the fact that from the first they recognized that the evangelization of the world was the most pressing of all the obligations that rested upon the Christian Church, and that the carrying out of this obligation was the "common affair" of the community. Up to the present time (1930) the Moravians have sent out nearly 3,000 missionaries, the proportion of missionaries to their communicant members being 1 in 12.[5]

In almost every place their endeavors bore fruit, so that before long they had three members on the mission field for every one at home. And all of this was accomplished by men with little formal, and no theological, education. In this respect they differed radically from the Halle missionaries, all of whom were men of some erudition. Like the early apostles,

---
[5] Charles H. Robinson, *History of Christian Missions* (New York: Scribners, 1915), p. 50.

they were "unlearned and ignorant men," and like them, they were despised by the cultured people of their day. The first two missionaries to Greenland were gravediggers. Of the first two missionaries to the West Indies, one was a potter and the other a carpenter. But they were men of passion and piety. What they lacked in knowledge they made up in zeal. When Sorensen was asked if he were ready to go to Labrador, he replied: "Yes, tomorrow, if I am only given a pair of shoes." When they went out they were provided with their fare. On reaching their destination they were expected to fend for themselves. They took their wives and little ones with them. They lived and died and were buried in the land of their adoption. For years they bore the stigma of their humble origin. It was only the unanswerable power of their humility, courage, industry, and endurance that gradually overcame the prejudice of the cultured classes of Europe.

After almost two hundred forty years the Moravians still maintain their missionary commitments in various parts of the world. They have four main home bases: in West Germany, England, Denmark, and the United States. Supporting agencies are found in four European countries.

These two missions, the Danish-Halle and the Moravian, occupied the center of the stage throughout the whole of the eighteenth century. Towards the close (1797) the *Netherlands Missionary Society* got under way.

During the nineteenth century some fifteen additional continental societies were organized. Germany led the way with five: *Berlin Missionary Society* (1824), *Rhenish Missionary Society* (1828), *Gossner Mission* (1836), *Leipzig Mission Society* (1836), and the *Hermannsburg Mission* (1849). Between 1821 and 1874, the four Scandinavian countries organized six societies. In France the *Paris Evangelical Missionary Society* came into being in 1822. The *Basel Evangelical Mission Society* (Switzerland), dating back to 1815, was the earliest of them all.

All these missions continue to function. The German societies took a severe beating during the first World War and again during World War II. At present German missionaries number about thirteen hundred.

The Evangelical Awakening

We have already noted that the missionary movement on the continent grew out of the Pietist movement of the seventeenth century. Now we are to trace the origin of the British missionary movement to the Evangelical Awakening under John Wesley and George Whitefield in the eighteenth century. These revivals were not two separate and distinct movements; rather they were two phases of one event—a mighty outpouring of spiritual power which eventually affected the whole of Christendom in the first decades of the eighteenth century. The leading figures in the Pietist movement were Spener, Francke, and Zinzendorf. The great preachers of the Evangelical Awakening were Wesley and Whitefield in England and Jonathan Edwards and Whitefield in America. The connecting link between the two phases was Wesley's personal contact with Zinzendorf and the Moravians and Whitefield's study of the works of Francke.

John Wesley spent several years in Georgia (1735-1737) under the auspices of the *Society for the Propagation of the Gospel.* He had hoped to do some missionary work among the Indians, but the white settlers in Savannah claimed so much of his time and strength that the Indians were neglected. Even his work among the settlers was disappointing. His legalistic approach to Christian ethics and the unbending manner in which he administered church discipline led to a virtual revolt among his parishioners. Wesley left Georgia a disillusioned man. But all was not lost. While in Georgia Wesley was introduced to Spangenberg and his Moravians, whose simple faith, personal piety, and joyous spirit were in direct contrast to his own brand of holiness. Especially was he impressed with their complete assurance of salvation—something he himself had never achieved. His sense of spiritual inadequacy was greatly accentuated when he beheld, during a storm at sea, the quiet joy and serene peace which possessed the hearts of the Moravians in the face of death.

Back in England Wesley kept up his contacts with the Moravians. On May 24, 1738, while attending an informal prayer meeting at Aldersgate Street, the light dawned and John Wesley experienced the peace of heart which he had sought so long. This simple yet profound experience, which was to change the whole course of Christendom, was described by Wesley in his journal: "I felt my heart strangely warmed. I felt that I did trust Christ, Christ alone, for salvation; and an assurance was given me that he had taken away my sins, even mine, and saved me from the law of sin and death."

Seeking to understand further the doctrines of the Moravians, Wesley visited *Herrnhut,* where he conferred for several days with Zinzendorf. Immediately upon his conversion Wesley began his evangelistic ministry— probably the greatest in the history of preaching—which lasted forty years and included an average of three or four sermons a day. His organizational genius resulted in the formation of the great Methodist Church, first in England and later in America. It is no exaggeration to say that he saved England from moral and religious disaster and laid the foundations of the modern missionary movement launched by Carey.

Early British Missions

We generally regard British missions as beginning in 1792 with the famous William Carey, the father of modern missions. Strictly speaking, this is not correct. Prior to that time there were three societies, all of them designed originally to operate within the colonial framework of North America.

The first was the *Society for the Propagation of the Gospel in New England,* founded in 1649. As its name implies, it was organized with the Indians of North America in mind. An original endowment of twelve thousand pounds was invested in land and the proceeds used to support missions in the New World. Its first missionary was *John Eliot,* who had been in Massachusetts since 1631 and who gave half a century to the evangelization of the Indians of that colony. The mission continued its work in New England until the War of Independence.

The *Society for Promoting Christian Knowledge* was organized in 1698 as an independent mission within the Anglican Church. A leading figure in its formation was *Thomas Bray,* Rector of Sheldon and Commissary in Maryland of the Bishop of London. It was not intended in the beginning to be a missionary venture. Its original purpose was to strengthen the religious life of the white colonists in the New World. This was to be done by the dissemination of Christian literature and by augmenting the meager libraries of the colonial clergy. As it branched out into many different parts of the world it became, for all intents and purposes, a missionary agency.

Through the years the SPCK has engaged in a variety of activities, mostly in the fields of education and literature. During a time of crisis in the eighteenth century it came to the rescue of the Danish-Halle Mission in South India. For over two hundred sixty years it has been a supporting mission, providing an ever increasing stream of high grade Christian literature not only for Anglicans but for others as well. Since 1835 it has been doing its own publishing. Today it has bookstores all around the world.

The *Society for the Propagation of the Gospel in Foreign Parts,* commonly known throughout the world as the SPG, is the oldest, and was for nearly a century the only, specifically missionary agency of the Church of England. The major difference between the SPG and its equally famous sister mission, the *Church Missionary Society,* is that the former is High Church and the latter, Low Church.

Here, as with the SPCK, Thomas Bray was instrumental in bringing it into being. The SPG was founded by royal charter in 1701 with a twofold purpose: to minister to the spiritual needs of the English settlers overseas, many of whom were in danger of lapsing into heathen ways for lack of religious instruction; and to evangelize the indigenous population, who were heathen to begin with.

During the entire eighteenth century the SPG maintained a rather modest program on a very restricted budget. During that time its activities were confined to the American colonies and the West Indies. Nevertheless, as will be seen in the chapter on missions in North America, the SPG filled a pressing need for chaplains and missionaries in colonial America.

VI

Origin of Protestant Missions
in England and USA: A.D. 1750-1850

If Western colonialism is said to have begun with Vasco da Gama, Protestant missions may be said to have been launched by William Carey. What Luther was to the Protestant Reformation, Carey was to the Christian missionary movement. Though there were missionaries before him, it is altogether fitting that William Carey should be known as "the father of modern missions."

Many factors contributed to the inauguration of the "Great Century" of modern missions. The famous East India Companies tapped the riches of the Indies and laid the foundation of world trade. They also paved the way for European colonization which, in the providence of God, greatly facilitated the worldwide mission of the church. The invention of the steamboat made ocean travel faster and safer. Of more immediate interest to William Carey were the voyages of Captain James Cook.

Religious factors were no less potent. The Pietist Movement in Germany and the Evangelical Awakening in England and America have already been mentioned. Even before Carey's time there were stirrings of missionary interest in England. In 1719 Isaac Watts wrote his great missionary hymn, "Jesus Shall Reign Where'er the Sun." Several of Charles Wesley's compositions also bear a missionary theme. In 1723 Robert Millar of Paisley wrote *A History of the Propagation of Christianity and the Overthrow of Paganism,* in which he advocated intercession as the primary means of converting the heathen. The idea soon caught on. Twenty years later prayer groups were to be found all over the British Isles. Their chief petition was for the conversion of the heathen world.

In 1746 a memorial was sent to Boston inviting the Christians of the New World to enter into a seven-year "Concert of Prayer" for missionary work. The memorial evoked a ready response from Jonathan Edwards, who the following year issued a call to all believers to engage in intercessory prayer for the spread of the gospel throughout the world.

Almost forty years later, in 1783, Edwards' pamphlet was introduced to the churches in England by John Sutcliff in the Northamptonshire Ministerial Association. Following the reading of the pamphlet, he made a motion that all Baptist churches and ministers set aside the first Monday of each month for united intercession for the heathen world. It read:

> Let the whole interest of the Redeemer be affectionately remembered, and the spread of the Gospel to the most distant parts of the habitable globe be the object of your most fervent requests. We shall rejoice if any other Christian societies of our own or other denominations will unite with us, and we do now invite them to join most cordially heart and hand in the attempt. Who can tell what the consequences of such a united effort in prayer may be?[1]

About this time *William Carey* (1761-1834) came on the scene. At fourteen years of age he apprenticed himself to the shoemaker at Hackleton. Following his conversion at eighteen he left the Church of England to join a "nebulous body of Dissenters" and immediately began preaching in nearby churches. Later he was persuaded to join the Baptists. At twenty-six he was formally ordained by John Sutcliff, John Ryland, and Andrew Fuller. During these years he mended shoes and taught school on week days, and preached on Sundays. In his spare time he devoured every book he could lay his hands on. Doubtless it was from his father and grandfather, both schoolmasters, that he inherited his passion for learning. He taught himself Latin, Greek, Hebrew, Italian, French, and Dutch! He denied that he was a genius; he simply claimed to be a plodder.

Strangely enough, it was the reading of *The Last Voyage of Captain Cook* that first aroused in William an interest in missionary work. Thereafter he read every book that had any bearing on the outside world, including Guthrie's *Geographical Grammar*. It is certain that he read Jonathan Edwards' *Life and Diary of David Brainerd*. He was familiar with the Danish-Halle Mission, John Eliot of New England, and the Moravian missionaries. He made his own map of the world on which he inscribed every bit of pertinent information he could find. Surely there never was another cobbler's shop like Carey's. Picture the village cobbler in his leather apron, his books by his side, his map on the wall, and his beautiful flowers in the window.

In 1792 Carey published his eighty-seven-page book, *An Enquiry into the Obligations of Christians to Use Means for the Conversion of the*

---

[1] H. B. Montgomery, *Prayer and Missions* (West Medford, Mass.: The Central Committee of the United Study of Foreign Missions, 1924), p. 78.

Heathens. Believed by some to be the most convincing missionary appeal ever written, Carey's *Enquiry* was certainly a landmark in Christian history and deserves a place alongside Martin Luther's Ninety-five Theses in its influence on subsequent church history.

Carey was no armchair strategist. He was concerned with action, not theory. His immediate aim was the formation of a society that would send missionaries abroad. This was not easy, for the Baptists among whom Carey moved were staunch Calvinists. At a ministerial meeting in North-amptonshire when Carey proposed that they discuss the implications of the Great Commission, Dr. John C. Ryland retorted: "Young man, sit down. When God pleases to convert the heathen, He will do it without your aid or mine."

Undaunted, Carey used every opportunity to press home upon the church of his day the needs and claims of the non-Christian world. He was not altogether alone. There were a few who shared his vision, among them John Sutcliff, Andrew Fuller, Samuel Pearce, and others; but even they counseled caution and delay in the execution of the plan. The idea was too new, too startling; and the obstacles seemed insurmountable.

On May 30, 1792, at the Baptist Ministers' Association at Notting-ham, Carey preached his epochal sermon on Isaiah 54:2, 3, in which he coined the now familiar couplet: "Expect great things from God; attempt great things for God." The sermon had a profound effect on his hearers. The following day Carey pled for immediate action; but the brethren, while acknowledging the "criminality of their supineness in the cause of God," faltered when they faced the immensity of the task. The meeting broke up, but not before Carey persuaded them to include in the minutes a resolution that at the next meeting they would present a definite plan for the formation of a "Baptist society for propagating the gospel among the heathen." That meeting occurred on October 2 in Andrew Fuller's chapel in Kettering. The matter appears not to have been mentioned in the full public meeting of that day; but in the evening a small group of twelve ministers and one layman gathered with William Carey in the spacious home of Widow Wallis, known for its hospitality as the Gospel Inn. Again Carey pressed for action, and again the brethren wavered. After all, who were these men, ministers of poverty-stricken churches, to undertake a mission so beset with difficulty, so fraught with uncertainty? At the crucial moment, when all hope seemed gone, Carey took from his pocket a booklet entitled *Periodical Account of Moravian Missions.* With tears in his eyes and a tremor in his voice he said: "If you had only read this and knew how these men overcame all obstacles for Christ's sake, you would go forward in faith." That was it. The men agreed to act. The minutes of the meeting record their decision to form *The Particular Baptist Society for Propagating the Gospel among the Heathen.* Reynold Hogg was appointed treasurer and Andrew Fuller, secretary. The mission was to be supported by individual subscriptions. Every person subscribing ten pounds at once, or ten shillings and sixpence annually, was considered a member. Then and there the thirteen men subscribed a total of thirteen pounds, two shillings and sixpence. Carey was no longer alone in his plans for the evangelization of the world. "The ability of Ryland, the influence of Fuller, the eloquence of Sutcliff, and the enthusiasm of Pearce were now linked unreservedly with the faith and courage of Carey."[2]

It was one thing to pass a resolution to form a mission; it was another to get the mission under way. Difficulties abounded on all sides, pertaining to family, finance, and field. Carey's father considered him mad. His wife refused to accompany him. But one by one the problems were solved; and after some delay and not a little discouragement, William Carey sailed for India on June 13, 1793. He was accompanied by a reluctant wife, four children, and two companions. Five months later he arrived in India, the land to which he gave forty years of unbroken service.

Back home in Europe and America, largely through the labors and letters of Carey, missionary societies came into existence: the *London Missionary Society* (1795), the *Scottish and Glasgow Missionary Societies* (1796), the *Netherlands Missionary Society* (1797), the *Church Missionary Society* (1799), the *British and Foreign Bible Society* (1804), the *American Board of Commissioners for Foreign Missions* (1810), the *American Baptist Missionary Union* (1814), and the *American Bible Society* (1816). It is difficult to exaggerate the influence of William Carey on the missionary enterprise of the nineteenth century. Few will wish to deny him the title of "father of modern missions."

In America

About this time there was a quiet but far-reaching movement of the Spirit of God on this side of the Atlantic. The call to preach the gospel to all nations came to *Samuel J. Mills* while he was following the plow on his farm in Connecticut one day in 1802. Four years later, in obedience to the heavenly vision, he entered Williams College at Williamstown, Massachusetts, to prepare for the Christian ministry. There he kindled a fire whose sparks were destined to be carried to the ends of the earth. A group of kindred spirits—James Richards, Francis Robbins, Harvey Loomis, Gordon Hall, and Luther Rice—known as the Society of the Brethren met frequently in a grove of maples near the campus for prayer and discussion. One day on their way to prayer they were caught in a sudden thunderstorm. Taking refuge in the lee of a nearby haystack, they had their usual time of prayer for the heathen world, following which they stood to their feet and said, "We can do it if we will." They thereupon resolved to

---

[2] F. Deaville Walker, *William Carey: Missionary, Pioneer, Statesman* (Chicago: Moody Press, 1925, p. 89.

become America's first foreign missionaries and signed a pledge to that effect. Henceforth they were known as "the Haystack Group."

After graduation several of them went to Andover Seminary, founded in 1808 by the Old Calvinists and the followers of Samuel Hopkins because of dissatisfaction with the liberalism of Harvard. This young school, the inheritor and preserver of New England Puritanism and the evangelical tradition of Jonathan Edwards, became the fountainhead not only of evangelicalism in New England but also of Christian missions overseas. Here they were joined by Adoniram Judson from Brown University, Samuel Newell from Harvard University, and Samuel Nott, Jr., from Union College. Under the leadership of Judson, the brilliant valedictorian, they formed the Society of Inquiry on the Subject of Missions.

On June 28, 1810, Judson, Mills, Nott, and Newell walked six miles to Bradford to present to the General Association of the Congregational Ministers of Massachusetts a memorial in which they offered themselves for missionary service and solicited the advice, direction, and prayers of the "Reverend Fathers." The young men gave their testimonies, after which the matter was referred to a committee of three. The following day the committee approved the purpose of the young men and recommended the formation of a foreign mission board. The report was immediately and unanimously adopted. Nine men were appointed to constitute the original Board of Commissioners for Foreign Missions. The first annual meeting of the board was held at Farmington, Connecticut, on September 5, 1810, with five commissioners present. They discussed and adopted a constitution of fourteen articles and elected officers for the following year, including a Prudential Committee of three members. They also prepared an *Address to the Christian Public* to enlist support for the new enterprise. Such was the humble beginning of the American foreign missionary movement, which today provides almost 70 percent of the worldwide Protestant missionary force and about 80 percent of the finances.

From the beginning the board was concerned for home as well as foreign missions. At its second meeting (Worcester, Massachusetts) it expressed the hope that "this Board will not lose sight of the heathen tribes on this Continent." Beginning in 1817 and extending to 1883, missions were conducted among the Indians, especially the Cherokees, Chickasaws, Choctaws, and Dakotas. All told, fifteen tribes were evangelized in as many states.

Foreign missions posed more difficult problems. The Prudential Committee corresponded with the directors of the London Missionary Society, and even sent Adoniram Judson to London to inquire more specifically about fields of service and methods of work. At one point the suggestion was made that the LMS might support Judson and his colleagues until they became self-supporting. He also inquired about the feasibility of joint support by the two societies. Wisely, the LMS suggested that the American Board maintain its own identity and autonomy, and the Americans accepted the suggestion. Acting on the recommendation of the LMS, the Prudential Committee decided on Burma as its first mission field. At the third annual meeting, held in Hartford in September, 1812, the committee designated four types of field that called for missionary activity: (1) peoples of ancient civilizations; (2) peoples of primitive cultures; (3) peoples of the ancient Christian churches; and (4) peoples of the Islamic faith.

It was at the second annual meeting of the board that the four young men, Judson, Nott, Newell, and Hall, were actually appointed as missionaries of the board. As usual, finance was a problem. Only fourteen hundred dollars had been received and this was not enough to pay the cost of passage. The committee deliberated anxiously. Should they proceed with their plans or wait for additional support? At last, on January 27, 1812, they voted to send the four men but to detain the wives until sufficient funds were on hand. Perhaps the LMS would come through after all. It was a brand new venture; they oscillated between faith and fear. But their fear was shortlived. When it became known that the young missionaries had actually booked passage, gifts flowed in from all quarters. Within three weeks more than six thousand dollars was received, enough to provide for outfit, passage, and a year's salary in advance!

The first party consisted of eight missionaries: Judson, Newell, and Nott, with their wives, Gordon Hall, and Luther Rice. The five men, all graduates of Andover Theological Seminary, were ordained in the Tabernacle in Salem on February 6, 1812. It was a most impressive service. The church was crowded, and at times the entire assembly "seemed moved as the trees of the wood are moved by a mighty wind."

Two weeks later the Judsons and the Newells set sail from Salem on the *Caravan*. The other members of the party left from Philadelphia on the *Harmony* on February 24. It took them four months to reach India. The first American mission had been launched. Other fields opened in rapid succession. Ceylon (1816), the Near East (1820), China (1830), and Madura (1834) were among the earliest.

Between Salem and Calcutta Judson changed his views on baptism, and on arrival was immersed by the Reverend William Ward, one of Carey's colleagues at Serampore. With characteristic honesty, Judson resigned from the Congregational Board and offered his services to the Baptists in America. This providentially led to the formation, in May, 1814, of what is now the American Baptist Foreign Mission Society. Judson became its first and most famous missionary. In the meantime, Judson and his wife, ordered out of India by the East India Company, made their way in a "crazy old vessel" to Rangoon, where they arrived on July 13, 1813. The second American mission was under way.

Other mission boards were organized in rapid succession by the *Methodist Episcopal Church* (1819), the *Protestant Episcopal Church* (1821), the *Presbyterian Church* (1831), the *Evangelical Lutheran Church*

(1837), and others later on. Today almost every Protestant denomination of any size has its own foreign mission board. The 1980 *Mission Handbook: North American Protestant Ministries Overseas* lists 714 sending and supporting organizations engaged in overseas operations. The operating budget of these organizations totaled $1.15 billion. Together they support fifty-three thousand full-time missionaries in nearly two hundred countries. This means that North Americans now represent 70 percent of the total number of Protestant missionaries in the world and provide an even higher percentage of the overall missionary budget.

PART TWO

Around the World

VII

Expansion of Protestant Missions in the Nineteenth Century

In his monumental seven-volume *History of the Expansion of Christianity* Kenneth Scott Latourette devoted three volumes to the nineteenth century, which he referred to as "The Great Century." Indeed it was. Never before in the history of the Christian church had such a concerted, organized, herculean effort been made to take the gospel to the ends of the earth.

Protestant missions from England got under way during the closing years of the eighteenth century. The first foreign mission board in the United States was organized in 1810. As the century progressed, one after another of the Protestant countries began sending missionaries to the "heathen world." By the end of the century every Protestant country in the world was represented on the mission field.

Cross and Flag. In Latin America the Spanish colonial system broke up between 1810 and 1824; but in other parts of the world—Asia, Africa, Oceania, and the Middle East—the missionary advance coincided with the rapid expansion of European power. Three major groups were involved in the invasion—the diplomat, the merchant, and the missionary. In the eyes of the nationals they came to represent three forms of imperialism—political, economic, and cultural.

Geographically the cross followed the flag. The very first Protestant missionaries of the Danish-Halle Mission went to Tranquebar, at that time a Dutch colony on the east coast of India. Later, in the nineteenth century, British missionaries followed the Union Jack to India and Africa. Dutch and German missionaries were found in large numbers in the East Indies. The Scandinavian countries had no colonies; consequently their missionaries were not concentrated in any one region. American missionaries represented the widest geographic spread of all. They ended up in all major regions of the world, but were particularly numerous in the Far East. In Latin America, apart from one or two small Anglican missions, they had the continent to themselves.

From a chronological point of view the shoe was on the other foot; the flag followed the cross. The missionaries were well established in Oceania long before Britain and France imposed their colonial rule on that part of the world. It was the missionaries, not the colonialists, who explored the vast unknown areas of Central Africa and there opened "a path for commerce and Christianity." In fact, it was the missionaries who invited the European powers to intervene in Africa to stop the iniquitous slave trade carried on by the Arabs. And in areas already under some form of colonial or quasi-colonial rule the missionaries often chafed at the bit to extend their endeavors beyond the areas regarded as safe by the colonial administrators.

Interestingly enough, North Africa was the last major region of the world to attract the attention of the churches in the West. For over 150 years missionaries passed North Africa on their way to the Middle East, India, and Southeast Asia. It was not until the 1880s that the first Protestant missionaries took up work in North Africa.

Four Kinds Of Mission. As the modern missionary enterprise got under way several different kinds of mission emerged. The earliest societies were interdenominational. The London Missionary Society and the American Board of Commissioners for Foreign Missions were in this category, though later on they became, for all practical purposes, Congregational boards. The earliest societies in Germany were also in this category. Later, as the missionary movement gained momentum, each denomination organized its own board of missions, supported and controlled by the denomination. In a class by itself was the Church of England, which ended up with ten or eleven independent societies, none of which was the official society of the denomination.

A third kind of mission, the faith mission, came into existence about the middle of the century. These missions appeared first in the British Isles. The earliest was the Zenana and Medical Missionary Fellowship (now BMMF International), organized in 1852, followed by the British Syrian Mission (later the Lebanon Evangelical Mission and now the Middle East Christian Outreach) in 1860, and the China Inland Mission (now the Overseas Missionary Fellowship) in 1865. Others followed in rapid succession. By the end of the century there were some two dozen of these faith missions in Britain.

On this side of the Atlantic the earliest faith mission was the Woman's Union Missionary Society (now merged with BMMF International), begun in 1860. The Christian and Missionary Alliance was established in 1887, and the China Inland Mission opened an American branch in 1888. Other well-known missions followed: The Evangelical Alliance Mission (1890), SIM International (1893), and the Africa Inland Mission (1895).

Though their organizational structure and their patterns of support were quite different, these three kinds of mission had much in common so far as methods of work were concerned. All three engaged extensively in evangelistic, medical, and educational work. In this way their well-balanced programs tried to meet the needs of the whole man—body, mind, and soul.

In time a fourth kind of mission emerged—the specialized mission. These missions usually ministered to a certain class of people, such as the Jews, the Indians, the Eskimos, the deaf, the blind, the military, orphans, women, children, leprosy patients, etc.; or they engaged in some particular kind of work—development of literacy, distribution of literature, radio broadcasting, aviation, social service, relief work, etc. Some of these were sending missions; others were simply supporting agencies.

The *Encyclopedia of Modern Christian Missions,* published in 1967, lists 1,437 missionary agencies based in the West. The 12th edition of the *Mission Handbook: North American Protestant Ministries Overseas,* published in 1980, lists 714 sending and supporting agencies in North America alone. Such has been the growth of the missionary movement in the past 275 years.

The Bible Societies. Special mention should be made of the Bible societies, without which the missions would have been greatly handicapped. In time each of the Protestant countries of the world organized its own Bible society; today sixty-six of them belong to the United Bible Societies, with headquarters in Stuttgart. Through the years four of these Bible societies have made an enormous contribution to Christian missions around the world: the British and Foreign Bible Society (1804), the National Bible Society of Scotland (1809), the Netherlands Bible Society (1814), and the American Bible Society (1816).

These Bible societies are unique. Never before in the history of the world have so many organizations been dedicated solely to the translation, publication, and distribution of one book. Through the years they have worked very closely with various missions, regardless of their ecclesiastical affiliation, their theological orientation, or their geographical location. Actually the Bible societies are responsible only for the publication of the Scriptures. The translation work is done by missionaries, with the advice and supervision of the Bible societies' linguistic experts. When it comes to distribution, the Bible societies depend heavily on the local churches. In recent years less distribution has been done by hired colporteurs and more by volunteers.

The Scriptures are always published without note or comment, making possible almost total cooperation on the part of the missions. They are sold rather than given away, ensuring that they will be read rather than used for other purposes. They are always sold considerably below cost, at a price that the people in the Third World can afford. The Bible societies, like the missionary societies, depend on the contributions of the churches in the homelands.

Missionary Characteristics. What was the caliber of the nineteenth-century missionaries? From an academic point of view they represented a wide spectrum, all the way from semi-literate artisans to university graduates. Missionaries from Germany and Scotland were much better trained, many of them being university men. The same was true of the early missionaries from the United States. Most of them were graduates of the finest colleges and seminaries on the East Coast; they established some of the most prestigious educational institutions on the mission field, especially in the Middle and Far East.

On the other hand the missionaries from England were not so well educated. From 1815 to 1891 the Church Missionary Society sent out 650 missionaries, of whom only 240 were college graduates. Moreover, most of them were laymen, not ordained ministers. The first band of missionaries from the London Missionary Society sailed for the South Seas in 1796. There were thirty in the party; only four of them were ordained; the rest were artisans. It should be remembered, however, that then as now colleges were not nearly as numerous in England as in the United States; consequently there were fewer college graduates to offer for missionary service.

When the faith missions came on the scene in the latter half of the century they contributed greatly to the number of missionaries with an inferior education. Hudson Taylor, the father of the faith mission movement, made a special appeal for persons with "little formal education." Consequently very few of the faith mission missionaries were university graduates. For the most part they were the products of the Bible schools that started about the same time.

What about their spiritual qualities? What they may have lacked by way of intellectual prowess they made up for in Christian character. Almost without exception the missionaries of the nineteenth century were men and women of deep conviction and compassion. They believed that the heathen were lost without a knowledge of Jesus Christ. They spared no pains to take the gospel to the lost and dying "before it was too late." Pearl Buck, whose biographies of her missionary parents would not lead one to believe that she was exactly in sympathy with missionary work, had this to say about missionaries:

> The early missionaries were born warriors and very great men, for in those days religion was still a banner under which to fight. No weak or timid soul could sail the seas to foreign lands and defy death and danger unless he did carry religion as his banner, under which even death itself would be a glorious end. To go forth, to cry out, to warn, to save others, these were frightful urgencies upon the soul already saved. There was a very madness of necessity —an agony of salvation.

How Missionaries Were Received. What kind of reception did the missionaries receive? In the conduct of their work they encountered indifference, suspicion, hostility, persecution, and imprisonment. Times without number their homes were looted, their buildings burned, their churches desecrated, and their lives threatened. Thousands returned home broken in health. Other thousands died prematurely of tropical diseases. Hundreds became martyrs. And all of this they endured without reserve and without regret. Their compassion knew no bounds. They literally fulfilled the words of Christ: "Love your enemies, bless them that curse you, do good to them that hate you, and pray for them which despitefully use you, and persecute you" (Matt. 5:44, KJV). They were neither saints nor angels, but they were unusually fine Christians. They were the salt of the earth and the light of the world.

The hardest thing of all to bear was the reaction to their message. As a rule the missionaries were not wanted, not liked, and not trusted; consequently their message was rejected. It is a mistake to think that the "heathen in his blindness" is just waiting for the missionary to bring him the light. He is blind all right, but he doesn't know it; consequently he is in no hurry to embrace the light. In country after country the missionaries had to wait many years for the seed to take root in good ground. It required endless patience and stamina to win the day.

Adoniram Judson, America's first and greatest missionary, landed in Rangoon in 1813. From the beginning his life was beset with difficulties and frustrations calculated to break the strongest spirit; but in spite of all the adversities he persevered until, after six long years, he won his first convert. Robert Morrison, the first Protestant missionary to China, took seven years to win his first convert. The Primitive Methodists in Northern Rhodesia (Zambia) labored for thirteen years before the first African came forward for baptism. In Thailand it was even worse. The American Congregational missionaries arrived in 1831 and labored for eighteen years without baptizing a single convert. They became weary in well-doing and withdrew in 1849. The American Baptists had a similar experience. They baptized a few Chinese converts but not a single Thai. After seventeen years of futile effort they withdrew and did not return until after World War II. The American Presbyterians entered in 1840 and refused to leave, but it took them nineteen years to win their first Thai convert!

Hardships Endured. Death claimed an abnormal number of missionaries, especially in Africa. The big killers were malaria, yellow fever, typhus, and dysentery. The story of missions in Africa is an amazing tale of adventure, endurance, privation, sickness, weakness, and death. The pioneer missionaries penetrated the heart of that great unknown continent through peril, toil, and pain; and the trail they blazed was marked by blood, sweat, and tears.

In his farewell address to the Church Missionary Society before setting out for Uganda, Alexander Mackay said: "Within six months you will probably hear that one of us is dead. When the news comes, do not be cast down; but send someone else immediately to take the vacant place." How prophetic his words were! Within three months one of the party of eight was dead; within a year five had died; and at the end of two years Mackay himself was the sole survivor. In the face of overwhelming odds he struggled on for twelve years until he too was felled by the fever.

West Africa came to be known as "the white man's grave." When Adlai Stevenson II visited Africa in the 1960s he was dumbfounded at the number of missionary graves he saw. His reaction was: "My God, I didn't know so many missionaries died here." In Sierra Leone the Church Missionary Society lost fifty-three missionaries in the first twenty years. In Liberia the losses were even higher. The first American Methodist missionary, Melville B. Cox, arrived in Liberia in 1833 but died within four months of his arrival. His last words were: "Let a thousand fall before Africa be given up."

Not a few missionaries were called upon to seal their testimony with their blood. Not many violent deaths occurred in Africa, for the simple reason that the European powers stopped the intertribal warfare and imposed their own form of peace on the entire continent. The colonial presence provided the missionaries with a certain degree of protection. The same was true of India where, apart from the Sepoy Mutiny, there were few missionary martyrs. Not so with China, where almost every decade there was a major anti-foreign outbreak. The businessmen and the diplomatic corps in the treaty ports were under the protection of the foreign concessions, but the missionaries upcountry were exposed to the fury of the Chinese mobs as they went on the rampage. In the Boxer Rebellion of 1900 no fewer than 189 missionaries and their children lost their lives. Nobody knows how many Chinese Christians were killed. Certainly China proved to be the most resistant of all the major fields of the world, with the single exception of the Muslim world.

Some Outstanding Missionaries. One reason for calling the nineteenth century "The Great Century" is that it produced so many great missionaries. No other period in Christian history produced such a galaxy of missionary giants. *An Initial Bibliography of Missionary Biography,* published by the Missionary Research Library of New York in 1965, lists 2,286 full-fledged biographies; most of them belong to the century under review. There is room here to mention only a few of the most outstanding missionaries in different parts of the world.

We must begin with William Carey, the father of modern missions, who spent forty years in India, during which time he translated the Scriptures into thirty-five languages and dialects of India and Southeast Asia. Adoniram Judson spent thirty-seven years in Burma; he translated the Bible into Burmese and completed his monumental *Burmese-English Dictionary.* By the close of his life the church in Burma had seven thousand members and Judson had the oversight of 163 missionaries. Robert Morrison spent twenty-seven years preparing the way for the evangelization of the most populous nation on earth. His great life's work was the translation of the Bible into the ancient Wenli language of China and the publication of his massive six-volume *Chinese Dictionary*. These three men— Carey, Judson, and Morrison—by their prodigious literary labors placed all later missionaries forever in their debt.

Of the various countries of the world, China led the way with a group of missionary giants second to none. The list is a long one. It includes S. Wells Williams, James Legge, W. A. P. Martin, Karl Gützlaff, Hudson Taylor, Griffith John, David Hill, Timothy Richard, and Karl Reichelt, to mention only a few.

India, likewise, was blessed with some outstanding pioneers: Alexander Duff, Reginald Heber, John Scudder, James Thoburn, William Miller, Christian Schwartz, and others.

Three outstanding missionaries laid the foundations of the Christian church in Japan: James Hepburn, Guido Verbeck, and Samuel Brown. Verbeck was a born linguist who spoke Japanese with a fluency and accuracy that amazed his missionary colleagues and charmed his Japanese friends. He was at once educator and evangelist, orator and translator, brilliant statesman and humble Christian worker. He helped the Japanese government build a modern system of education based on Western learning. He assisted in framing the Meiji Constitution. A man without a country, he was awarded the highest of all decorations, the Order of the Rising Sun; and when he died he was given a state funeral.

Horace Underwood and Henry Appenzeller, one a Presbyterian and the other a Methodist, landed in Korea on Easter Sunday, 1885. Together they laid the foundations of the two great churches that emerged in Korea. A third-generation member of the Underwood family acted as interpreter for the United States Army during the armistice negotiations at Panmunjom in the early 1950s.

In the South Seas three Johns stand out from the rest: John Paton, John Patteson, and John Geddie. The famous Ludwig Nommensen spent fifty-six years in Sumatra, during which he witnessed the birth and growth of the great Batak Church, whose early members had been cannibalistic headhunters.

In the Middle East the American Congregationalists made a significant contribution to the cause of Arab nationalism. Cyrus Hamlin founded Robert College in Istanbul. Daniel Bliss established the Syrian Protestant College, which later became the American University of Beirut. Speaking in 1920, Emir Feisal bore testimony to the influence of that institution when he said: "Dr. Daniel Bliss, the founder of the college, was the grandfather of Syria; his son, Dr. Howard Bliss, the present president, is the father of Syria. Without the education this college has given, the struggle for freedom would never have been won. The Arabs owe everything to these men." Two other giants were Eli Smith and C. V. VanDyck, who together translated the Bible into the difficult classical Arabic language.

And what shall be said about Africa? The best-known missionary of all time was David Livingstone who, by his travels in Central Africa, exposed the Arab slave trade as "the open sore of the world" and managed to "open a path for commerce and Christianity" in that unknown continent. His father-in-law, Robert Moffat, became "the apostle to Bechuanaland," where he spent fifty years. His chief task was the translation of the entire Bible and the founding of the great church in that land. Other well-known pioneers in Africa include Dan Crawford, François Coillard, James Stewart, Donald Fraser, Alexander Mackay, Mary Slessor, and a host of others.

Missionary Accomplishments. By all odds the missionaries of the nineteenth century were a special breed of men and women. Single-handedly and with great courage they attacked the social evils of their time: child marriage, the immolation of widows, temple prostitution, and untouchability in India; footbinding, opium addiction, and the abandoning of babies in China; polygamy, the slave trade, and the destruction of twins in Africa. In all parts of the world they opened schools, hospitals, clinics, medical colleges, orphanages, and leprosaria. They gave succor and sustenance to the dregs of society cast off by their own communities. At great risk to themselves and their families they fought famines, floods, pestilences, and plagues. They were the first to rescue unwanted babies, educate girls, and liberate women. Above all, they gave to the non-Christian world the most liberating of all messages—the gospel of Christ. They converted savages into saints; and out of this raw material they built the Christian church, which is today the most universal of all institutions. By the end of the century the gospel had literally been taken to the ends of the earth. "Never before in a period of equal length had Christianity or any other religion penetrated for the first time as large an area as it had in the nineteenth century."[1] The emissaries of the cross were to be found in all habitable parts of the globe, from the frozen wastes of Greenland to the steaming jungles of Africa. Churches, chapels, schools, and hospitals were scattered with great profusion from Turkey to Tokyo, from Cairo to Cape Town, from Monterrey to Montevideo, from Polynesia to Indonesia. There were, to be sure, a few areas of the world where there were no resident missionaries, but that was because of government restrictions, not because the church lacked either the will or the power to press forward with the task of world evangelization. Included in the Christian church, for the very first time, were representatives of "every tribe and tongue and people and nation" (Rev. 5:9, RSV). Latourette was right when he called the nineteenth century "The Great Century."

---

[1] Kenneth Scott Latourette, *The Great Century in the Americas, Australasia and Africa* (New York: Harper, 1953), p. 469.

VIII

Development of Protestant Missions in the Twentieth Century

The turn of the century marked the development of three important movements destined to have an important bearing on the course of Christian missions: the Faith Mission Movement, the Bible Institute Movement, and the Student Volunteer Movement. All three began during the latter half of the previous century but did not come to full fruition until the 1900s. All three came in time to be predominantly North American phenomena. The Faith Mission Movement and the Bible Institute Movement are still with us; the Student Volunteer Movement ended in the 1930s.

Faith Mission Movement. The term *faith mission* has been applied to a number of interdenominational agencies which, because they have no "captive constituency," must to an unusual degree look to the Lord for the supply of their needs. They themselves, however, would be the last to claim that they have any monopoly on faith. Their missionaries have no guaranteed income, though they do have a support scale which they try to maintain. They do not go into debt, nor do they solicit funds. They prefer to make their needs known to the Christian public and look to the Lord to move in the hearts of His people.

The faith missions have never regarded themselves as being in competition with the mainline denominations. However, the denominational missions have tended to regard the faith missions as something of a Cinderella and refer to them as "sects." Every faith mission has a statement of faith which each member is expected to sign. In this way they preserve their conservative, evangelical stance.

One of the outstanding characteristics of the faith missions has been their *enduring quality*. Several of them are over one hundred years old and still going strong. Others are close to the centennial mark. Not a single mission brought into existence in the nineteenth century has folded.

Another feature has been their *steady and dynamic growth*. Today the faith missions are among the largest in the world, some with a membership approaching one thousand. Wycliffe Bible Translators has 4,200 members; Campus Crusade for Christ International has over 6,000 staff members working in 150 countries.

Still another feature has been their *creativity*. Most of the innovations in twentieth-century missions have been introduced by the faith missions, including radio, aviation, Bible correspondence courses, gospel recordings, tapes, cassettes, saturation evangelism, and theological education by extension. "Hidden peoples" is the latest innovation.

Through the years the faith missions have derived most of their support from the independent Bible, Baptist, and community churches and their recruits from the Bible schools. In their overseas work they have concentrated on evangelism and church planting. In the medical field they have maintained scores of hospitals and hundreds of clinics. In the educational field they have established and maintained thousands of elementary schools, especially in Africa, but very few high schools and no colleges. In theological education they have been content with Bible schools. Only in recent years have they established a few seminaries.

Bible Institute Movement. The Bible Institute Movement got under way in the 1880s and, even more than the Faith Mission Movement, became overwhelmingly a North American phenomenon. S. A. Witmer in his book *Education with Dimension*, published in 1962, listed 247 Bible institutes and colleges in the United States and Canada. Today the figure is considerably higher, with over fifty reported in Canada alone. The earliest schools were Nyack (1882), Moody (1886), Ontario (1894), and Barrington (1900). From the beginning the Bible schools emphasized the need for home and foreign missions as well as evangelism and Bible teaching.

In recent years many of these schools have added sufficient liberal arts subjects to the curriculum to enable them to grant the B.A. degree. Today there are 96 members of the American Association of Bible Colleges (AABC), with a total enrollment in the fall of 1981 of 36,254. In addition there are 29 schools in process of applying for membership.

In spite of the changes that have come about, the Bible colleges continue to provide most of the candidates for the faith missions. Over the years schools such as Columbia Bible College, Nyack College, Multnomah School of the Bible, Prairie Bible Institute, Ontario Bible College, Lancaster Bible College, and others have produced a steady supply of missionaries for the foreign field. Moody Bible Institute has chalked up a fantastic record. Since 1890 over 5,800 Moody alumni have served under 255 mission boards in 108 countries of the world. Of this number over 2,300 were still in active service in 1981. This means that one out of every eighteen

North American missionaries in the world today is an alumnus of Moody Bible Institute. And the flow continues unabated; 85 Moody alumni left for the field in 1981.

Though not as numerous or as large as the North American schools, the Bible schools of Europe and the British Isles have played a major role in the preparation of missionaries. Today there are approximately forty Bible schools on the Continent and twenty-nine in the United Kingdom, with a total of 3,000 students. Several of these schools with a long history have made a significant contribution to the missionary movement, among them Spurgeon's College in London (1856), Bible Training Institute in Glasgow (1892), and Redcliffe Missionary Training College in Chiswick (1892).

Student Volunteer Movement. Another mighty movement of the Holy Spirit was the Student Volunteer Movement. It too began in the 1880s. Its inception and much of its early success were due to the missionary vision of Robert P. Wilder, a graduate of Princeton University; the spiritual power of D. L. Moody, the greatest evangelist of the nineteenth century; and the organizing genius of John R. Mott, then a student at Cornell University. It all began in the summer of 1886 when one hundred university and seminary students at Moody's conference grounds at Mount Hermon, Massachusetts, signed the Princeton Pledge, which read: "I purpose, God willing, to become a foreign missionary." In 1888 the movement was officially organized in New York City as the Student Volunteer Movement for Foreign Missions, with John R. Mott as chairman and Robert Wilder as traveling secretary. In no time at all the movement spread to colleges and universities all over the United States and Canada and even to foreign countries. The watchword of the movement, coined by Wilder, was: "The evangelization of the world in this generation."

One of the outstanding features of the movement was the quadrennial missionary convention, the first of which was held in Cleveland, Ohio, in 1891. Through the years tens of thousands attended these conventions, hearing the call of Christ to missionary service and signing the Princeton Pledge. The Des Moines Convention of 1920 was the highwater mark, after which the movement began to decline. The last convention was held in Indianapolis in 1936, by which time the Student Volunteer Movement was virtually a spent force; but in fifty years it had been instrumental in sending 20,500 students to the foreign mission field, most of them from North America. In a very real sense the Student Missions Fellowship of Inter-Varsity Christian Fellowship is the successor of the Student Volunteer Movement.

Demise of Colonialism. Since its beginning in 1945, membership in the United Nations has increased from 51 to 157 countries. Most of these new countries are located in the Third World, where missions have always operated. The collapse of the vast colonial system in Asia and Africa has been the most significant event of the twentieth century. It has not only changed the balance of power in the United Nations and around the world, but it has profoundly affected the cause and course of Christian missions at home and overseas. Specifically, three major changes have occurred: The image of Christianity has changed; the status of the national church has changed; the role of the missionary has changed.

Christianity in the Third World has always been regarded as a "foreign religion," but worse still it was identified with colonialism. Now that the colonial system no longer exists, that stigma has at last been removed. The missionaries entered with the colonialists. It is fortunate they did not leave with them, or the identification would have been complete. Now Christianity can stand on its own feet, free from the "entangling alliances" with the European empires of yesteryear. No longer can the missionaries be accused of "cultural imperialism," nor can the national Christians be called the "running dogs of foreign imperialism."

The status of the national church has likewise changed. The churches, with few exceptions, have received their independence. They are no longer tied to the "mother" churches in the West. For the first time they are free to act as they wish. Their leaders are now on a basis of absolute equality with the missionaries. Indeed, they can refuse to accept missionaries if they want to. The church leaders are now masters in their own houses, subject only to the authority of the Holy Spirit, not to the directions and dictates of the missionaries.

This, of course, means that the role of the missionary has also changed. He began by being the master. Then he was reduced to the role of partner. Now he is the servant, not only of the Lord, but of the national church as well. This is not an easy role to play; but play it he must, for the time has come.

With the advent of independence the great ethnic religions of the East have taken a new lease on life. They are passing from the defensive to the offensive. Some are demanding that they be declared the official religion of the country. Others are calling for the expulsion of the foreign missionaries. Still others are urging their governments to pass anti-conversion laws designed to cripple the witness of the national church. Some are even sending missionaries to the West to convert us. As a result there is a great and growing interest in our country in Oriental mysticism, transcendental meditation, yoga, and Zen Buddhism.

Rise of Communism. Since World War II, Communism, the implacable foe of all religion, has made important gains in Asia and is infiltrating Africa and Latin America. China, Mongolia, North Korea, Vietnam, Laos, and Cambodia are all closed to missionary work. Both Russia and China are fishing in troubled waters in the unstable countries of Africa. As for Latin America, the countries there have long been ripe for revolution. In some countries Roman Catholic priests are flirting with guerrilla bands who are attempting to overthrow the reactionary governments. Wherever the Communists extend their rule, both church and mission are bound to suffer. Communism is not the monolithic international superstructure we once thought it was; but it is still too early to announce its demise.

Missionary Retrenchment. This recent postwar period has seen a marked decline in missionary interest and activity on the part of the main-line denominations in the United States. With few exceptions they have retreated all along the line. The following statistics tell the story of six of our largest denominations;

Overseas Task Force	1971	1979
American Baptist Convention	290	200
United Presbyterian, USA	810	359
Presbyterian Church, US	391	259
United Methodist Church (including EUB)	1,175	938
Protestant Episcopal Church	138	69
United Church of Christ	356	160
Total	3,160	1,985

There have been several contributing factors in this situation: (1) Now that the national churches have achieved both independence and maturity, the missions, as a matter of policy, have gradually and purposely reduced their overseas forces. (2) With nationalism making life and work on the mission field more and more difficult, to say nothing of the problem of closing doors, the home boards are not recruiting candidates in the same numbers as before. (3) With a lower enrollment in the liberal seminaries, candidates for pastoral ministry and for missionary service are both in short supply. (4) Many of the mainline denominations have experienced a marked drop in contributions to the administrative budget—to the point where staff members have been laid off. The more conservative church members are opposed to the increasing commitment on the part of the leaders to civil rights, nation building, and even revolution. For the present, many have decided to withhold their gifts. (5) Theological liberalism, especially neo-universalism, is slowly but surely cutting the nerve of the Christian mission. If it is true that all men are already saved without a knowledge of Jesus Christ, there is no compelling reason for the church to be in any great hurry to share the gospel with the world, especially when our own needs are so great.

It should be noted that not all mainline denominations are in retreat. The more conservative churches are holding their own and some of them, such as the Southern Baptists, are forging ahead, a fact which confirms the conviction that theology plays a major role in Christian missions.

While the mainline denominations are in retreat the conservative evangelicals, with few exceptions, are doing well. The older and larger missions with a membership approaching one thousand find it difficult to go beyond that point. The main reason for this is that every year the rolls are reduced by death and retirement, which nearly offsets the influx of new members. The younger and smaller missions continue to grow, some of them rather rapidly. The New Tribes Mission, founded in 1942, now has

950 missionaries. Wycliffe Bible Translators, founded in 1935, has 3,500 workers. Some missions were not established until after World War II. Already they have a membership of between one and two hundred. In this category are the Greater Europe Mission and the Far Eastern Gospel Crusade.

Short-Term Programs.   Two new programs were developed during the 1960s; short terms abroad and the summer missionary project. Short terms abroad was actually begun long before 1960, but only in recent years has the program burgeoned. Both programs have attracted a good deal of attention. Both seem to fit the mood of today's youth. Both have been made feasible by the rapid transportation of the jet age and the affluence of American society. So popular are these programs that in some missions half the new recruits each year are short-termers. In fact several mainline denominations and at least one faith mission will no longer accept career missionaries when they first apply. Only after they have served a term or two overseas are they eligible to become career missionaries.

The summer missionary project is even more popular than short terms abroad. Every summer thousands of college students serve overseas under the auspices of some mission board. They pay their own transportation and sometimes are responsible for their own room and board. They serve in scores of different capacities and usually manage to make a solid contribution. On their return to campus at the end of the summer they share their experiences and enthusiasm with their fellow students. Some Christian colleges report that the summer missionary project has completely changed the attitude of the student body toward foreign missions.

It is still too early to make a final evaluation of these two programs, but according to the latest information 25 percent of all short-termers become career missionaries. In some missions the figure is much higher. In a twenty-five-year period between 1949 and 1974 OMS International sent out 108 persons on a short-term basis. The average stay was two years and two months. Of the 108 short-termers, 64 became career missionaries under OMS, 3 volunteered for a second term, and 4 joined other missions as career missionaries. Thus, 63 percent of the short-term missionaries from OMS International continued in mission work. In addition, another 15 are currently in the pastorate. The Free Methodists have chalked up a similar record. In the first ten years of their program called Volunteers in Service Abroad, more than 1,000 persons took part. In a recent five-year period 62 percent of the new career missionaries had participated in some phase of VISA's outreach.

According to a recent survey the primary motive for short-term missionary programs is twofold: To better understand the missionaries' aims and goals, and to develop an appreciation for Christians in another culture. Ninety-eight percent of those surveyed indicated that these insights were more important than helping the missionaries. On the whole they returned home well satisfied with their experience. Only 3.1 percent were turned off, and a tiny 0.4 percent said they would discourage others from going into missionary work. Apparently they received a good impression of the missions under which they served. Between 54 percent and 73 percent gave them high marks, describing them as "extremely productive," "progressive," "contemporary," "creative," and "innovative."

Missionary Radio. For almost a hundred years the church in its missionary meetings has been singing, "Give the winds a mighty voice." These familiar words took on new meaning when the first missionary radio station, HCJB in Ecuador, went on the air on Christmas Day in 1931 with a tiny 250-watt transmitter which barely covered the city of Quito. Since those humble beginnings we have progressed to the place where there are now approximately sixty-five radio stations owned and operated by various missionary agencies, to say nothing of tens of thousands of Christian programs aired every week over commercial stations. Some of these stations are among the most powerful in the world.

The activity of the Far East Broadcasting Company (FEBC) based in Manila is typical of what is being done in missionary radio today. Founded in 1945, FEBC is presently using twenty-eight transmitters to broadcast the gospel for 1,900 program hours each week in ninety-one major languages and dialects of the world. Broadcasting facilities are located on the island of Luzon in the Philippines, the Seychelles in the Indian Ocean, Cheju Island off the coast of Korea, Saipan in the Pacific, and in San Francisco. FEBC has its own recording studios in Tokyo, New Delhi, Bangalore, Jakarta, Hong Kong, Bangkok, Saipan, Seoul, and Singapore. Cooperating studios belonging to other missions throughout Asia make tapes in the languages of their respective countries and send them to Manila for broadcasting. Mail is received at an average of thirty thousand letters a month from a hundred countries around the world. And FEBC is only one of sixty-five missionary radio stations!

A similar story could be told of other stations: ELWA in Liberia (Sudan Interior Mission); HCJB in Ecuador (World Radio Missionary Fellowship); HLKY in Korea (National Council of Churches); KLKX in Korea (The Evangelical Alliance Mission); and Trans World Radio in Monte Carlo, Swaziland, Cyprus, Sri Lanka, Guam, and Bonaire. In Japan the Pacific Broadcasting Association prepares radio and television programs that are aired over commercial stations. Station RVOG in Ethiopia (Lutheran World Federation) was commandeered by the Military Council in 1977.

Bible Correspondence Courses. Along with radio broadcasting go the Bible correspondence courses. Many of the broadcasting stations operate their own Bible Institute of the Air. Through the years millions of persons have enrolled in these courses. The Light of Life Correspondence School, which promotes Bible studies in twenty-four languages of India, has itself enrolled over a million students since it began in the 1940s. These courses have two great advantages: They are usually offered free of charge, and they can be studied in the secrecy of the home. Even in Muslim lands, where people would not dare enter a church, there are tens of thousands now studying the Word of God by means of Bible correspondence courses.

During the 1960s three important developments took place: Church Growth, Evangelism-in-Depth, and Theological Education by Extension.

Church Growth. The first of these developments—Church Growth— grew out of the Institute of Church Growth, originally located in Eugene, Oregon, and later transferred to Fuller Theological Seminary in Pasadena, California. Dr. Donald A. McGavran, former missionary to India, was the founder and for many years the director of the Institute of Church Growth. He has done more than any other missiologist to arouse both the home churches and foreign missions to the paramount importance of *growth* in Christian work. Growth with McGavran is always spiritual growth. He is not interested in more and bigger budgets, buildings, or bureaucracies. Growth to him is gaining converts, discipling the nations, multiplying churches—in a word, *church* growth. That, to him, is the end and aim of all missionary work worthy of the name. Other forms of work are valuable and have their place, but preaching the gospel and building the church should always be given first place.

Three auxiliary enterprises have been brought into existence: a monthly publication entitled *Church Growth Bulletin,* the Church Growth Book Club, and William Carey Library. Some of the masters' theses produced at Fuller are published by the William Carey Library. Every year Church Growth Workshops are organized in various parts of the United States for the benefit of missionaries on furlough and pastors of American churches.

Evangelism-in-Depth (EID). The second development—Evangelism- in-Depth—was the brainchild of Dr. R. Kenneth Strachan, former General Director of the Latin America Mission. Expressed in simple terms, EID is an attempt to mobilize the entire resources of the churches in a given country in order to bring the gospel in verbal or written form to every family in that country. The idea caught fire and spread to other parts of the world, where it was called by various names: New Life For All (Nigeria), Christ For All (Zaire), Mobilization Evangelism (Japan), Evangelical Advance (Guatemala). Dr. George W. Peters coined the phrase "Saturation Evangelism" and used it to describe all these various movements.

The philosophy underlying EID is based on four presuppositions: (1) Abundant reaping results from abundant sowing. (2) Christians can and must work together in evangelism. (3) When Christians pool their resources God multiplies them. (4) A dedicated minority can make an impact on an entire nation.

The genius of EID is summed up in the word *mobilization.* Dr. Strachan, after making an intensive study of the propaganda methods of the Communists, Jehovah's Witnesses, and other dynamic groups, enunciated the following principle: "The growth of any movement is in direct proportion to the success it obtains in the mobilization of the totality of its membership for the constant propagation of its beliefs."

Theological Education by Extension (TEE). The third movement was Theological Education by Extension. This was not a beautiful theory developed in a spiritual vacuum in the homeland and then exported to the mission field. Rather it grew out of an existential situation in Latin America where, because of rapid church growth, the existing seminaries were not doing an adequate job, with the result that nearly sixty thousand pastors were without any formal training in Bible or theology. Obviously something different, something drastic, had to be done.

These pastors were older men who already had churches and could not leave their farms, shops, and families for any extended period of time. If they were to get any kind of training, the seminary would have to go to them; they could not go to the seminary.

It all began with the Presbyterians in Guatemala in 1960. In this, as in many other projects, Ralph Winter was the guiding spirit. From there it spread to other countries of Latin America and eventually to Africa and Asia. During the past five or six years scores of TEE workshops have been conducted on three continents. The Committee for Assisting Ministry Education Overseas (CAMEO) has assisted in the organizing and financing of these workshops.

The cornerstone of the decentralized seminary is the programmed textbook. This enables the student-pastor to study in his own way, on his own time, and at his own pace. Periodically he and the other student-pastors meet with the seminary professor in some central place for a short period of counsel, encouragement, supervision, and testing—not for learning; that is supposed to have been done by the student beforehand.

New Interest in Missions. In the middle sixties there was a time when interest in missionary work, especially on the college campus, was very low. Mission leaders had a difficult time finding recruits. In the past few years, however, the situation has improved. Once again the Christian mission has become a viable option.

This welcome change is due to a number of factors, one of which is the famous Urbana Missionary Convention held every three years by the Inter-Varsity Christian Fellowship. In 1981 fourteen thousand college students attended Urbana. IVF leaders are hoping that 5,000 students will go into full-time missionary service by the end of the century.

Another factor is the fine work done among university students by such groups as Inter-Varsity Fellowship, Navigators, and Campus Crusade for Christ. An increasing number of seminary freshmen come from this source each year. Many of them come from a "pagan" background and were introduced to Jesus Christ for the very first time after they got to college. These young people often make better disciples than the youth reared in evangelical homes and churches to whom Christianity is "old hat." These new converts are still in the glow of their first love and are willing to follow Christ to the ends of the earth.

Probably the most potent factor is the gracious moving of the Holy Spirit among the youth of our nation. No one can study the Jesus Movement without thanking God that He has once again visited His people. Everywhere there is a new interest in religion, even in intellectual circles. The Charismatic Movement has invaded the mainline denominations, including the Roman Catholic Church. As a result Bible study groups are meeting not only in homes but in shops, schools, factories, offices, banks, etc. all over the country. Bibles by the millions are being sold every year. And the amazing thing is that all this has happened without any human leader or any man-made organization. In the next ten years thousands of these young people will find their way to Bible colleges and seminaries; many of them will end up on the mission field. Missions and revival have always gone together. The revival now taking place is bound to result in more recruits for the mission field. Indeed, some have already arrived. Several mission boards now report that they have more accepted candidates than they can send out.

Internationalization of Missions.   The modern missionary movement based in the Western world has always been a multinational undertaking involving all the Protestant countries of Christendom. In the early part of the century only one out of every three missionaries in the world was an American; today the ratio is two out of three. The reason for the increase is not difficult to find. German missions were hard hit during World War II and to date have not recouped their losses. Great Britain, which used to be one of the larger sending countries, is in the throes of a religious depression not seen since before the Wesleyan Revival. Moreover, Britain, robbed of her empire, is economically unable to sustain her overseas commitments on anything like the former scale. It is only proper that the United States with its vast resources should bear the responsibility for a larger share in world evangelization. We thank God that the USA has "come to the kingdom for such a time as this."

In this connection it should be noted that certain faith missions which formerly were based in Britain have in the postwar period opened branches in North America. Included in this category are BMMF International, the Japan Evangelistic Band, Scripture Union, and North Africa Mission. In other instances the traffic has moved in the other direction. Several faith missions originally based in the United States have recently branched out into other parts of the world and now have supporting and recruiting offices in several Western countries. Wycliffe Bible Translators, Mission Aviation Fellowship, Gospel Recordings, and Trans World Radio belong to this group.

Several specialized agencies, whose work has been confined to the United States, have in recent years become international in scope. The list is a long one: Bible Club Movement, Youth for Christ, Gideons, Christian

Businessmen's Committee, Child Evangelism Fellowship, Word of Life Fellowship, High School Evangelism Fellowship, Young Life, Navigators, and Campus Crusade for Christ. Some of these are engaged in direct missionary work; others are only indirectly involved; but all are making a significant contribution to the cause of Christ around the world.

Christian Literature. Time and again we have been told that the missionaries taught the people to read, but the Communists gave them literature. This is one of those half-truths which can be so misleading to the uninformed. Missionaries have always given high priority to the printed page. William Ward, Carey's colleague in Serampore, was a professional printer and operated the first mission press in North India. The first thing the American missionaries did when they arrived in the Middle East in the early 1820s was to write home for a printing press. Shortly after the Communists came to power in Russia, Arthur J. Brown could report: "Today one hundred and sixty presses are conducted by the Protestant mission boards in various parts of the world, and they issue annually about four hundred million pages of Christian literature."[1] From that day to this in all parts of the world, mission presses have been pouring out a veritable Niagara of Christian literature.

And the work goes on. Today several agencies are engaged solely in the production and distribution of Christian literature overseas: Christian Literature Crusade, Evangelical Literature Overseas, Literature Crusades, World Literature Crusade, Operation Mobilization, and Moody Literature Ministries. The last-named organization is now producing and distributing gospel literature in 184 languages in over a hundred countries. In addition, Moody Institute of Science has made its science films available in 27 languages to missionaries in 132 countries.

Third World Missions. Too long we have subscribed to the notion that world evangelization is "the white man's burden." This grew out of the eighteenth and nineteenth centuries, when Western missionaries roamed the world preaching the gospel, translating the Scriptures, and planting churches—all on their own. Only in the South Pacific were the nationals involved in the enterprise. In recent decades, however, the "younger" churches of the Third World have begun to assume responsibility for missionary work at home and overseas.

Today there are 15,250 non-Caucasian missionaries serving in cross-cultural situations. As might be expected, Asia has led the way, with Korea, Japan, and the Philippines in the vanguard. One church in Manila, Grace Gospel Church, is supporting fifty missionaries at home and overseas. India has a large home-mission ministry among the many tribes of the northeast. In several countries of Asia interdenominational missionary associations have been formed, similar to the Interdenominational Foreign

---

1 Arthur J. Brown, *The Why and How of Foreign Missions* (New York: Missionary Education Movement, 1921), p. 127.

Mission Association in the USA. In 1970 six autonomous churches joined to form the Christian and Missionary Alliance Fellowship of Asia whose purpose is "to fulfill the command of Jesus Christ by promoting the program of foreign missions."

In 1973 the first All-Asia Mission Consultation was convened in Seoul with twenty-five delegates from fourteen countries. Out of this grew the Asia Mission Association in 1975. That same year the East-West Center for Missionary Research and Development was formed, also in Seoul. Its stated purpose is to train at least 10,000 Asian missionaries by the year 2000.

In August 1976 some 1,600 Chinese from all parts of the world assembled in Hong Kong for the Chinese Congress on World Evangelization. Convened originally with the idea of mobilizing support for the evangelization of the Chinese in China and overseas, it ended by emphasizing the responsibility of Chinese Christians to take the gospel to the ends of the earth. A second congress was convened in Singapore in 1981, at which time the delegates hammered out a ten-year program to promote evangelism and church growth. They expressed special concern for the spiritual welfare of their compatriots—some 40 million of them outside China.

In January 1977 the Evangelical Fellowship of India sponsored the All-India Congress on Mission and Evangelization. The Congress brought together 374 participants from all over India and 25 invited observers from India, Korea, Japan, Sri Lanka, England, and the United States. The official report, *The Devlali Letter,* has already been published in over 20 Indian languages. Out of the Congress have come thirteen separate projects which will be implemented in the coming years.

The churches in Africa and Latin America, after a late start, are beginning to make their contribution. Brazil has provided 75 percent of all the missionaries from Latin America. In Africa the Evangelical Churches of West Africa[2] are supporting 260 missionary couples engaged in home and foreign missions, mostly among the unreached tribes of Nigeria.

This is, without doubt, one of the most exciting developments in twentieth-century missions.

---

[2] Originally founded by, and presently affiliated with, SIM International.

IX

Missions in the Muslim World

"The explosion of the Arabian peninsula into the conquest and conversion of half the Mediterranean world is the most extraordinary phenomenon in medieval history."[1] So said Will Durant. Certainly the greatest threat ever faced by the Christian church came from the sudden rise and rapid spread of Islam in the seventh century.

Mohammed, the founder of Islam, died in A.D. 632. After his death his followers conquered and unified the warring tribes of Arabia, and in the flush of easy and rapid victory they went out on their mission of conquest and conversion.

With lightning speed they conquered Damascus, Antioch, Jerusalem, Caesarea, and Alexandria. By 650 the Persian Empire had been destroyed. They then turned west and swept across North Africa, where they destroyed nine hundred churches—one quarter of all the churches in Christendom. By 715 the greater part of Spain was in their hands. Crossing the Pyrenees and penetrating into France, they were stopped by Charles Martel in 732 at the Battle of Tours. Later they made significant gains in the East, advancing into Central Asia and through the Khyber Pass into the Punjab in northwest India. Then came a five-hundred-year stalemate.

A second tide of Muslim conquest occurred in the thirteenth and fourteenth centuries when the Ottoman Turks and the Mongols of Central Asia became followers of the prophet Mohammed. They went on the rampage, pillaging and destroying everything in their path. By the fifteenth century the Ottoman Turks had invaded Greece and the Balkans. Constan-

---

1 Will Durant, *The Age of Faith* (New York: Simon and Schuster, 1950), p. 155.

tinople fell in 1453. By a series of incursions the Muslims overran North India and in the sixteenth century established the famous Mogul Empire, which endured until the arrival of the British.

From India, Islam spread down the peninsula of Malaysia and across the straits to Indonesia. From there it spread east and north to the Philippine Islands, where its northern march was stopped on the island of Mindanao by the Roman Catholics moving south. Islam is still in possession of the lands it conquered centuries ago. More recently, in the twentieth century, Islam has made great progress in East and West Africa, where it is competing with Christianity for the soul of Africa.

Several factors make Islam unique among the religions of the world: (1) With more than seven hundred million adherents, it is the largest of the non-Christian religions. (2) It is the only non-Christian religion that makes any claim to be universal. (3) It is the only non-Christian religion that has any sense of world mission. (4) It is the only great ethnic religion that is younger than Christianity. (5) It is the only religion that has fought and conquered Christianity in certain large areas of the world. Except for Spain, Christianity has not recouped its losses. (6) Through the centuries it has proved to be by far the most resistant of all the non-Christian religions.

Certainly it is correct to say that of all the non-Christian peoples in the world today, the Muslims are the most difficult to win to Christ. The Scottish Presbyterians have labored around the perimeter of Arabia for over eighty years and today have a church of about thirty members. In North Africa, west of Egypt, after almost a hundred years of work, there is not one organized indigenous church of any size. R. Park Johnson, a Presbyterian missionary in the Middle East for many years, said: "So confined is the Muslim that in some countries of the Middle East a follower of Islam who changed his religion would in effect be tearing up his birth certificate, citizenship papers, voting registration, and work permit, and would become like a man without a country."[2]

Why the Muslim Soil Is So Barren

A number of factors enter into the picture. Taken together they constitute a formidable obstacle to the acceptance of the gospel.

1. **Islam is younger than Christianity.** This made it possible for Mohammed to borrow heavily from both Judaism and Christianity. Consequently it has more in common with Christianity than any of the other great religions. It has just enough of Christianity to inoculate it against the real thing.

Islam believes in four revelations from God: the Law of Moses, the Psalms of David, the Gospel of Jesus, and the Koran of Mohammed. This

---

[2] R. Park Johnson, *Middle East Pilgrimage* (New York: Friendship Press, 1958), p. 142.

means that the Muslims accept the Old Testament and the Gospels as divine revelations. This excellent point of contact should be to the missionary's advantage, but the Muslims believe that each succeeding revelation is greater than the preceding one. This makes the Gospel of Jesus more authoritative than the Law of Moses, but it also makes the Koran more authoritative than the Gospels. If the Koran differs from the Gospels—and it does—the Koran is correct and the Gospels are wrong.

2. **Islam denies the deity and the death of Christ.** Jesus is mentioned many times in the Koran and always given honorable treatment. He is referred to as the son of Mary, as a great prophet, even as a sinless person. The Koran acknowledges that He worked miracles. But the Jesus of the Koran differs from the Jesus of the Gospels in two important respects: His deity and His death are both denied.

The doctrine of the deity of Christ is utterly and completely abhorrent to the Muslim. For God to have a Son He must have a wife; the very suggestion is blasphemous. Moreover, there can be only one God, not two. The worship of any god but Allah is idolatry, and idolatry in the Koran is the unpardonable sin. If the missionary but mentions the deity of Christ the fanatical Muslim is likely to spit on his shadow to show his utter contempt for such a blasphemous statement.

With regard to His death, the Koran teaches that Jesus did not end His life on a cross. That too is unthinkable. God, the sovereign ruler of the universe, would never permit His prophet to come to such an ignominious end. Such a tragedy would be libelous to the character of God. He would not, He could not, tolerate such a diabolical deed. Therefore Jesus did not die on the cross. At the last minute a substitute appeared and Jesus was raptured away.

There appears to be no way around these two obstacles. The Christian missionary can find many points of similarity between Christianity and Islam, and certainly he will want to make full use of these; but sooner or later he must come to the central theme of the gospel—the cross. At that point he runs into a stone wall. He can remove many offending things, but he can never do away with the offense of the cross. That and the deity of Christ are hurdles that can never be removed.

3. **Islam's treatment of defectors.** All religions, including the broadest of them—Hinduism—look with disfavor on the devotee who changes his religion. But it remained for Islam to devise the Law of Apostasy, which permits the community to kill the adherent who defects from the faith. This law, of course, is not spelled out in the Constitution, nor is it applied by the government; but it has the sanction of the Koran: "Whoso shall apostatise from his religion, let him die for it, and he is an infidel."[3] In Islam conversion is a one-way street. A person can convert *to* Islam but not *from* Islam.

---

3 *The Koran: Surah* 2:214.

4. **The solidarity of Muslim society.**   In Islam there is no such thing as the separation of church and state. Religion in inextricably bound up with politics. To convert to Christianity is to become an apostate from the faith and a traitor to one's country.

> Islam is more than a religion. It is a complete code of life, a political system, an economic system. It is everything. Islam is a great practical religion because it is complete. A Muslim is one who has surrendered himself to God and to God's laws, and who has formed a society with other Muslims.[4]

There is no doubt that this solidarity acts as a deterrent to the Muslim contemplating conversion to Christianity.

> There is a great solidarity among Moslems and this is welded by a fanatical devotion to religion which may be likened to faith and patriotism combined. It is not difficult for any one of us to realize how hard it would be should we become, in the eyes of our fellow nationals, traitors to our country. Add to this the shame of becoming an apostate in the eyes of our co-religionists, and we get a picture of what it means for a Moslem to leave the faith of his fathers, and adopt a religion which has been considered an implacable enemy of all that from infancy the Moslem has been taught to hold most dear and sacred.[5]

It was this fact that prompted British colonial officials to declare Muslim areas off bounds to Christian missionaries in certain parts of the world. They wanted to avoid communal riots. Hence they played it safe and kept the missionaries away.

It is true, of course, that Christian churches in the Middle East enjoy certain rights and privileges as religious minorities. They may baptize their children, marry their young, and bury their dead. Church services are permitted provided they are confined to church buildings, but any attempt to "proselytize" would inevitably lead to trouble. For this reason the churches have kept almost completely to themselves and through the centuries have developed a "ghetto" complex. They have made no attempt to share their faith with their Muslim neighbors, nor do they look with favor on such activities on the part of Protestant missionaries from the West.

5. **The public practice of religion.**   Unlike his Christian counterpart in the West, the Muslim wears his religion on his sleeve. Islam is a religion that permeates all of life and is practiced more in public than in private.

> No one acquainted with Moslem peoples can fail to be impressed with the large place which religion occupies in their life. It is doubtful whether any people, unless it be the Jews, have taken religious observances as seriously as have the Moslems. In the case of the Mohammedan world. religion has seemingly affected every detail of life with its prescriptions and requirements.[6]

---

[4] Freeland Abbott, *Islam and Pakistan* (New York: Cornell University Press, 1968), p. 181.

[5] Nazmul Karim, "Pakistan and the Islamic State," *Muslim World,* Vol. 43, Number 4 (October 1953), p. 254.

[6] Charles Watson, *What Is This Moslem World?* (New York: Friendship Press, 1937), p. 53.

One of the Five Pillars of Islam is prayer. There are five prescribed times for prayer each day. When the call to prayer goes out from the minaret every devout Muslim gets out his prayer mat, faces Mecca, and prays, regardless of where he is or what he is doing at the time. The peasant in the field, the teacher in the classroom, the merchant in the bazaar, the traveler on the road, the prisoner in the jail—all fall on their knees, bow their heads to the ground, and recite their prayers. It is a moving sight to see fifty thousand Muslims, all dressed in white robes, kneeling together in an act of public, corporate prayer.

This is not something that happens once or twice a year on high days or holy days. It happens five times every day of the year. The lone individual who remains standing when all his compatriots are kneeling is sure to invite attention. There is no way for the Christian convert, or the person contemplating a new life in Christ, to be lost in the crowd. He cannot travel incognito.

6. **The memory of the Crusades.** To Christians in the West the Crusades were a bad dream, of which we have only the faintest recollection; but to the Arabs they are the greatest proof of the Christian hatred for Islam. Eight hundred years of history have failed to obliterate the Crusades from the memory of the Arabs. To this day they continue to fester in the body politic in that part of the world.

The Crusades were, without doubt, the greatest blunder ever made by the Christian church. The most calamitous result was the alienation of the entire Muslim world. The fact that the church would resort to war to regain the holy places of Palestine was itself a denial of its own faith. Once the victim of aggression, the church now became the aggressor. Such a course of action was a denial of the teaching of Christ and contrary to the practice of the early church.

Moreover, the atrocities committed by the Crusaders in the name of Christ left an indelible scar on the Muslim mind. When Jerusalem was captured in 1099 the Crusaders, not content with wiping out the one-thousand-man garrison, proceeded to massacre nearly seventy thousand Muslims. The surviving Jews were herded into a synagogue and burned alive. The Crusaders then repaired to the Church of the Holy Sepulchre, where they publicly gave thanks to Almighty God for a resounding victory. To this day Christianity's reputation for cruelty and revenge is a millstone around the neck of the Christian missionary in the Middle East. Some Arab writers still refer to Christians as Crusaders. Needless to say, Campus Crusade for Christ had to adopt another name when it moved into the Middle East.

Cracks Appearing in the Muslim Soil

In spite of the hardness of the soil in the Muslim world there are signs, however small, that cracks are beginning to appear.

1. **Human rights on the march.** Long before President Carter commenced his campaign for human rights, the United Nations adopted a Universal Declaration of Human Rights. Article Eighteen deals with the problem of religious freedom. A stronger statement one could hardly wish for:

> Everyone has the right of freedom of thought, conscience, and religion; this right includes freedom to change his religion or belief, and freedom, either alone or in community with others, and in public or private, to manifest his religion or belief, in teaching, practice, worship, and observance.

Most of the member states have signed this Declaration, including many Muslim states. This does not mean, of course, that they are all prepared to implement the Article; but it is significant that they have at least signed it. In declarations of this kind there is always a gap between the promise and the performance, just as in the more recent Helsinki Agreement signed by thirty-five nations of Europe. However, there can be no doubt that religious freedom is the wave of the future. Every country, communist or Muslim, will sooner or later have to come to terms with this reality if it wants to stay abreast of the modern world.

Arnold Toynbee has argued that the time has arrived when the intelligent man has the information and ability to choose his own religion regardless of his inheritance, and that he will increasingly make his own choice. This being so, Muslim governments cannot continue very long to treat their nationals like children. The time will come when they will be forced to make concessions to religious liberty.

2. **Increased contact with the West.** Every year thousands of Muslims, mostly students, visit Europe and the United States. They come for travel, business, higher education, and technical training. While here they see our open society, our spirit of toleration, our sense of fair play, and, above all, our freedom of religion. They cannot but be impressed with the pluralistic society found here in the West. The world over, educated people tend to be more tolerant than their uneducated compatriots. With more and more Muslims getting a higher education, the spirit of tolerance is bound to spread to Muslim countries.

If it were not for the immense influence of the mullahs (teachers of the religious law and doctrines of Islam) in the smaller towns and villages, freedom of religion would be much greater than it is. High government officials are often embarrassed when public opinion forces them to crack down on Christian activities in their countries. Muslim missionaries are free to carry on their activities in Christian countries. How long can they refuse to allow Christian missionaries to do the same in their countries?

3. **The political climate is changing.** Not so long ago Saudi Arabia was almost a forbidden country. Today there are tens of thousands of Western technicians helping the government bring the country, with its fabulous oil riches, into the twentieth century. In time, modernization on

such a mammoth scale is bound to change the political climate of that country. Already one Christian pilot has landed his plane at Mecca!

When Bangladesh was part of Pakistan it was a Muslim state, based on the teachings of the Koran. As soon as independence was achieved, Mujibur Rahman, the new prime minister, declared that Bangladesh was to be a secular state. Several of the more fanatical Muslim parties were dissolved. If genuine freedom of religion comes to Bangladesh, will we see large numbers turning to Christ? It is difficult to tell, but the chances are good. The same is true of Afghanistan. For centuries it was a Muslim state based on the Koran. Following the coup in 1973 a new Constitution was drawn up which makes no mention of the Koran. The Soviet invasion of Afghanistan in December 1979 changed that situation completely. It remains to be seen what will happen when the USSR withdraws.

4. **Increasing penetration by Christian radio.** At one time Muslim governments could keep their people sealed off from all contact with the outside world. This is no longer possible. The Christian gospel is now being beamed into Muslim countries by radio. Powerful broadcasting stations in the Seychelles, Monaco, Cyprus, and Monrovia have daily programs aimed at the Muslim world. Muslims who would not visit a church have no aversion to listening to the Christian message in the seclusion of their own homes. Every week letters of appreciation are received telling of interest and blessing.

5. **Bible study by correspondence.** In 1960 the Gospel Missionary Union in Morocco placed an ad in the local newspaper offering a free correspondence course on the Christian religion. It was the first time anything like that had been done, and the missionaries had no idea what kind of response they would get. Imagine their surprise when eighteen thousand people signed up for the Gospel of John. A few years later the North Africa Mission used the same plan and twenty thousand responded in Tunisia. Operation Mobilization had a similar experience in Iran. Thousands signed up for a Bible correspondence course. So heavy was the work that missionaries had to be taken away from their own work to correct papers. A similar report comes from Bangladesh, where over fifty thousand persons, half of them Muslims and half Hindus, have enrolled in Bible correspondence courses since 1960.

This is a strong indication that under the surface there is a deep hunger for spiritual reality in the Muslim world. Given complete freedom of religion, how many of these Muslims would embrace the Christian faith? Obviously the governments do not want to run the risk, but they cannot keep the lid on forever.

6. **Doors open and close.** Like the rest of the world, the Muslim world is in a state of flux. One door opens and another closes. Southern Sudan closed in 1964 during the seventeen-year civil war. Missionaries were invited back in the mid-1970s. Somalia opened its doors to Christian missions in 1953 but closed them again twenty years later. In 1973 most of

the non-professional missionaries in Afghanistan were ordered out. Some were allowed to remain and several have been permitted to enter for the first time in recent years. Libya, Iraq, and Syria are still closed, but non-professional missionaries—called "tent-makers"—can enter under secular auspices. In Saudi Arabia there are thousands of American technicians, some of them dedicated Christians, who are making a silent but significant impact on that backward country.

7. **Freedom brings fruit in Indonesia.** Indonesia is the one Muslim country where there is genuine freedom of religion, and the results are most gratifying. We have won more converts from Islam in Indonesia than in all the rest of the Muslim world combined.

The ideological basis of the Indonesian state is expressed in the five principles known as *Pantjasila:* belief in a Supreme Being, just and civilized humanity, the unity of Indonesia, guided democracy, and social justice. Although Islam is the dominant religion (85 percent), the government recognizes three other religions: Hinduism, Buddhism, and Christianity.

Islam in Indonesia tends to be rather tolerant and recognizes two kinds of Muslim—nominal and fanatical. There are two reasons for the large number of converts in Indonesia. First, the farther the Muslim community is from the heartland of Islam—the Middle East—the less fanatical it is. Secondly, throughout history the people of Indonesia have changed religions several times. Animism gave way to Hinduism, Hinduism to Buddhism, Buddhism to Islam. Now Islam is yielding converts to Christianity. There is an underlying feeling that Islam, like the other religions, is a foreign import, which, of course, it is.

8. **Growing optimism in mission circles.** Through the centuries Christians have tended to regard the Muslim world as an impregnable fortress against which the Christian gospel has no effective weapons. That attitude is changing. In recent years there has been a growing sense of cautious optimism. The idea is being expressed that perhaps God's time for the evangelization of the Muslim world has come. During the past two years several special workshops on Missions to the Muslims have been held in various parts of the country, and books on the subject are beginning to appear. Christians are being urged to pray as never before for the conversion of the Muslims, that the Holy Spirit will open their hearts and minds to receive with meekness the engrafted Word which is able to save their souls (James 1:21).

Speaking of the Arab world, Harry Genet, former TEAM missionary in Beirut, said:

> Over the last decade increasing exposure to the rest of the world, migration to larger cities, and secular higher education, have all been undermining Islam's dominance in society. An increasing openness in exploring Christian belief has surfaced simultaneously. The Middle East, once widely regarded as impregnable, is clearly shifting into the winnable camp.[7]

---

[7] "Penetrating the Muslim World," *Moody Monthly*, May 1974, p. 63.

No one can deny that the Middle East today is on the move. It remains to be seen to what extent Islam can retain its hold on the minds of men in the next few decades.

X

Missions in Asia

Christianity began in Asia and was carried to Europe by Paul and his companions about the time that Buddhism was introduced into China from India. There it flourished and grew into a large tree as set forth by Christ in His parable of the mustard seed in Matthew 13:31-32. For a time it flourished in Mesopotamia until the Muslims destroyed the Persian Empire. After that Christianity in Asia declined steadily until it became a minority religion.

Some General Observations

1. **Asia is the most densely populated portion of the globe.** Half the world's population lives in an arc between Karachi and Tokyo. Two countries have enormous populations—China with 990 million and India with 700 million. Since the Communists came to power in 1949 the population of China has *increased* by some 480 million people, which equals the combined populations of the USSR and the USA. Some of the largest cities in the world are found in this region. The 1970 census gave metropolitan Tokyo a population of 22 million—twice that of Greater New York. Shanghai has 10 million and Bombay 7 million. These cities are not only large, they are congested beyond anything known in the West. Of Calcutta's 8 million people, 250,000 live and die in the alleys, without so much as a roof over their heads.

2. **Asia is the home of the great ethnic religions.** Hinduism is the dominant religion of India, where it claims some 83 percent of the people. Buddhism died out in the land of its birth—India. In its Theravada form it

123

spread south and east to Sri Lanka, Burma, Thailand, and Indochina. Mahayana Buddhism spread north and east to China, Korea, and Japan. Today it is the most widespread religion in Asia. Taoism is native to China and Shinto to Japan. Confucianism, which began in China, spread to all parts of the Far East, where it has greatly influenced the culture of the entire region.

3. **Asia was the scene of the earliest missionary efforts.** The apostle Thomas is said to have reached India in A.D. 52 and labored there for twenty years before his martyrdom near Madras. The Mar Thoma Church in South India is named after him. The great Nestorian Church took the gospel to India and later to China, where it flourished for two hundred years during the T'ang Dynasty (618-907). The earliest Roman Catholic missionaries went to this part of the world. The Franciscans were in China during much of the fourteenth century. The first Jesuit missionaries landed in India in 1542, labored in Japan in the sixteenth century, and gained entrance into China in the seventeenth century.

When Protestant missions got under way their first missionaries also went to Asia. The Danish-Halle Mission worked in India during most of the eighteenth century. William Carey, the first missionary from the English-speaking world, spent almost forty years in India, during which time he helped to translate the Scriptures into thirty-five languages of India. The first American missionary, Adoniram Judson, served in Burma, where he laid the foundation of the great Baptist Church. The first Protestant missionary to China, Robert Morrison, began work in Canton in 1807. When China opened five treaty ports in the 1840s a dozen Protestant societies entered China during the first decade.

During the 1920s there were approximately sixteen thousand missionaries in China, half of them Roman Catholic. This was more than in any other country in the world. In India the figure was slightly lower. Through the years Asia has attracted more missionaries than Africa or Latin America. Tens of thousands of missionaries lived and died in Asia, and literally hundreds of millions of dollars for mission work have been invested in that part of the world.

4. **Results in Asia have not been commensurate with the efforts.** The Catholics have been in this part of the world for almost 500 years and the Protestants have been there for 275 years, but after all this time only 3 percent of Asia is professing Christian. China yielded 3 million Roman Catholic Christians and only 1 million Protestant Christians, less than 1 percent of the population. India did a little better but not much—2.9 percent of the population, divided among Roman Catholics, Syrian Orthodox, and Protestants. After 125 years in Japan we garnered only 1 million converts out of a population of 118 million. It is a staggering fact that there are more non-Christians in India and China than there are Christians in the whole world. Results in Thailand have been distressingly small—only one tenth of 1 percent of the people are professing Christians.

Fortunately we did much better in other countries. European missionaries, mostly Dutch Reformed, had considerable success in Indonesia, where large churches are quite common, the Batak Church of Sumatra having over a million members. Other churches have a membership running into hundreds of thousands. On the island of Java Christians are fewer and churches are smaller. In Sulawesi almost 90 percent of the Minahasa are Christians. In recent years, as a direct result of the revival of the late sixties, many churches have doubled or trebled their membership.

The Roman Catholics made their greatest gains in the Philippines where today they claim 82 percent of the population. The Protestants and the Independent Catholics, both dating back to the turn of the century, make up another eight percent. The American Baptists did well in Burma, but they won few converts among the Burmese. The American Presbyterians continued the mission in Thailand when others became discouraged and left. The Christian and Missionary Alliance, for many years the only Protestant mission in Vietnam, ended up with a strong church of over 60,000 members.

It was in Korea, however, that we met with the greatest numerical and spiritual success. Three American missions carried the heavy end of the load: Presbyterians, Methodists, and OMS International. Today the Christians represent almost 22 percent of the population, the vast majority of them being Protestants. The churches are strong in every respect. In 1977 over a million new members were added to the church rolls in Korea. One Presbyterian church in Seoul has 40,000 members and an Assembly of God church has 200,000.

5. **Coverts have come mostly from the lower classes.** This is especially true in India, where 60 percent of the Christians came originally from the "Untouchables," now known as the Scheduled Classes. These conversions were the result of mass movements that took place much earlier. Many of these people have improved their lot in life since becoming Christians, but their standard of living is still quite low. Their presence in the churches helps to explain, at least in part, the great poverty that plagues the church in India.

Over 97 percent of all the Christians in Burma have come not from the Burmese, who are Buddhists, but from the tribespeople, who are animists. A similar situation exists in Indonesia, where the Batak Church of Sumatra is made up almost entirely of tribespeople who were formerly animists. In China the situation was slightly better. Very few of the literati, or Mandarin class, ever embraced the Christian faith. Most of the Christians came from the humbler walks of life. Japan was an exception to this phenomenon. There the early Christians were members of the military elite, the *samurai,* whose stamp remains on the Japanese church to this day. The churches there are made up mostly of the middle and upper middle classes. Consequently, though they are quite small, they are blessed with a well educated ministry.

Reasons for the Paucity of Results

1. **The presence of ancient, well developed civilizations.** It was here that the Christian missionaries encountered civilizations that are three, four, or five thousand years old. The Indus civilization in India antedates the Aryan civilization which began in 1500 B.C. The Chinese had *one dynasty* that endured for 900 years! Little wonder that they smile with amusement when we celebrate our Bicentennial.

The people of Asia are justly proud of their cultural heritage and are not prepared to exchange it for any other. Indeed, they regard their civilization as superior to ours in everything but technology. China in particular is proud of her long history, her advanced civilization, and her enormous population. In all three she leads the world. For well over a thousand years China shed the light and luster of her ancient civilization over most of Asia. She lent to everyone; she borrowed from no one. Even Japan owes much of her civilization to China.

So far as the Chinese were concerned there was only one civilized country in the world—the Middle Kingdom. All others were beyond the pale; hence they were called "barbarians." China's civilization reached its zenith during the Dark Ages, when the lights all over Europe were going out. Changan, the capital of the T'ang Dynasty, was probably the most sophisticated city in the world of that day. With such a history and such a civilization, China can be forgiven if she entertained ideas of her own greatness.

When the missionaries from the West arrived in China in the nineteenth century they found themselves up against a stone wall. Their physical appearance alone—blue eyes, blonde hair, and white skin— was enough to scare the wits out of the illiterate peasantry. For want of a better term they called them "foreign devils." As for the literati, they regarded the missionaries with undisguised hostility because their Western learning posed a threat to their own power and prestige as guardians of Chinese culture. With every weapon at their disposal they fought the presence of the missionaries.

2. **Competition from ancient, highly developed religious systems.** The religions of Asia have their own founders, philosophers, teachers, and reformers. They have their own beautiful and richly adorned temples, stupas, pagodas, and monasteries. People from all parts of the world travel to India to see its famous temples. The Taj Mahal is one of the most strikingly beautiful edifices in the world. Moreover, they have their sacred rivers, their sacred mountains, and their sacred scriptures. They also have their holy men: fakirs, swamis, yogis, and gurus. And, of course, they have their gods and goddesses by the millions. They even have their own saviors and their bodhisatvas.

The Hindus believe that their ancient scripture, the Rig Veda, was revealed by God to the seers. So sacred is this book, according to the ancients, that if a Sudra—a member of the lowest caste—were to take its words on his lips his tongue was to be cut out. And if he allowed himself to listen to its words, his ears were to be filled with molten lead. It comes then as no surprise that the Hindu is satisfied with his *Bhagavad Gita* and the Buddhist with his *Lotus Gospel.*

The same was true of the Confucian scholars in China. On one occasion the literati memorialized the throne, requesting the emperor to outlaw the Christian religion. After studying the New Testament for himself the emperor replied: "There is no need to outlaw this religion. To say that the salvation of the world was accomplished by a criminal on a cross is so patently foolish that no Chinese will believe such a doctrine. We have nothing to fear from this new religion."

So attached were the Chinese to their own traditions that after having heard the gospel message they replied: "We would sooner go to hell with our Confucius than go to heaven with your Jesus."

3. **Opposition due to deep-seated, longstanding social and religious customs.** In every culture there are practices and prejudices which are inimical to the Christian gospel. India, China, and Japan each had one major obstacle to the acceptance of Christianity. In each case that single obstacle was primarily responsible for the paucity of results in those countries.

In India it was the caste system. For thousands of years the outstanding feature of Indian social life was the caste system, by which Hindu society was divided into four broad socio-occupational groups. At the top were the *Brahmins,* the traditional priests and intellectual leaders; next were the *Kshatriyas,* the warriors and rulers; then the *Vaisyas,* the traders and merchants; and finally the *Sudras,* the servants and laborers, who performed all the menial tasks for the other three groups. Below this structure were the *Pariahs,* better known as the "Untouchables."

Every Hindu is a member of a particular caste by accident of birth. Throughout his entire life he remains a member of the caste into which he was born. He can go neither up nor down in the scale. His only hope of improving his condition is in the next incarnation. The only way to do that is to accept his *karma* and fulfill his duty—*dharma*—to the best of his ability. By accepting his fate in this life he may possibly improve it in the next.

Along comes the Christian missionary, who declares that all men have been created in the image of God and are, therefore, members of the one great human family. Moreover, in Christ there is neither Jew nor Greek, slave nor free, male nor female; all are one in Jesus Christ.

This concept is totally unacceptable to the Hindu. All men are *not* equal. Some are higher and others are lower in the social scale, and this by the inexorable law of *karma.* Scavengers can never associate with scholars; butchers can never associate with Brahmins—any time, any place, for any purpose. To do so would break caste, and to break caste is to be an outcaste. The Sudra is just as desirous as the Brahmin to stay within his caste; for only by so doing can he hope eventually to effect his own salvation. To break caste in this life is to set himself back and hinder his progress toward *Nirvana.*

The question is often asked: "Can a Hindu become a Christian without breaking caste?" And the answer is: "No! To become a Christian *is* to break caste, and that by *their* definition, not ours." When a Hindu becomes a Christian he is regarded *by other Hindus* as an outcaste and treated as such.

In each of the four main castes there are hundreds of subcastes. Carpenters and fishermen belong at the bottom of the lowest caste—the Sudra. And Jesus was a carpenter and some of His disciples were fishermen. To ask a high and haughty Brahmin to believe that the Savior and Sovereign of the world was a carpenter is to confront him with an idea that is utterly repugnant to his way of thinking. Little wonder that more Brahmins did not come to Christ.

It should be noted in passing that "Untouchability" has been outlawed in India. Caste, however, continues to be a problem, especially in the smaller towns and villages. In the larger cities the acid of modernity is eating away at the caste system, but it will be a long time before it completely disappears.

In China the great stumbling block was ancestor worship, which has been practiced for thousands of years. In the Confucian ethic the greatest single virtue was filial piety. On one occasion the sage said: "If a person will not revere his own father, he will not revere anyone." And filial piety extends to the dead as well as to the living, for both are members of the extended family. The souls of the departed are dependent for their sustenance on the food and other offerings made to them by the living, principally by the eldest son. If he neglects his duty, their souls will perish. To neglect the souls of the dead is hardly less criminal than to murder the bodies of the living.

The early missionaries regarded ancestor worship as a form of idolatry. They therefore preached against it, and the Chinese church leaders did the same. The first taunt thrown at a new convert by his friends and relatives was: "So, you no longer want your elders?" That was the last word in defamation. For a son to neglect his father, living or dead, was to commit the unpardonable sin in the eyes of the Chinese.

If the missionaries had been able to find a functional substitute for ancestor worship, the number of Christian converts would doubtless have been greater than it was.

In Japan the situation was even worse. In addition to ancestor worship they had emperor worship. Shinto is the national religion of Japan. In 1889 Shinto was divided into two parts. One, known as Sect Shinto, was regarded as a religion. It dealt with rituals, prayers, divination, and charms. The other was State Shinto, which was not supposed to be a religion but a national cult which every patriotic Japanese was required to accept. State Shinto was supported by the government, enforced in the schools, and later exploited by the militarists. Shrines were converted into national monuments. Priests were civil servants under the Home Office. According to Japanese mythology the first emperor, Jimmu Tenno, was the great-great-grandson of the Sun Goddess and was thought to be divine. All his descendants likewise were divine. Thus State Shinto culminated in emperor worship.

Consequently in Japan the Christian convert had to reject both ancestor worship and the worship of the emperor, thereby incurring the wrath of the government as well as that of his relatives. During World War II hundreds of Japanese pastors were imprisoned when they refused to pay homage to the emperor. To be accused of being a traitor to one's country is a very serious charge, especially in time of war. Few people in the homeland have any idea what it costs to be a Christian in such non-Christian countries as India, China, or Japan.

4. **Christianity's close ties with colonialism.** In the whole of East Asia only one country did not become the victim of Western imperialism—Thailand. Britain, France, Spain, Holland, and the United States all had colonies. Even before the Western governments moved in and took over, the powerful East India Companies had staked out their claims and made their fortunes. India, Pakistan, Bangladesh, Burma, Malaysia, and Sri Lanka were all parts of the British Empire. France occupied the three countries that made up Indochina. Holland had the Netherlands East Indies. The Spanish occupation of the Philippines lasted for over three hundred years until the United States took over the islands at the turn of the century.

The tie-in between the gospel and the gunboat was closest in China. After centuries of isolation China was forced to open her doors to Western commerce by the Treaty of Nanking that followed the Opium War (1839-1842). Five treaty ports were opened, and into those treaty ports went the missionaries with their Bibles and the merchants with their opium. To make matters worse, the missionaries, the only bilingual people on the scene, acted as interpreters when the Treaty of Nanking was drawn up. For a hundred years the unholy alliance between the gospel and the gunboat was a source of embarrassment to the missionaries.

5. **The exclusive claims of Christianity.** If Christianity had posed as one religion among many it would have found greater favor; but it presented itself as the only true religion, thereby dismissing all other religions as false. Such a view was totally unacceptable to the religious leaders of Asia.

Hinduism, the most tolerant of all religions, would gladly have made room for Christianity. It already had thousands of gods in its pantheon; to add one more was of no consequence. In fact many Hindus were quite willing to regard Christ as one of the many *avatars* of Vishnu, along with Krishna. But to insist on the uniqueness of Christ was not only in poor taste, it was completely foreign to their way of thinking. Mahatma Gandhi had the greatest admiration for Christ as a person and was quite willing to acknowledge Him as one of the world's greatest teachers, but never as the unique Son of God. He was unable, he said, to place Jesus on a "solitary throne." Gandhi likened truth to a tree and the various religions to branches of the tree. As many branches are required to make a tree, so it takes many religions to express the full truth regarding God, man, and salvation. "For me the different religions are beautiful flowers from the same garden, or they are branches of the same majestic tree."[1]

The same was true, though to a lesser extent, with Buddhism and Confucianism. Buddha never claimed to be inspired, nor did he leave behind any infallible guide for faith or morals. Original Buddhism had neither gods nor saviors. Every man was expected to work out his own salvation as best he could. The Chinese, for all their xenophobia, were not against a new religion simply because it was foreign. "The concept of a universal order on earth had made the Chinese tolerant of *any* religion as long as it posed no threat to that order. Thus, they found it difficult to grant to the Christian faith the uniqueness that it claimed."[2]

Another aspect of Christianity that appeared strange to the Chinese was its emphasis on the sinfulness of man. For over two thousand years Confucianism had taught that human nature is essentially good and requires only self-cultivation to bring it to perfection.

Little wonder then that Christianity, with all its strange doctrines and its claim to uniqueness, should have been rejected by the people of Asia.

The Impact of Christianity on Asia

To what extent has Christianity influenced the culture of Asia? This is a big question and one that cannot be answered in a few pages. Christian missionaries tend to overemphasize the impact that Christianity made on the continent of Asia. On the other hand anti-foreign nationalists often go to the other extreme and deny that Christianity has had any appreciable effect on Asia. The truth probably lies somewhere between these two extremes. One thing seems fairly certain. The overall impact of Christianity on Asian society was much larger than the number of converts actually won to Christ would seem to indicate.

Obviously Christianity made its greatest impact where it has been the longest and where it made the largest number of converts—the Philippines. The Christianization of the islands began with the arrival in 1564 of Father Legaspi and the Augustinian friars, followed later by the other religious

---

[1] M. K. Gandhi, *Christian Missions: Their Place in India* (Ahmedabad: Navajivan Press, 1941), p. 126.

[2] Charles Corwin, *East to Eden? Religion and the Dynamics of Social Change* (Grand Rapids: Eerdmans Publishing Company, 1972), p. 83.

orders. They opened schools at all levels and taught the doctrines of Christianity and the arts of Western civilization. The women were raised from practical slavery to virtual emancipation by the introduction of the Christian concept of the family. Spanish officials married Filipino women and the children were reared in the Christian faith. A combination of religious passion and military conquest enabled the Roman Catholics to effect the conversion of the islands during the first century of occupation. Some of the credit for this achievement belongs to Philip II of Spain, who made the spread of the Christian faith the chief aim in the colonization of the islands named after him. To the Roman Catholic Church must go the credit for stopping the spread of Islam from Indonesia through the archipelago. The Muslims advanced from the south, the Roman Catholics from the north. They met on the island of Mindanao, where today there are some two million Muslims, known as Moros.

Beginning about 1900 American missions entered the Philippines and have been at work there in large numbers ever since. Today the Christians represent about 90 percent of the population, making the Philippines the only "Christian" country in Asia. The vast majority of these are claimed by the Roman Catholic Church. Spanish culture and American influence remain strong. The modern Filipino is a mixture of Western and Oriental, with the Oriental predominating.

It is difficult to assess the impact of Christianity on a country as large and diverse as India with 700 million people, fourteen major languages, and over five hundred minor ones. Christianity has made its greatest impact in the south where the Syrian Orthodox churches have been in existence for well over fifteen hundred years. Many of their members came originally from high-caste Hindu background and still enjoy a certain degree of prestige in the community. The strength of the Christian community varies greatly from state to state. Nagaland is almost 100 percent Christian but the Nagas are a small tribe and have no influence outside their own restricted community in the northeast. Goa is 36 percent Christian—entirely Roman Catholic. Kerala is next with 21 percent and Manipur with 20 percent.

About 70 percent of all the Christians in India live in the four southern states and Goa. Of these, 75 percent live in villages. Accordingly, the Indian church is predominantly rural and poor. Christianity has had very little influence on the tens of millions of people in the Ganges Valley.

It is largely to British influence that India owes its open society with its democratic institutions. To what extent these are the result of Christianity it is difficult to say. Modern Hinduism has seen three major attempts at reform: the Brahmo Samaj, the Arya Samaj, and the Ramakrishna Movement. All three were to some extent influenced by Christianity.

Ram Mohun Roy, founder of the Brahmo Samaj, never became a Christian; but he was on friendly terms with Alexander Duff and William Carey. Through them he was introduced to the Christian religion. After searching Sanskrit, Greek, and Hebrew literature, he wrote: "The consequence of my long uninterrupted researches into religious truth has been that I have found the doctrines of Christ more conducive to moral principles and better adapted for the use of rational beings than any other which have come to my knowledge."[3]

And what about Mahatma Gandhi, the most influential person in India in the present century? He had close contacts with evangelical Christians in England, South Africa, and India, and his knowledge of Christian doctrine was considerable. His concept of nonviolence *(satyagraha)*, which he used so effectively against the British Raj, he got from the Sermon on the Mount, not the *Bhagavad Gita.*

No missionary knew India better or loved it more than did E. Stanley Jones. Most of his sixty-year ministry was spent among the intellectuals of India, who came to respect him greatly. From his first two books, *The Christ of the Indian Road* and *Christ at the Round Table,* one gets the impression that Christianity had deeply influenced the thinking of India and was at the bottom of many of its reforms.

> Call the roll of the reforms that are sweeping across India, and whether they be economic, social, moral, or religious, they are all tending straight toward Jesus Christ and his thought. Not one of them is going away from him, that is, if it be a reform and not a reaction.[4]

It is correct to say that nowhere in the non-Christian world is Jesus Christ more highly revered than in India. Somehow His gentleness, integrity, and spirituality have appealed to the soul of India. It is not too much to say that Christ is more highly regarded in India than in some circles here in the West.

K. N. Panikkar in his book *Asia and Western Dominance* was highly critical of Christian missions and predicted their demise once the colonial era came to an end. India has been independent now for over thirty years, and while the missionary forces have been greatly reduced, the Christian church is as viable as ever. Stephen Neill is correct when he says:

> It can be maintained with some confidence that if every foreign missionary and every cent of foreign support were withdrawn, the churches, though weakened at certain points, would still maintain their existence, and would continue to expand, though perhaps more slowly than in the past. . . . The faith of the village Christian is in many cases unenlightened, but it is real; it is most unlikely that he will ever forsake this religion in favor of any other.[5]

Christianity was introduced into China on four separate occasions. Not once did it take root permanently. Opposition came mostly from the

---

[3] Daniel J. Fleming, *Building with India* (New York: Missionary Education Movement, 1922), p. 75.

[4] E. Stanley Jones, *The Christ of the Indian Road* (New York: Abingdon Press, 1925), p. 212.

[5] Stephen Neill, *The Story of the Christian Church in India and Pakistan* (Grand Rapids: Eerdmans Publishing Company, 1970), p. 167.

scholar-gentry class, the most powerful segment of Chinese society. The closest that China ever came to becoming Christian was during the Taiping Rebellion in the middle of the nineteenth century. The rebellion, which lasted almost fifteen years and took at least twenty million lives, was a quasi-Christian movement led by a "convert" named Hung Hsiu-ch'uan. The Roman Catholics, who might have been expected to support that kind of movement, opposed it because its leader was a Protestant. The Protestants repudiated Hung because he resorted to violence and included in his theology many bizarre doctrines which could only be regarded as heretical.

Finally the Western powers helped the central government to suppress the movement and Hung and his cohorts came to an untimely end. It is interesting to speculate what might have happened to China had the rebellion succeeded. Would China have become Christian? If so, would that have been a good thing under the circumstances? Charles P. Fitzgerald, one-time cultural attaché to the British Embassy in Peking, thinks Christian missions missed the boat when they failed to support Hung and the Taipings. "Protestants temporized, sent emissaries to inquire, doubted and debated, and finally rejected the T'ai Ping prophet as an imposter, and so lost their share in the only Christian movement which ever had a chance of converting the mass of the Chinese people."[6]

The impact of the West on China in the nineteenth century was enormous, all the more so because her civilization was so old and her population so large. The gospel as well as the gunboat was responsible for the impact. By the turn of the century China was ready to come to terms with the West and institute the reforms necessary to bring her into the family of nations. K'ang Yu-wei (1857-1927), one of China's greatest scholars and reformers, took a leading role in those reforms. Though he never became a Christian he acknowledged on one occasion: "I owe my conversion [to reform] chiefly to the writings of two missionaries, the Reverend Timothy Richard and the Reverend Doctor Young J. Allen."[7]

Speaking of the missionaries and their work in China, John Fairbank said:

> The influence of mission schools and hospitals, of missionary ideals and activities in seeking out the common man, translating Western literature, initiating women's education, assisting in ancient tasks of charity and famine relief and in new tasks of modernization, was considerable.... The missionary movement, whatever its spiritual-doctrinal results in this period, was a profound stimulus to China's modernization.[8]

---

[6] Charles P. Fitzgerald, "Opposing Cultural Traditions, Barriers to Communication," in Jessie G. Lutz, *Christian Missions in China: Evangelists of What?* (Chicago: D. C. Heath, 1965), p. 97.

[7] Cyrus H. Peake, *Nationalism and Education in Modern China* (New York: Columbia Unversity Press, 1932), p. 15.

[8] John King Fairbank, *The United States and China* (Cambridge, MA: Harvard University Press, 1971), p. 178.

It is worth noting, in this connection, that the very first Chinese student to America, Yung Wing, was brought here by missionaries in 1847 and graduated from Yale in 1854.

Sun Yat-sen, who was instrumental in bringing down the ancient empire, was a baptized Christian. It was his belief that the Republic of China could not long endure unless the righteousness for which the Christian religion stands was at the center of its national life. Chiang Kai-shek, also a practicing Christian, used his influence to promote Christian ideals in Chinese society. When he launched his New Life Movement in the 1930s he appointed a missionary to be in charge. The Sino-Japanese War broke out just as he was beginning to effect his reforms. Given two decades of peace there is no telling what Chiang, with his Christian ideals, might have done for China.

From a numerical point of view the Christian mission in China was disappointing. The number of professing Christians never quite reached 1 percent of the population. But here again, their influence was considerable. In the early 1930s some 35 percent of those listed in *Who's Who in China* received at least part of their education in a Christian school. In the 1920s, 90 percent of all registered nurses were Christian.[9] In line with this is the testimony of a non-Christian foreign newspaper correspondent who had many opportunities for wide observation. He said that "Christianity had produced a special type of human being in China, more alert, more modern, and more committed to the public welfare."[10] Another experienced foreign newspaperman, who described himself as a "friendly sceptic," declared that "Christianity provided the impetus for most of the really constructive social work in China in the 1930s."[11]

There are those who go farther and suggest that even the Communists were influenced by Christian missions. John Fairbank observes that "on a small scale, the missionaries were the Communists' predecessors."[12] And Fitzgerald states:

> The Chinese Communists took these things at second hand from the practice of the Russian Party, but in other respects they sought to imitate the work of missions, and have at long last, in the fulness of power, acknowledged the debt. . . . It is hard to doubt that some of these characteristics come from Christian examples, not from the manners of the Russian Communist Party.[13]

What about Japan, the most dynamic society in Asia? The early missionaries were very influential people. Thirty percent of their converts were from the powerful *samurai*, the military and intellectual elite who

---

[9] Kenneth Scott Latourette, *A History of Christian Missions in China* (New York: Macmillan, 1929), p. 362.

[10] George E. Sokolsky, *The Tinder Box of Asia* (Garden City, NY: Doubleday, Doran & Co., 1932), p. 21.

[11] H. J. Timperley, *The China Quarterly* (summer 1936).

[12] Fairbank, *The United States and China*, p. 178.

[13] Fitzgerald, "Opposing Cultural Traditions," p. 102.

were interested in all kinds of social and political reforms. To this day the Japanese church comprises the middle and upper classes, in contrast to the church in India, which represents the other end of the social spectrum. For over a hundred years Christians have been in the forefront of reform movements. Many of them were decorated by the government. Outstanding among them was the world-famous Toyohiko Kagawa, who devoted his entire life to social reform. He was one of the founders of the trade union movement in Japan.

The American occupation of Japan following World War II had a profound influence on the entire nation which now seems to be irrevocably committed to the democratic way of life. For almost half a century Japan was our chief opponent in Asia. Today she is our staunchest ally. Between 1945 and 1960 an enormous amount of evangelistic activity took place in Japan. In 1958 the secretary of the Bible Society wrote: "The Bible is becoming the book of the people. It has been placed by the newspapers at the head of our classical literature."[14] In 1977 it was reported to be a best seller.

When it comes to the reception of the gospel, however, the Japanese must be numbered among the more resistant people of the world. Local churches are without exception small even by Asian standards. There are no mass meetings, no thronging crowds. The average church has fifty members. To date Christianity has not succeeded in penetrating Japanese culture to any great extent. Christmas is celebrated with great gusto but largely for commercial purposes. Richard Drummond summed it up as well as anybody when he said:

> There is good reason to believe that the Christian faith and church are now accepted by the nation as an authentic part of Japanese life. Christianity probably no longer appears as something spiritually alien, at least to most people in the cities.[15]

It is in Korea that Protestant missions have made their greatest gains. Not only is the number of Christians high (about 22 percent of the population), but the quality of church life is also very high. Many of the leading educators and politicians are practicing Christians. Half of the men in the armed forces are professing Christians. The Billy Graham Crusade in June 1973 attracted four and a half million people in six cities. Dr. Graham was overwhelmed by his reception and declared the crusade to be the greatest in his twenty-five years of preaching on six continents. If the present rate of church growth continues, it is quite possible that by the turn of the century Korea may be a predominantly Protestant country, the only one in Asia.

---

14 *Worlds Apart,* p. 98.
15 Richard H. Drummond, *A History of Christianity in Japan* (Grand Rapids: Eerdmans Publishing Company, 1971), p. 364.

The Christian church in Korea has always been to the fore in the fight for civil rights—first with the Japanese, later with the Communists, and more recently with the dictatorial regime of President Park Chung Hee. With great courage church leaders, Roman Catholic as well as Protestant, have spoken out against the repressive measures which followed the demise of democracy in October 1972, when President Park suddenly declared martial law, suspended the Constitution, banned all political activity, and dissolved the National Assembly. Not a few church leaders have been imprisoned; others are awaiting trial. Few churches in modern history have suffered as consistently and as courageously as has the Korean church, and the end is not yet.

XI

Missions in Africa

The continent of Africa is divided into two clearly defined regions, North Africa and Sub-Sahara Africa, otherwise known as Black Africa. North of the Sahara Desert the people are Arab and Berber by race and Muslim by religion. For this reason the five states in the north have more in common with the Middle East than with the rest of Africa. In this chapter we are concerned only with Black Africa.

The population of Black Africa is approximately 400 million, divided among forty-four independent countries. Most of these countries are small and have a population of fewer than 10 million. Six countries may be considered large: Nigeria (80 million), Ethiopia (33 million), South Africa (26 million), Zaire (32 million), Sudan (20 million), and Tanzania (20 million). Together these six countries represent one half of the 400 million people in Black Africa.

In the last twenty years the political configuration of Black Africa has changed almost beyond recognition. In the heyday of Western imperialism all of Africa except Ethiopia and Liberia was parceled out among the European powers. Germany lost her colonies after World War I, which left Britain and France as the two colonial giants, each with a dozen or more colonies. Belgium had the Congo and Ruanda-Urundi and Portugal had Angola and Mozambique. All thirteen French colonies received their independence in 1960. The British colonies were granted independence one by one over the span of a decade or more, beginning with Ghana in 1957.

Politically, Africa still has its problems; but they stem from within and are occasioned largely by lack of internal cohesion—party politics divided along tribal lines. Democracy was tried but soon abandoned in favor of one-party rule—all too often headed by a self-appointed dictator. The independence that was expected to solve all their problems has turned out to be a mirage. In most African countries the people have fewer freedoms than they did under colonialism. However, at least they have the satisfaction of knowing that they are ruled by their own people. All this turmoil has, of course, adversely affected both church and mission in that part of the world.

The earliest missionaries to Africa were Roman Catholics who accompanied the Portuguese explorers along the coast of Africa during the fifteenth century under Prince Henry the Navigator. They served as chaplains to their own compatriots and as missionaries to the Africans. They established thriving missions in West Africa and as far south as Zaire and Angola. On the east coast they penetrated inland as far as present-day Zimbabwe. For a time these missions thrived, but by the end of the eighteenth century they had all but disappeared.

When Protestant missions got under way about the turn of the nineteenth century, they approached the continent from four different directions—west, south, east, and up the Congo River.

In the early years the going was hard, deaths were numerous, and results were meager.

> The European arm of this missionary movement . . . was a costly business. In the first twelve years of its work from 1828 at Christiansborg, Accra, the Basel Mission lost eight of nine men from fever. The CMS lost fifty-three men and women in Sierra Leone between 1804 and 1824. The Methodists in the fifteen years following 1835 had seventy-eight new appointments, men and wives in the Gambia, Sierra Leone and the Gold Coast; thirty of these died within a year of arrival.[1]

The story of missions in Africa in the nineteenth century is an amazing tale of adventure, endurance, privation, sickness, weakness, and death. With such crippling casualties the missions during the latter half of the century were able to do little more than maintain a holding operation. Under such conditions it is little wonder that converts came slowly.

> Each of the pioneer missions was disheartened by its inability to make numerous and lasting conversions. The Primitive Methodists [in Northern Rhodesia] for example waited thirteen years to make their first convert. Moreover, he, and five other students who followed him, soon lapsed into apostasy, and the Primitive Methodists were compelled to wait patiently until a new group of catechumens could be prepared slowly for baptism. For all missions these were barren, pioneer years.[2]

The period of rapid growth began about 1900. From 1900 to 1950 the Christian population increased about sixty times. From 1950 to the

---

[1] T. A. Beetham, *Christianity and the New Africa* (London: Pall Mall Press, 1967), p. 11.

[2] Robert I. Rotberg, *Christian Missionaries and the Creation of Northern Rhodesia, 1880-1924* (Princeton: Princeton University Press, 1965), p. 42.

present the growth rate has been even faster. Today the whole of Black Africa is on the move spiritually, away from animism, which has nothing to offer an educated person, to something more satisfying to mind and soul.

The educated African today has really only two options—Christianity or Islam, both of which are world religions with a world brotherhood. We often hear that Islam is making converts three and four times faster than Christianity. It is doubtful if this was ever true. Certainly it is not true at the present time. In some parts of the continent the Muslims may have the edge on us, but in other parts we are far ahead of them in the race for the mind of Africa.

Although the growth of Islam has slowed down in recent years, it remains Christianity's greatest rival in Africa. It still makes a strong appeal, for the following reasons: (1) It poses as the "black man's religion"—supposedly indigenous to Africa, though it is not. (2) Islam was not identified with the European colonial system though through the Arabs it was connected with the slave trade of an earlier era. (3) Islam has made good use of lay missionaries, principally teachers and merchants who settle down and become part of the local community. (4) Islam makes fewer ethical and moral demands on its adherents. Polygamy, an almost insurmountable problem to the Christian church, is no problem at all to Islam, for all devout Muslims are permitted to have four wives at one time. (5) Some branches of Islam are now extensively engaged in social and humanitarian service, taking a leaf from the missionary's book.

Christianity has made more converts in Black Africa than in all the rest of the Third World combined. In spite of the fact that we had a late start in Africa as compared with Asia, we have made converts much faster. Accurate statistics are difficult to obtain. Moreover, church growth is so rapid that any estimate is out of date in a year or two. According to reliable estimates the population of Black Africa is around 400 million. Of this figure 200 million are Christians, 125 million are Muslims, and about 75 million are still animists. This means that 50 percent of the people of Black Africa are professing Christians, compared with about 3 percent for the continent of Asia. It should be noted that Christians outnumber Muslims.

The ratio of Christians to the total population is highest in south Africa, lowest in west Africa, and somewhere in between in central and east Africa. Countries with the highest ratio of Christians, including Roman Catholics, are: Congo, 99 percent; Central African Republic, 90 percent; Lesotho, 87 percent; Zaire, 86 percent; Namibia, 84 percent; Swaziland, 83 percent; South Africa, 83 percent; and Angola, 83 percent.

In west Africa the ratio drops drastically. In seven countries it is below 10 percent. The Big Five include: Ghana, 63 percent; Nigeria, 46 percent; Liberia, 42 percent; Togo, 30 percent; and Benin, 20 percent.

The Christians are broken down into four major groups: Roman Catholics with eighty-seven million; Protestant with eighty-three million; Separatists or Independent with twenty million; and Copts with ten million.

The oldest are the Copts, who belong to the Ethiopian Orthodox Church, which dates back to the fourth century. The African Independent Churches are to be found all over Africa, but the largest concentrations are in South Africa, Nigeria, Zaire, Ghana, and Kenya. Altogether there are some seven thousand separate groups in this movement. They are divided into two major groups—Ethiopian and Zionist. The Ethiopian type is due in large measure to the color bar and emphasizes the African character of the church. The Zionist type is a much more significant and elaborate expression of the African mind. Both types have developed an indigenous form of ritual which includes hand-clapping, dancing, native music, and faith healing.

The Protestants, who through the years have lagged behind the Roman Catholics, have more recently been making phenomenal gains. This is due largely to the great emphasis placed in recent years on mass evangelism, which under various names has been carried out with excellent results in Nigeria, Zaire, Ghana, and other countries. Everywhere churches have been revived, pastors and leaders have been given special training (theological education by extension), and laymen at all levels have been mobilized for mass evangelism.

Along with evangelism goes Bible translation, an area in which Protestant missionaries have always excelled. Bible translation can be a nightmare in a continent with 860 tribes, each speaking its own language. In most cases the language had to be reduced to writing before translation could begin. When translation was completed and the book published, the people had to be taught to read the script invented for them by the missionaries. It was a long, laborious, and costly operation, requiring infinite patience and not a little linguistic skill. By December 1980 the complete Bible was available in 100 languages, the New Testament in another 158, and portions in still another 241, making a grand total of 499 languages for the entire continent.

Factors Conducive to Growth

Each major area of the world has its own peculiar set of circumstances. Sometimes these are conducive to the acceptance of the gospel and sometimes they are not. The missionaries in Africa had their problems to be sure, but the overall situation was favorable to the spread of Christianity.

1. **An enormous amount of missionary effort.** There are more missionaries per capita in Africa than anywhere else in the world. To begin with, Black Africa attracted missions from *all* the major sending countries

—England, Scotland, Ireland, Germany, Switzerland, Scandinavia, United States, Canada, Australia, and New Zealand. Moreover, in this part of the world we find all *kinds* of missionary agencies—mainline denominations, faith missions, Pentecostals, Seventh-Day Adventists, Quakers, and indigenous movements. Before the evacuation in the early sixties there were two thousand Protestant missionaries in Zaire, which at that time had a comparatively small population of only twelve million. Paul reminded the Corinthians that he who sows bountifully will also reap bountifully. This has certainly been the case in Black Africa.

2. **Colonialism, a blessing in disguise.** In Asia colonialism was a serious hindrance to the spread of the gospel, but in Africa the story was different. In spite of its many shortcomings, colonialism there had some things in its favor. It terminated intertribal warfare and the infamous slave trade, both of which were decimating the population, and imposed a much-needed peace on the entire continent. Moreover, the colonial governments favored missionary work in many ways. In the early years they made land grants for schools and mission stations and later subsidized mission schools. Without such aid the missions would not have been able to maintain all their Christian schools. The colonial officials, representing as they did the paramount power in the colonies, enjoyed a good deal of personal prestige in society. Some of this prestige rubbed off on the missionaries, for they too belonged to the white race.

3. **The structure of African society.** The tribal structure of African society made it easy for the missionaries to acquire power. For centuries all major decisions were made by the tribal chiefs and the members of the tribe simply obeyed orders. When the Africans became Christians and were to a certain extent "detribalized," it was only natural that they should transfer their allegiance to the missionaries. Hence the great influence of the missionaries in Africa. This should be borne in mind when the nineteenth-century missionary in Africa is criticized for acting like the "great white father."

4. **A huge investment in education.** When the early missionaries arrived in Africa they found an almost totally illiterate society. Indeed, the vast majority of African languages had no written form. The missionaries had to start from scratch—inventing scripts, writing textbooks, and opening schools. For many decades they were the sole purveyors of education. The British did as good a job as anyone in Africa, but in 1923 only one hundred of the six thousand schools in British Africa were government schools. As late as 1961, 68 percent of all the school children in Africa were still in mission schools. All schools are now nationalized.

This imposed a heavy burden on the missions; nevertheless it afforded them a unique opportunity to mold the character of several generations of Africans. The connection between the church and the school was very close. In the bush schools—of which there were tens of thousands—the evangelist was also the teacher. He taught not only the three Rs but also the Bible and Christian doctrine. Today there is hardly a leader in any walk of life who did not receive at least part of his education in a mission school. With so many people being exposed to Christianity over such a long period of time during the most formative years of their lives, it is no wonder that so many of them embraced the Christian faith in one form or another.

5. **Little opposition from indigenous religions.** The great ethnic religions which posed such problems for the missionaries in Asia were not found on the continent of Africa. Africa is the heartland of animism and the people there knew little else until the coming of Islam and Christianity.

Reduced to its simplest form, animism is the belief in spirits. Spirits abound everywhere—in the atmosphere, in trees, mountains, houses, and in human beings. There are two kinds—good and evil. The evil spirits are by far the more active; consequently they must be constantly placated or they will inflict all manner of pain and misfortune on human beings.

Animism has produced no books and no temples; nor has it produced any great leaders, thinkers, or scholars. Of course, it has its medicine men, witch doctors, and devil dancers. While these are powerful figures in the local tribe, they are no match for the missionary doctors and teachers. Animism cannot withstand the inroads of Western learning. People with a modern education find it difficult to continue to practice the superstitious rites connected with animism. This is obviously one reason why modern Africans are deserting animism by the millions every year.

6. **The prestige of the missionary.** We have noted that in Asia the missionary was looked down on by the Brahmins of India and the Confucian scholars of China. In Africa, however, the situation was reversed. There the missionary was regarded as belonging to a "superior" race. Even the simple trinkets he used to pay his carriers and guides—beads, shells, nails, combs, mirrors, etc.—were objects of the greatest curiosity. Their possession marked the proud owner as a person on his way to "civilization." And what shall be said of the more ingenious inventions of Western technology which were introduced by the missionary: reading, writing, and arithmetic, not to mention agricultural tools, medical instruments, alarm clocks, rifles, typewriters, adding machines, etc.? When the simple, illiterate Africans saw the missionary and all the accoutrements of Western civilization which he brought along, they must have felt like the Lycaonians of Paul's day when they exclaimed: "The gods have come down to us in the likeness of men!" (Acts 14:11, RSV). The nineteenth-century missionary did not have to *act* like a tin god, he *was* a tin god! This was in stark contrast to China, where he was called a "foreign devil" and treated as a "barbarian."

7. **The African's deeply religious nature.** In spite of their primitive form of animism, the Africans have always believed in a Great Spirit in the sky. He was called by different names in different tribes, but his existence was recognized by all. Indeed, his presence was never far away, for the

Africans live close to nature and the veil between the seen world and the unseen world is paper thin. They have no hangups regarding the supernatural. They are not like the Theravada Buddhists, who deny the existence of all gods. Nor are they like the Hindus, who believe that everything is god. Nor are they like Western men of science, who are locked into a closed system. The African carries religion in his soul and constantly communes with the unseen powers of the universe. In the vicissitudes of his daily life he may be preoccupied with spirits and demons, but in his more sober moments he recognizes the presence and power of the Great Spirit who lives in the sky, who sends the sunshine and the rain, who watches over crops and cattle, who has the power of life and death, and who can both protect and punish man. When the missionary, therefore, brought to the Africans a clear knowledge of the One True God, Maker of heaven and earth, and Jesus Christ His only Son, the African mind found it easy to embrace such a doctrine.

The Impact of Christianity on Africa

To what extent has Christianity affected the culture of Africa? When a powerful, highly developed civilization comes into contact with a weaker, less highly developed civilization, the former tends to swamp the latter. This is what has happened in Black Africa.

When that higher civilization is backed up by all the apparatus of a colonial administration based on economic and military power, it is bound to have a detrimental effect on the indigenous culture.

Moreover, when education, the most potent instrument for the molding of the national character, is in the hands of the representatives of that higher civilization, the less developed culture is sure to be undermined.

The missionaries' contribution to the modernization of Africa has been prodigious. It is no exaggeration to say that without the groundwork laid by them, especially in the area of education, not a single country in Black Africa would be independent today. No one knows this better than do the Africans themselves.

The first country to achieve independence was Ghana in 1957. Its first president in one of his early announcements said: "We owe much to the missionaries, and we will continue to welcome them to our country." Prime Minister Balewa of Nigeria, in his Motion for Independence made in Parliament in January 1960, said: "We are grateful to the missionaries who have done so much to assist in the independence of Nigeria. . . . Missions can look back with satisfaction on many notable educational successes, and indeed there are, I am sure, some honorable members present who are a living testimony to this." Jomo Kenyatta, one-time leader of the Mau Mau Movement, later president of Kenya, more than once went on public record to thank the missionaries for their contribution to Kenya's independence and to invite them to stay and help him build a better country.

In most non-Christian countries Christians tend to have an influence out of all proportion to their numbers, and not without reason. They are often better educated than their compatriots. They are usually conscientious and trustworthy. They make good neighbors and loyal citizens. They are fair and honest in their business dealings. It is true that in the higher echelons of politics they might suffer some form of discrimination on account of their faith. This is especially true when they are a tiny minority. But on the other hand, even as business clerks and government workers they are often preferred to their non-Christian neighbors. In not a few countries the highest government officials are practicing Christians. They are making an honest effort to bring Christian principles to bear on the social, economic, and political problems of the day. At one time or another in recent years Liberia, Ghana, Nigeria, Chad, Zaire, Uganda, Tanzania, and Zambia all had Christian presidents.

Many Africans fear that their culture will in time be completely swamped by Western culture. They are making every effort to preserve all that is good. The Christian church is doing the same. It is trying to indigenize its liturgy, music, theology, and other features of its corporate life. In the words of John Mbiti, Africa's leading theologian, "The missionaries Christianized Africa; now it's time for the Africans to Africanize Christianity." The next ten or fifteen years will be crucial to the future image of Christianity in Africa.

XII

Missions in Latin America

A good deal is heard these days about the population explosion; but nowhere in the world is the population increasing faster than in Latin America, where the growth rate is around 3.5 percent as compared with the world rate of 2 percent. In some of the countries it is a whopping 4 percent or more. This high growth rate is due in part to Catholic influence and the continued opposition to birth control on the part of the Catholic church.

The people of Latin America, now numbering about 383 million, can be divided into three major groups: people of pure Spanish blood; people of pure Indian blood; and people of mixed blood, known as *mestizos.* There are about 30 million Indians. In the Andes countries of Peru, Bolivia, and Ecuador they constitute the bulk of the population. Two countries in Central America have large Indian populations—Mexico and Guatemala. On the other hand there are countries like Argentina and Uruguay whose population is almost entirely European in descent. In Brazil one-fourth of the population is *mulatto,* a mixture of Portuguese and Negro blood.

The Indians have never been successfully assimilated by Spanish culture. They retain their own customs, traditions, and languages and live mainly by agriculture, which they carry on by methods both primitive and unproductive. Illiteracy among them is extremely high, and medical services are practically unknown. Housing is wholly inadequate. Three centuries of Iberian rule, while it brought many material benefits to Latin America, resulted in untold sufferings to the Indians, sufferings which to this day have not been redressed. Though nominally Roman Catholic, these Indians are still more pagan than Christian.

Roman Catholic Missions in Latin America

South America is the only continent that is completely dominated by the Roman Catholics. The Roman Catholic Church has been there ever since the Spanish and the Portuguese arrived at the beginning of the sixteenth century. Until the Protestant missionaries entered South America in the mid-nineteenth century the Catholics had the field entirely to themselves.

Some of their missionaries were worthy disciples of Loyola and Xavier and faced hardship, danger, disease, and persecution in a heroic spirit deserving of high praise. Yet they were part of the military, ecclesiastical, and political system of the times, and their ardent missionary efforts were strangely mixed with the slaughter and subjugation of the Indians and the extortion of their land and wealth. Conversion was often forced and occurred en masse, resulting in baptized pagans entering the church in large numbers with consequences all too familiar in Latin America.

During the colonial period church and state were one. After the various republics gained their independence the church demanded and received preferential treatment that was spelled out in concordats drawn up by the Vatican. In return the Catholic hierarchy supported the military dictatorships and oppressive regimes. It did nothing to solve the problems or redress the grievances of the downtrodden masses.

The situation, however, has been improving in recent years. Cardinal Cushing of Boston took a personal interest in Latin America, and largely as a result of his influence, more and more American priests have been going there. Today between 45 and 50 percent of all American Catholic missionaries are serving in Latin America. As a result the image of the Catholic church is changing. The church is making an attempt to identify more closely with the common people in their poverty and oppression. Many of today's priests are progressive. A few are even revolutionary. Several Maryknoll missionaries were recalled from Guatemala when it was suspected that they were involved in guerrilla activities. Very significant is the changed attitude of the church to the reading of the Scriptures. In the past Bible colporteurs were persecuted and not a few of them wound up in prison. That day is gone. The church itself is now encouraging its own members to read the Bible. As a result Bible sales are soaring in all parts of the continent.

Today the Catholic church in Latin America is numerically strong but spiritually weak. In strength and numbers it varies from country to country. In Peru the church claims 99.3 percent of the population, but in Haiti the percentage drops to 65.7. The Vatican has diplomatic relations with all the republics except Mexico. The Catholics themselves identify four forms of Catholicism—formal, nominal, cultural, and folk.

We can find very easily all four Catholicisms in each of the twenty Latin American countries; but never in the same degree or in the same relation to one another. What can be affirmed of Peru and Bolivia, cannot be said of Chile and Argentina; and what may be observed in Colombia and Ecuador will be distinct from that noted in Mexico and Guatemala. Greater unity in greater diversity cannot be found in any area—religious, social, economic, or political —than can be found in Latin America.[1]

Protestant Missions in Latin America

When Protestants entered this part of the world they found themselves in a unique situation which has greatly affected their work and witness. The fact that the Roman Catholic Church had been there in full force for over three hundred years and laid claim to well over 90 percent of the population posed special problems for Protestant missions. Only in recent years—since Vatican II— are some of these problems being resolved.

Certain features of Protestant missions are to be noted.

1. **A Tardy Beginning.** Our earliest missionaries went to Southeast Asia, the Far East, and the Middle East long before they thought of taking the gospel to the lands south of the border. It was not until the middle of the nineteenth century that the first Protestant missionaries went to South America, and it was not until the 1870s that the movement built up any momentum. The Big Three were the United Presbyterians, the United Methodists, and the Southern Baptists. To this day these three boards have a large investment in Latin America. In more recent years they have been joined by the Assemblies of God, who also have a large stake in that part of the world.

2. **Preponderance of American Missions.** Missionaries from the United Kingdom number 601, whereas missionaries from North America number 10,830. European missions are conspicuous by their absence. There are several reasons for this. One, of course, is the fact that our Monroe Doctrine kept the European powers from meddling in the Western Hemisphere. Inasmuch as the cross tended to follow the flag, it was natural that British and European missions should avoid this part of the world. Another reason was the fact that in some circles Latin America was regarded as a Christian continent whose spiritual needs were adequately cared for by the Roman Catholic Church. Indeed, at the Edinburgh Missionary Conference in 1910, at the insistence of the Anglicans, it was clearly stated that Latin America was not to be considered as a mission field. Robert E. Speer and other American leaders opposed the idea, but the view prevailed.

3. **Conservative Missionaries Predominate.** It is no secret that some missionaries are liberal and others conservative in their theological orientation. In Korea the missionaries were largely conservative and produced a

---

1 William J. Coleman, *Latin-American Catholicism: A Self Evaluation* (Maryknoll, NY: Maryknoll Publications, 1958), p. 3.

very strong conservative church. In Japan the missionaries were mostly liberal and they produced a small liberal church. In other areas of the world the liberals and conservatives were found in more or less equal numbers, and each group produced a church after its own kind. Latin America is the only large region where conservative missionaries are found in large numbers, not only in the faith missions but also to a great extent in the mainline denominations. Consequently the Protestant churches in Latin America are among the most conservative in the world. C. Peter Wagner estimates that as many as 95 percent of the Protestants in Latin America are conservative evangelicals. This is one reason, doubtless the main reason, why the Ecumenical Movement has not been able to make more headway in Latin America.

4. **The Pentecostal Movement.** The Pentecostals now have adherents in all parts of the world. The largest denomination is the Assemblies of God, with almost a million members in the USA, and ten times that number overseas. Last year their growth rate was 14.2 percent. If they keep that up their total membership will double in seven years. This makes them the fastest growing denomination in the world.

It is in Latin America, however, that the Pentecostals have achieved their greatest gains. In 1900 there were approximately 50,000 Protestants in Latin America. By 1950 the number had climbed to the ten million mark. Twenty years later the figure had doubled to twenty million. Today the estimates run from twenty-five to thirty million. Referring to an exhaustive study called *Church Growth in Latin America* published in 1969, Peter Wagner says:

> When this information was made available, one of the findings that surprised many observers was that 63.3 percent of all Latin American Protestants were Pentecostals of one kind or another. This proportion has undoubtedly increased since 1969, and is likely well above the two-thirds figure by now.[2]

According to Wagner the Pentecostals are the largest group of Evangelicals in ten of the twenty republics of Latin America. In Chile they outnumber all others by nine to one. In Brazil the largest church, with 6,100,000 members, is the Assemblies of God. The second largest, with well over 900,000 members, is the Church of Christ in Brazil—another Pentecostal church. They are also the largest group in Argentina, Peru, Ecuador, Colombia, Panama, El Salvador, Honduras, and Mexico. "Whether you are a Pentecostal or not, you have to admit that the Pentecostals are doing something right in Latin America."[3]

How are we to account for the rapid growth of the Pentecostals? Several factors have been at work and each has, in its own way, contributed to growth. (1) The churches have been largely indigenous from

---

[2] C. Peter Wagner, *Look Out! The Pentecostals Are Coming* (Carol Stream, IL: Creation House, 1973), p. 26.

[3] Ibid.

the beginning. Some churches have had no missionaries at all. The Assemblies of God in Brazil, with a Christian community of almost six million, has 27,000 lay workers and 29,000 credentialed ministers but only 20 missionaries. (2) Through the years the churches have learned to pay their own way without the use of foreign funds. (3) They have made good use of lay witness. Every Christian is expected to share his faith with friends and neighbors. (4) Their lively church services, with plenty of indigenous music, hand-clapping, and testimonies, appeal to the emotional nature of the Latins. (5) They concentrate on the lower classes, who make up the bulk of the population. They take them in and make them feel at home immediately. (6) They have taken the gospel into the highways and byways. Open-air meetings, Scripture distribution, and public parades are regular features of their corporate witness. (7) They have emphasized the fullness—baptism, they call it—of the Holy Spirit as an experience to be sought, not simply a doctrine to be believed. (8) Divine healing in answer to believing prayer is a common occurrence. In a poor society where medical facilities are inadequate or non-existent, miracles of healing are a great drawing card.

5. **Protestant-Catholic Relations.** It is common knowledge that on the mission field there was no love lost between the Catholics and the Protestants. The rivalry between them was sometimes quite fierce, for they were competing for the same converts—the so-called heathen. But in Latin America the situation was different. There the two groups came into open, head-on conflict. It was not simply a case of competition but of direct opposition. When the Protestant missionaries appeared on the scene there were very few "heathen" to convert. More than 90 percent of the population was already "Christian." The Indians in some countries, like Colombia, were regarded as wards of the Roman Catholic Church and therefore off limits to the Protestant missionaries. The Protestant missionaries, therefore, sought converts wherever they could be found—usually among the nominal Roman Catholics. Naturally the Roman Catholic Church looked upon these activities as "proselytizing" and persecution ensued.

Protestants in Latin America are divided into three distinct groups. The first is represented by the Lutheran and Waldensian churches located in Argentina, Uruguay, and Brazil. The Catholic church has no quarrel with this small group, which is the result of European migration. The second group comprises those Evangelical churches resulting from Protestant missionary work over the past century. The third group is the Pentecostal churches which have developed largely on their own without outside help. The Roman Catholic Church is not happy with these last two groups, which the hierarchy claims are the result of "proselytizing."

Before we condemn the Catholics out of hand, we should remember that every Christian group regards its own constituency as composed of *bona fide* Christians and is resentful of any attempt on the part of others to take them away. The mainline denominations tend to resent the activities of the faith missions; and the faith missions, on their part, resent the intrusion of charismatic groups who invade their ranks and run off with "their" Christians. This being so, it is not surprising that the Roman Catholic Church in Latin America should look with disfavor on the "proselytizing" activities of the Protestant missionaries. Given their political clout and ecclesiastical power, it is not difficult to understand why the Catholics persecuted the Protestants.

The Protestants, on the other hand, felt quite justified in their activities when they saw the low level of the spiritual life manifested by the Catholics, the vast majority of whom never go to church except at Christmas and Easter.

> It is not surprising that Protestant churches have regarded this as a field in which they may legitimately work; attempts to meet the needs of those who have been left in such total spiritual destitution can hardly be regarded as "proselytization" in any bad sense of that word.[4]

The ecumenical overtures of the Roman Catholic Church have posed problems for the Evangelicals, who are divided into three camps at this point. There is a rather small group that welcomes the new stance and is happy to cooperate with the Catholics in many matters, including Bible translation. There is a second group of ultraconservatives who cannot believe that recent changes are anything but cosmetic, designed to catch the Evangelicals off guard. No major dogmas have been changed; therefore the new image is false. Between these two extremes are to be found the majority of Evangelicals, who at this point are simply confused. They left the Catholic church when they became Evangelicals and for this they paid a high price. Yesterday they were "heretics." Today they are "separated brethren." While they have done nothing to merit the new name, they are thankful that persecution has ceased. They are not sure that cooperation is the right thing, and they do not know where it might lead. They are rather uneasy about the whole situation.

6. **Patterns of Church Growth.** Much attention has been paid to church growth in Latin America. This is particularly true since the appearance in 1969 of *Church Growth in Latin America*.[5] It is estimated that the Protestant community throughout Latin America is growing at 10 percent a year, which means that it doubles every eight years. If this trend continues Latin America could easily become a predominantly Protestant continent by the year 2000; but that is not likely to happen.

The growth pattern, however, has not been uniform. The fastest growth has come in Brazil, Chile, and Colombia in South America, and in Mexico, El Salvador, and Guatemala in Central America. Other countries

---

[4] Stephen Neill, *Call to Mission* (Philadelphia: Fortress Press, 1970), p. 86.

[5] Read, W. R., Monterroso, V. M., and Johnson, H. A., *Church Growth in Latin America* (Grand Rapids: Eerdmans Publishing Company, 1969).

have not done so well, particularly Panama, Honduras, and Nicaragua. In spite of recent growth three countries still have a Protestant population of less than 3 percent—Ecuador, Peru, and Venezuela.

Nor have all the Protestant churches participated equally in the growth. In many countries the Pentecostals have outdistanced everyone else. In some countries the Seventh-day Adventists have done well. One church in Colombia, after 120 years of work, has a small membership of only 3500 baptized persons. Another in Honduras, after almost eighty years of work, reports a membership of only 3000.

Particularly disappointing has been the lack of growth among the faith missions. In 1969 they represented 32.4 percent of the missionary force but only 1.5 percent of the communicant members. There are several extenuating circumstances that should be borne in mind: (1) They got a late start as compared with the mainline missions. (2) Many of the faith missions have done extensive work among the Indians, who have proved to be very resistant to the gospel. Some of them are working *exclusively* among the Indians. (3) One very large faith mission, Wycliffe Bible Translators, is engaged in the technical work of Bible translation, which only indirectly and belatedly contributes to church growth.

7. **Work Among the Indians.** In other parts of the world the greatest response has come from the aborigines. This is not the case in Latin America. The Indians there, like those in North America, have proved to be impervious to the gospel. Missionaries have labored among them for years with little or nothing to show for their efforts. Their languages have been difficult to learn and Scripture translation has not kept pace with that in other parts of the world. Most of the translation work has been done by Wycliffe Bible Translators. Many of the Indian tribes are extremely primitive, live in isolated jungle areas of Amazonia and Mexico, and are wild and warlike, defying even government forces to subdue them. Only recently has there been a moving of the Holy Spirit among the Quechuas of Ecuador, where some 26,000 are reported to have turned to Christ in the 1970s. This was the first major breakthrough in the evangelization of the Indians of Latin America.

8. **The Liberal-Conservative Clash.** Though the liberals are outnumbered nine to one they are better educated, better organized, and certainly more vocal than the conservatives. In the past decade there has been a rapid development in theological thinking, from a theology of development to a theology of liberation. Some of the liberal theologians have come to the conclusion that only a Marxist revolution can successfully solve the deep-seated, long-standing social and economic problems of Latin America. "Marxist ideology in the left wing of the church is a fact of life in Latin America."[6]

---

6 C. Peter Wagner, *Latin American Theology: Radical or Evangelical?* (Grand Rapids: Eerdmans Publishing Company, 1970), p. 60.

The gulf between the liberals and the conservatives is rather wide. The liberals consider the conservative churches to be lacking in social concern, altogether too pietistic, and interested only in personal salvation. They are grateful for the contribution made by North American missionaries in the past but have grave doubts about the value of their continued presence in Latin America. The "gringos" can hardly be expected to understand, much less solve, the gargantuan problems of Latin American society.

Their point of view, however, is not entirely correct. The conservatives, including the Pentecostals, are increasingly concerned about the social implications of the gospel and are speaking out against all forms of exploitation. At the grassroots they are engaging in social action and seeking to solve the problems of society, at least within their own community, though understandably they are reluctant to adopt the revolutionary methods of the radical left. They believe they have theological as well as pragmatic reasons for wanting to work within the existing system rather than trying to overthrow it. But the gulf remains and it weakens the corporate witness of the Protestant church.

XIII

Missions in Europe

Ever since the beginning of the Holy Roman Empire, about A.D. 800, Europe has been regarded as a Christian continent. This is no longer true. Kenneth Scott Latourette, Hans Lilje, and other prominent churchmen and historians have warned that Europe is rapidly becoming de-Christianized.

Several factors have contributed to this sad state of affairs. Secularism and humanism were spawned by the Renaissance. German rationalism and higher criticism undermined the veracity and authority of the Holy Scriptures. Two world wars among the so-called Christian countries of the West and the failure of the Christian church in Germany to offer more than token resistance to Nazism hardly enhanced the image of Christianity in Europe. The rise of the USSR and the emergence of Communist governments in Eastern Europe have imposed severe restrictions on the activities of the church in those countries. The new theology and the new morality espoused by some Protestant leaders in Western Europe have removed the ancient landmarks and left nominal church members in a spiritual vacuum. Vatican II and the rapid changes taking place in the Roman Catholic Church have thrown the faithful into confusion. Non-Christian religions from the East, particularly Buddhism and Hinduism with their mysticism and esoteric rites, are attracting a good deal of attention. Muslims from Pakistan and North Africa are emigrating in large numbers to Europe in search of employment, higher wages, and a better way of life. As a result mosques are being built in the larger cities.

Religion in Decline

An estimated 160 million people in Europe make no profession of religion. Among those who still claim allegiance to Christianity there are few who take their religion seriously. France, though nominally Roman Catholic, is the most pagan country in Europe. Fear and superstition abound, especially in the rural areas, and more and more people are turning to spiritism, so much so that the Roman Catholic Church now regards France as a mission field. In England 60 percent of the population are baptized by the Church of England; 20 percent go on to confirmation; but only 6 percent remain as regular churchgoers. In the state churches of Europe the situation is even worse. Only 5 percent of the German Lutherans and 3 percent of the Swedish Lutherans attend church on a regular basis. By no stretch of the imagination can Europe be called a Christian continent. Oddly enough, the most virile form of Christianity is found in the Communist countries of Eastern Europe and the USSR.

It is difficult for Americans to understand and appreciate the difference between the religious situation in Europe and that in the United States. In the whole of Europe there is only one Christian radio station, and that was erected and is maintained by an American mission, Trans World Radio. It is possible to buy time on Radio Luxembourg and Radio Monte Carlo; but prime time is almost impossible to secure and when available is extremely expensive. Even in England the local churches cannot buy time on the British Broadcasting Corporation network. The Bible, available in so many editions and versions in the United States, is a rare book in many countries of Europe. During the last two centuries Europe has produced no great evangelists such as Charles G. Finney, Dwight L. Moody, or Billy Graham. In fact, mass evangelism as we understand it is an American phenomenon and not particularly appreciated by most European church leaders. The two largest confessional groups in Europe are the Anglicans and the Lutherans, both of which believe in baptismal regeneration. The emphasis is on religious education rather than individual conversion. The Methodists and the Baptists, who traditionally have preached repentance and faith as an integral part of the conversion experience, form a very small minority in Europe.

Europe as a Mission Field

It was not until recent years that Europe came to be regarded as a mission field, and even today the historic denominations in the United States are reluctant to accept this point of view. The only large historical denomination with missionary work in Europe is the Southern Baptist Convention. Most of the American groups now working in Europe are evangelical and evangelistic and understand the missionary mandate to include all unregenerate persons regardless of their ecclesiastical connections. Nominal Christians have as much need for the gospel as the so-called pagans of the non-Christian world.

At present there are 122 North American societies in Europe. Together they account for 3,054 missionaries. In addition there are 600 missionaries from Great Britain and others from several Commonwealth countries. The idea of Europe as a mission field did not really catch on until after World War II, when there was a sudden influx of missions from North America. Prior to that, however, there were several well-established America-based missionary societies in Europe.

Special mention should be made of the radio ministry of Trans World Radio, which began broadcasting from Monaco in 1960. Today it is beaming the gospel in thirty-one languages into all parts of Europe, Russia, North Africa, and the Middle East. TWR broadcasts seven days a week over short, medium, and long wave transmitters with a total of more than half a million watts. Studios in various parts of Europe and the Middle East furnish tapes which are mailed to Monte Carlo. A German branch, Evangeliums-Rundfunk, is now part of TWR and, with a staff of fifty full-time workers, produces five daily programs in German. The German branch is a work of faith and is entirely self-supporting. In some countries behind the Iron Curtain the German programs are the only spiritual nourishment available to German-speaking Christians.

In the state churches theological education is at the university level, and seminary graduates usually know more about Barth, Brunner, and Bultmann than they do about the Bible. There are twenty-nine Bible schools in the United Kingdom and forty on the continent. About half of the schools on the continent have been established in the postwar period by American missions. A leader in this field is the Greater Europe Mission with nine Bible schools and one seminary. If the people of Europe are ever to be reached with the gospel, it will have to be by Europeans themselves. An unsolved problem is the reluctance of the state churches to accept the humble Bible school graduates as "men of the cloth." This, however, is changing as an acute shortage of pastors is forcing some state churches to accept Bible school graduates as assistant pastors.

What is the best way to evangelize Europe—to work through the existing churches, many of which are state or quasi-state churches, or to start new churches? Most people would agree that cooperating with the existing churches is more desirable; but is it feasible? When Protestant missionaries first went to the Middle East in the early part of the nineteenth century it was with the idea of reviving the Eastern churches and evangelizing the Muslim population through them. The attempt was not very successful because the Orthodox churches did not wish to be revived and resented any attempt on the part of the Western missionaries to infiltrate their ranks. Something of the same situation exists in the state churches of Europe. It has not proved easy to cooperate with them for reasons which are both theological and cultural.

For the most part missionaries who are involved in church planting are working outside the state churches. Among the free churches and some independent groups they have been more successful. In some parts, where the free churches do not exist, the missionaries have had to start from scratch and build churches of their own. Most of the interdenominational missions in Europe are engaged in church planting.

Missionary work in Europe differs in many respects from that in other parts of the world. Illiteracy is no problem. Mission schools, which played an important role in the evangelization of Africa, are nonexistent. The same is true of medical work. Bible translation is no problem, since the Bible has been available in most of the languages of Europe for many years. Indeed, many of the European countries for decades have had their own Bible societies. Schools for missionaries' children are not needed; the children attend local public schools. This sets the missionaries free for evangelism, church planting, radio broadcasting, and theological education.

Protestant Europe

There are approximately 110 million Protestants in Europe. The two largest groups are the Lutherans (60 million) and the Anglicans (30 million). The Lutherans are found in Germany and the four Scandinavian countries. About 80 percent of the East German Protestants and approximately 50 percent of the West German Protestants are Lutherans. In Scandinavia 90 to 97 percent of the Protestants belong to the Lutheran church. Of the thirty million Anglicans, almost twenty-eight million are found in England; the remainder are divided among Scotland, Wales, and Northern Ireland. There are no Anglican churches on the continent and no Lutheran churches in the United Kingdom, except for expatriates.

The remaining Protestants, made up of Baptists, Methodists, Pentecostals, Mennonites, Presbyterians, and Reformed, are found in relatively small groups in various parts of Europe. The Waldensian Church, the oldest Protestant church in the world, is located in Italy. It has a constituency of thirty-five thousand.

Many of the Protestant churches are state churches, supported by state funds and subservient to government control. Under such a system all citizens, Christian and non-Christian, are required to support the church. Such an arrangement is a source of irritation to the non-Christians and a serious detriment to the initiative of the church members, who feel no obligation to give to the support of the church. The pastors on their part have no great urge to seek the lost, or even to fill the pews. Their position is secure and their income is guaranteed regardless of performance. In England both church membership and seminary enrollment are decreasing rapidly. Religion is at its lowest ebb since the days of John Wesley. The situation is much better in Scotland and Northern Ireland, where the Presbyterians are numerically strong and church attendance is high. Even so, England is much better off than the Scandinavian countries. In the Anglican Church there is a strong evangelical wing. In addition there are some six million non-Conformist church members in Great Britain, and church attendance among them is much higher than is the case with the Anglicans. Among the non-Conformists there are evangelical denominations, and in all denominations there are some evangelical churches and preachers.

Catholic Europe

Europe, with 252 million Roman Catholics, is still a predominantly Roman Catholic continent. However, 50 million of these 252 million are behind the Iron Curtain, leaving roughly 200 million Roman Catholics in Free Europe. The three largest concentrations are in France, Italy, and Spain. These three countries have attracted the largest number of missionaries from North America: France, 652; Italy, 248; and Spain, 346.

While strife within the church is increasing, tension between Catholics and Protestants is on the wane. Ever since John XXIII substituted the term "separated brethren" for "heretics," a general *rapprochement* has been taking place between Roman Catholics and Protestants in all parts of the world. Three archbishops of Canterbury have visited the Vatican. Pope John Paul II returned the compliment in 1982. There is a growing spirit of cooperation between the Roman Catholic Church (RCC) and the World Council of Churches (WCC). The General Secretary of the WCC has more than once visited the Vatican, and Pope Paul paid an historic visit to Geneva in June 1969. A Joint Working Committee is only one of many cooperative ventures of the two world bodies. While it is still too early to talk about the RCC joining the WCC, the RCC is now definitely part of the ecumenical movement.

The winds of change blowing through the Vatican have been felt to the ends of the earth, and Protestant missionaries in Roman Catholic countries are grateful for an increasing measure of religious liberty. This is particularly true in Italy and Spain and to a lesser degree in Portugal. The coup in 1974 brought new freedom to Portugal, and elections in 1977 restored democracy to Spain after forty years of dictatorship.

Communist Europe

Besides the USSR there are eight Communist countries in Eastern Europe: East Germany, Poland, Rumania, Czechoslovakia, Hungary, Bulgaria, Yugoslavia, and Albania. Three of these countries are predominantly Roman Catholic in religion: Poland, Hungary, and Czechoslovakia. Three are predominantly Eastern Orthodox: Bulgaria, Rumania, and Yugoslavia. Albania is 70 percent Muslim. In the USSR there are probably 40 million members of the Russian Orthodox Church and perhaps as many as 5 million Evangelicals.

The picture in Eastern Europe is spotty. The degree of religious freedom varies from country to country. Indeed, it may well vary from place to place in a given country, or it may change overnight without any apparent reason. There is considerable freedom in Poland, where even Sunday schools are possible. In East Germany Bibles are sold in state-owned stores. In Albania, the only self-professed atheistic state in the world, religion has been outlawed. In Rumania church growth has reached revival proportions, with the lion's share going to the Baptists and the Pentecostals. In one city a Baptist congregation grew from 600 to 1,500 in one year, with scores of young people meeting for prayer and Bible study to offset the pressures against religion in the universities. Church leadership is a continuing problem. The Baptists in Rumania have only 150 trained ministers for 1,035 congregations. Their seminary in Bucharest in 1977 had ten times more applications than it could accept. In the Orthodox Church interest in theological training is high, with 1,200 students in its university-level theological institutes and many more at the seminary level.

Throughout most of Eastern Europe the churches are filled to capacity and pastors are hard pressed to meet the demands of their vocation. They do not have anything like the religious freedom we have in this country; but they dearly appreciate the freedom they do have, and they show it by the support they give to church attendance. We think they need our help and prayers. If the truth were known, it is we who need their prayers.

After more than sixty years of repression religion is by no means dead in the Soviet Union. The largest church is the Russian Orthodox Church, with approximately forty million members. The All-Union Council of Evangelical Christians-Baptists, which includes Mennonites, Plymouth Brethren, and Pentecostals, represents a community of about five million. In recent years a rift has appeared among the Evangelicals, with a militant group known as the Initiators demanding full religious freedom and accusing their leaders of collaboration with the government. Some members of this dissident group have been arrested and others have been sent to labor camps in Siberia. In some instances their children have been placed in state institutions where they are indoctrinated with Communist ideology. Lutherans, found mostly in Latvia and Estonia, number approximately one million. The Roman Catholic Church reports 3,200,000 members. There are also small groups of Methodists and Adventists.

Doubtless the most effective outside aid now being given to the Christians behind the Iron Curtain is the radio ministry. The gospel is beamed into Russia, including Siberia, from powerful short-wave transmitters in Monte Carlo, Quito, Manila, Guam, and Korea. So effective are these broadcasts that they have attracted the attention of the Soviet authorities and been denounced in *Pravda*. In many isolated communities these Christian programs are the only spiritual nourishment available to the Evangelicals.

Christian leaders from the West are now permitted to pay short visits to most of these Communist countries. In some cases they have been invited to preach in the churches. In all cases they reported a warm reception from the church leaders and a deep hunger for the Word of God on the part of the Christians. Something of a breakthrough occurred in September 1977 when Billy Graham was permitted to hold a week of meetings in Hungary; but it will doubtless be some time before missionaries from the West are permitted to resume normal operations in that part of the world. Contrary to common belief the Bible is published and distributed openly and legally in all of these countries except Albania, but never in sufficient quantities to meet the growing demand.

History was made in May 1982 when Billy Graham accepted an invitation from Patriarch Pimen of the Russian Orthodox Church to visit the Soviet Union. During the week he was in Moscow he preached in the cathedral on Sunday morning and in the Baptist Church later in the day. On Tuesday he participated in a conference, "Religious workers for saving the sacred gift of life from nuclear catastrophe," attended by hundreds of religious leaders from various parts of the world. Also in attendance were representatives of the Soviet government.

Billy Graham's address, entitled "The Christian faith and peace in a nuclear age," included some strong biblical affirmations seldom heard in high circles of the Soviet Union. While in Moscow Graham had conferences with government officials as well as church leaders. In private and public he made a strong plea for religious freedom and for world peace.

On the whole his messages were well received in spite of the negative comments of the American newsmen. For years Graham has entertained the hope of one day being able to conduct a crusade in the Soviet Union. Such a hope, however, seems rather forlorn.

XIV

Missions in Retrospect

No enterprise known to man has ever been 100 percent successful. Man is a finite, fallen creature, and his most noble efforts are marred by imperfection and failure. The modern missionary enterprise is no exception. Stephen Neill expressed it well when he said:

> Christian missionary work is the most difficult thing in the world. It is surprising that it should ever have been attempted. It is surprising that it should have been attended by such a measure of success. And it is not at all surprising that an immense number of mistakes should have been made.[1]

To hear some people talk one would conclude that the entire missionary enterprise has been a total disaster. But before we can talk of disaster or even failure we must understand clearly what the missionaries were supposed to do. If they failed to do what they were supposed to do, then, of course, they failed; but they can hardly be faulted for failure in a given task if that task was never really part of the missionary mandate.

What Missionaries Did Wrong

1. **The missionaries had a superiority complex.** Almost without exception they considered Western civilization superior to any other. Worse still, they unashamedly equated civilization with Christianity. They referred to the people as "natives," and in their letters home depicted them as lazy, dirty, dishonest, irresponsible, and untrustworthy.

---

[1] Stephen Neill, *Call to Mission* (Philadelphia: Fortress Press, 1970), p. 24.

In defense of the missionaries, several observations are in order. The missionaries were not the only ones with a superiority complex. There were very few persons in the nineteenth century who did not share this point of view. Professors, clergymen, politicians, men of letters—all had a blind spot at this point. They assumed that Western civilization was superior to all others and expressed their views freely. In the United States this came to focus very sharply in the doctrine of "Manifest Destiny."

In the conduct of their daily work the missionaries were usually in contact with the lower classes who formed 80 to 90 percent of the population. In all honesty it must be said that these people, through no fault of their own, *were* poor, ignorant, dirty, superstitious, undernourished, and often diseased. When the missionaries wrote home they simply told it as it was. Their mistake was not in what they said but in what they left unsaid. They spoke only of the seamy side of life—the side they knew best.

Few people today realize what it meant for the early missionaries to cast in their lot with these underprivileged people. Curiously enough, modern, well-educated nationals have difficulty in identifying with their poor, illiterate compatriots living in the rural areas of their own countries. Very few of them, having completed their education in the West, settle down in the small towns and villages "to serve the people." Instead they tend to congregate in the larger cities where they can enjoy the amenities of modern civilization.

2. **The missionaries took a dim view of the "pagan" religions.** They were unnecessarily negative in their attitude towards these religions and often preached against idolatry in terms that were quite offensive to the listeners. The same truths could have been expressed in less abrasive terms. Without sufficiently investigating the indigenous religions they assumed that they were wholly false and rejected them out of hand. Later they discovered that such tactics were self-defeating and abandoned them. In the meantime the deed was done and the reputation lingers.

3. **They failed to differentiate between Christianity and Western culture.** They took with them a large amount of excess luggage: moral and social taboos, personal prejudices and predilections, ethical and legal codes, economic and political institutions—everything from the Magna Carta to Robert's *Rules of Order.* In so doing they placed on the necks of their converts a yoke that was more than they could bear. Christianity as it developed in the Third World ended up with a "Made in the USA" stamp on it. Little wonder that it came to be known as a "foreign religion" in Asia and the "white man's religion" in Africa. Certainly it bore all the earmarks of a Western institution.

4. **The missionaries exported denominationalism along with the gospel.** In the beginning they said they would not do this, but they soon forgot their good intentions. Before they were finished they reproduced every major denomination and many of the minor ones in the West. It was

particularly confusing to the Chinese when the Southern Baptist churches were in *North* China and the Northern Baptist churches in *South* China!

Denominational divisions and distinctions naturally have historic significance for us in the West, but many of them are practically meaningless to the emerging churches in the Third World. The convert from Hinduism, Buddhism, or Islam has probably paid a high price for his allegiance to Jesus Christ. It may have cost him his wife, family, and livelihood. He becomes an outcast among his own people. He naturally expects that his new-found faith will be his passport to the Christian church—any branch of it. He is surprised and disappointed when he is told that it is not enough to be a Christian; he must also be a Presbyterian or a Lutheran or a Baptist, as the case might be. And when missions compete with one another for the converts the scandal is increased.

5. **The missionaries failed to encourage the indigenization of Christianity.** It never entered their minds that Christianity could retain its essential core while at the same time being expressed in non-Western forms. They seemed to think that the form was essential to the substance and must remain forever Western in motif. They erected church buildings complete with spire, bell, and cross. They introduced hymns with Western words and Western tunes. Drums and dances, so dear to the African soul, were taboo. Instead they used musical instruments imported from the West. The liturgy was Western in style. The Roman Catholics were the greatest offenders at this point. They insisted that the Mass be said in Latin in every Roman Catholic church in the world. The Anglicans translated the Book of Common Prayer along with, sometimes before, the Scriptures. Vestments worn by officiating priests and bishops were the same as those worn in the West. An Anglican church service in New Delhi was identical with one in London. Even theological education was patterned after the classical kind so common in the West.

6. **The missionaries were guilty of paternalism.** It is easy to make a case against the missionaries on this score. The unhappy details are well known to everyone remotely interested in Christian missions. It should be remembered, however, that paternalism is not *always* bad. In the beginning it was natural, necessary, and inevitable, given the circumstances of the nineteenth century. This was especially true in Africa, where most of the early converts were fugitive slaves and miscreants from tribal society. The missionaries took them into their "residential" stations, after which they became virtual wards of the mission. The missionary in charge provided them with food, clothing, shelter, and security; taught them to read and write; gave them land, seed, and tools to make a garden; and taught them a trade. All they asked in return was obedience. If they did not accept the discipline of the community they were chastised. In rare cases they were even flogged. The greatest punishment was expulsion from the community. That was paternalism with a vengeance, but it is difficult to see how else the missionaries could have acted in those early years.

The real problem came when paternalism was continued long after it had served its purpose. It is simply a matter of record that the missionaries held on to power much too long. They can be forgiven for their treatment of the first generation converts; but what about the second and third generations? These were educated men with ability and experience who wanted to be masters in their own house. It was at this point that the missionaries completely misinterpreted the needs of the church and its new members. They continued to think of the Christians as children to be pampered, prodded, and protected, not as mature adults capable of holding office, exercising discipline, and administering the affairs of the church.

7. **The missionaries were unwise in their use of Western funds.** Too often they allowed their hearts to run away with their heads. Western funds were used all too freely and over too long a period of time, to the detriment of the developing churches. This situation, however, was not as simple as it might appear on the surface. To begin with, charity is a Christian virtue. Our Lord told us that it is more blessed to give than to receive. Again He said, "Freely ye have received, freely give." So if the missionary was generous with his money, he can hardly be faulted for being un-Christian in his conduct. Secondly, the Christians were usually very poor, at least by Western standards; and often their profession of Christianity barred them from getting or holding jobs. Thirdly, the missionaries, though woefully underpaid by stateside standards, were regarded as fabulously wealthy on the mission field. In these circumstances the temptation to solve problems by handing out money was exceedingly great. Most of us would have done the same thing.

8. **The missionaries were too closely identified with the colonial system.** Through no fault of their own the missionaries were part and parcel of the gigantic outward thrust of the European nations in the nineteenth century, whereby they acquired empires in all parts of Africa, Asia, and the South Seas. The colonial administrators and the Christian missionaries traveled on the same ships, served under the same flags, worked in the same countries, and were mutually helpful. The missionaries carried on a "civilizing" mission among the "natives." They helped to create a middle-class bourgeois society susceptible to Western influence and amenable to Western laws, thereby making it easier for the colonialists to administer the territories under their rule. The colonial governments reciprocated in kind, giving the missionaries land for their stations, subsidies for their schools, and protection in times of danger. From many points of view this was the greatest mistake made by the Christian missions in the nineteenth century.

What the Missionaries Did Right

Having documented the faults and failings of the missionaries, we should also discuss their victories and successes. Obviously they did *some* things right or we would not be where we are today.

When one remembers the paucity of their numbers, the scarcity of their resources, the raw material with which they had to work, the incredible problems pertaining to food, health, climate, language, and culture—to say nothing of the indifference, ingratitude, opposition, and persecution they encountered—one is astounded at the progress made and the victories won. The famous words of Winston Churchill after the historic Battle of Britain in 1940 can be applied with equal truthfulness to the missionaries of the nineteenth century: "Never in the history of human endeavor have so many owed so much to so few." What were some of their successes?

1. **The missionaries loved the people among whom they worked.** Even their paternalism was born of love. In all modesty they could say of their converts what Paul said of his: "So, being affectionately desirous of you, we were ready to share with you not only the gospel of God but also our own selves, because you had become very dear to us" (I Thess. 2:8, RSV).

They loved them as they loved their own children. In sickness and in health, in peace and in war, in adversity and in prosperity, in life and in death, the missionaries were always there—loving, helping, caring, sharing. To be with their converts they were willing to be separated from their own children nine months of the year. They had many faults, but lack of love was not one of them. Of all the people who went to the East in those early days, the missionaries were the only ones who went to give and not to get.

> The great Thomas Gajetan Ragland, pioneer of itinerating evangelism in South India, died in 1858. More than forty years after his death a missionary asked a pastor who had been trained by him about Ragland's methods in the preparation of his students for the ministry. The old man thought for a few moments, and then said quietly, "He loved us. He loved us very much. Yes, very much he loved us."[2]

Their self-sacrificing love carried them to great lengths. Time and again they placed their own lives in jeopardy to protect the lives of others. When typhus, yellow fever, bubonic plague, and other dreadful epidemics swept the community, missionary doctors and nurses remained at their posts to tend the sick and bury the dead.

2. **The missionaries developed a genuine appreciation for the indigenous cultures.** Missionaries have often been accused of undermining the local culture and replacing it with Western culture. It is true that they introduced Western learning; and in some cases, notably China, it ultimately undermined the old classical system of education. But it is not true to say that the missionaries set out to destroy the indigenous culture. They, more than anyone else, tried to preserve the best in those cultures.

---

[2] Ibid., p. 49.

In many cases it took time for the missionaries to become accustomed to a strange culture; but once the adjustment was made, they soon acquired an appreciation for it. William Carey did for the Bengali language what the famous Chinese scholar Hu Shih did for the ancient Wenli of China. He invented a beautiful, free-flowing colloquial style that replaced the old classical form, thereby making it more intelligible and attractive to modern readers. Carey also showed his appreciation for Indian culture by translating the two great Hindu epics, *Ramayana* and *Mahabharata,* into English. James Legge, missionary to Hong Kong, did the same with the *Four Books* and the *Five Classics* of China.

Long before the modern anthropologists began to roam the world the missionaries were studying the cultures of the people among whom they worked. One such missionary was the English bishop, Robert H. Codrington, who studied the Melanesians of the Pacific. He wrote several books on their languages and cultures, including his famous classic, *The Melanesians.* Codrington is especially known for his discussion of *mana*—belief in a supernatural power which is both nonphysical and nonpresent, being unrelated to spirits or gods. This phenomenon is found in many parts of the world, but Codrington's study greatly clarified it, and his work in this area marks an important base line in the anthropological study of religion. Edwin W. Smith, missionary in South Africa, became president of the Royal Anthropological Institute and author of several books, including *African Ideas of God* and *The Golden Stool.*

3. **The missionaries learned the indigenous languages.** The greatest compliment anyone can pay a people is to learn their language. Here again the missionaries showed the way, for they more than any other group took the pains to acquire a knowledge of the language. In primitive parts of the world this was no easy task. In many instances the language had no written form. After learning the oral language the missionaries, starting from scratch and without the aid of primers or dictionaries, invented a written script; then they taught that script to their converts. This was a long, painful process and required many years of arduous intellectual work.

There are 860 known languages and dialects in Africa. A hundred years ago fewer than twenty had a written form. Since then five hundred have been reduced to writing—all the work of missionaries. Let no one imagine that all African languages are primitive. Dan Crawford discovered in Central Africa a language that had nouns in twelve genders and verbs with thirty-two tenses!

4. **The missionaries translated the Scriptures.** Few people know what a gargantuan task Bible translation can be. It takes the average missionary the best part of ten years to become proficient enough to undertake translation work. He must know not only the finer points of the language, including grammar, syntax, and morphology, but he must be thoroughly acquainted with the culture of the people. That is why the

British and Foreign Bible Society will not consider the publication of a manuscript unless the translator has lived in that culture for ten years.

The technical problems of translation are legion. Take a simple Bible verse: "The crucible is for silver, and the furnace is for gold, and the Lord tries hearts" (Prov. 17:3, RSV). What does the missionary do when neither silver nor gold is used in that culture, and when the people have never seen a crucible or a furnace? For "hearts" he may have to substitute "bowels," "kidneys," "liver," or some other organ. Bible translation requires the wisdom of Daniel and the patience of Job.

Today Bible translators are trained linguists; in the early days they had no technical expertise at all. They had to do the best they could with the tools and talents they had. Their monumental achievements are nothing short of a miracle. Today the entire Bible is available to 90 percent of the world's population. The New Testament is available to another 5 percent. At least one book of the Bible is available to still another 3 percent. This leaves only 2 percent of the world's population without any portion of the Word of God; and Wycliffe Bible Translators, with more than forty-four hundred members on the job, are hoping to finish the task by the year 2000. As of December 31, 1981, the Scriptures had been translated into 1,739 languages and dialects of the world. If the missionaries had done nothing more than translate the Holy Scriptures they would have put the world forever in their debt.

5. **The missionaries provided modern scientific education for the peoples of the Third World.** In country after country the first schools to be opened were mission schools. In other countries the missions were the first to offer Western learning, which in no time at all was in great demand all over Asia. It was in female education that the missions blazed a trail. In the nineteenth century such education was unknown east of Suez and all kinds of opposition developed. When Isabella Thoburn opened the first school for girls in India she had to go from door to door imploring the parents to permit their daughters to attend her school. One indignant Hindu father retorted: "You want to educate my daughter? Next you'll want to educate my *cow*." Fortunately, some progress in this respect has been made since that time. In the 1970s the prime minister of India was a woman!

In China the story was much the same. Unrelenting opposition came from the literati, who felt that Western education posed a threat to their favored position. But the missionaries persevered even when their buildings were ransacked by rampaging students. They operated thousands of elementary schools and hundreds of high schools, as well as thirteen full-fledged Christian universities.

6. **The missionaries were the first to believe in the potential of the "natives."** When the Spanish came to the New World, the colonists took a dim view of the savage Indians. Almost to a man they considered them to be subhuman and quite incapable of acquiring the rudiments of civilization. Only the missionaries disagreed. The papal bull, *Sublimis Deus,* prom-

ulgated on June 9, 1537 stated: "We consider that the Indians are truly men and that they are not only capable of understanding the Catholic faith, but that they exceedingly desire to receive it." Las Casas, John de Zumàrraga, and other missionaries devoted a lifetime of service to the social and cultural emancipation of the Indians of Mexico and South America.

In Africa the story was much the same. It was the missionary, not the anthropologist, who first saw the potential in the "natives" and did his best to help the African realize that potential.

> On one count the missionaries who went to Africa, whatever their other blunders, were uncompromising. They insisted that there was nothing in the world which the African could not achieve if he was given the opportunity. They believed this when nobody else believed it. And they acted on their belief. And the white missionary proved his case. He it was who demonstrated that "Black is Beautiful," long before anyone else dreamt of such an idea.[3]

7. **The missionaries opened hospitals, clinics, and medical schools.** Along with education they introduced modern scientific medicine. In the beginning they had to fight the witchdoctor and the medicine man—to say nothing of the fear and superstition of the illiterate populace. One missionary doctor in Cameroon waited eight years before the first African had the courage to commit himself to the tender mercies of the white doctor. But patience paid off and perseverance won the day. One or two successful surgical operations broke down opposition and dispelled fear. After that the people came in droves, many of them in the last stages of disease.

In the bush country missionaries opened clinics and dispensaries. Often they did not bother with a building. Under the open sky they pulled teeth, set bones, lanced boils, washed wounds, and dispensed pills. In the larger cities they established some of the finest hospitals in the world. In China they operated 270 hospitals—not many for a population of 500 million, but these accounted for more than half of all the hospitals in the country. Today India has 450 hospitals in the Christian Medical Association.

The Christian Medical College and Hospital in Vellore, India, is one of the most prestigious institutions of its kind in the world. It was founded by Dr. Ida Scudder, who began her work in 1900. Her first building was a vacant shed, and her original equipment consisted of two books, a microscope, and a few bones. On the staff today are 391 full-time doctors, 418 graduate nurses, and 207 paramedical workers. In training are 376 medical students, 276 nursing students, and 147 post-graduate students.

8. **The missionaries introduced social and political reforms.** This they did by indirect rather than direct methods. Like the early church they did not, indeed they could not, launch a frontal attack on the social and

---

[3] Max Warren, *I Believe in the Great Commission* (Grand Rapids: Eerdmans Publishing Company, 1976), p. 110.

political systems of the day. Quietly, consistently, unobtrusively, they went about their business of teaching and preaching the most revolutionary message the world has ever known. By precept and example they inculcated the ideas and ideals of Christianity—the sanctity of life, the worth of the individual, the dignity of labor, social justice, personal integrity, freedom of thought and speech—which have since been incorporated into the Universal Declaration of Human Rights drawn up by the United Nations.

Untouchability and widow-burning in India, footbinding and concubinage in China, and the destruction of twins in other parts of the world have now been outlawed by government decree; but it was the missionaries who first inveighed against these evils, often at great cost to themselves.

9. **The missionaries formed a bridge between East and West and helped to bring the two together.** World understanding is essential to world peace, especially in this nuclear age when it is possible to destroy an entire civilization in a matter of minutes. Kipling declared that East and West would never meet—but they have, and the missionaries made the greatest contribution. They not only carried Christianity and Western civilization to the ends of the earth, they also brought the great civilizations of the East to the peoples of the West.

Lord Macauley, one of England's greatest literary lights in the nineteenth century and author of the Minute on Education of 1835, which determined India's educational course for more than a century, took a very dim view of Indian civilization. After confessing that he had no knowledge of Eastern languages he went on to say:

> I have never known one among them [Orientalists] who could deny that a single shelf of a good European library was worth the whole native literature of India and Arabia. The intrinsic superiority of the Western literature is, indeed, fully admitted by those members of the Committee who support the Oriental plan of education.[4]

Contrast with this the attitude and understanding of William Carey, whose appreciation of Indian culture led him to produce his monumental *Dictionary of All Sanskrit-derived Languages*.

In China the missionary's admiration for Chinese civilization was great indeed. Bishop James W. Brashford ranked Confucius, along with Socrates, Epictetus, and Marcus Aurelius, among the greatest teachers of mankind. In his book *The Lore of Cathay*, W. A. P. Martin went to the defense of Chinese civilization, stating: "Never have a great people been more misunderstood." S. Wells Williams' famous book *The Middle Kingdom* remains to this day a standard work on nineteenth-century China. On his return from China, Williams became Yale University's first professor of Chinese literature. James Legge, translator of the Confucian classics, on his

---

[4] Michael Edwardes, *A History of India: From the Earliest Times to the Present Day* (Norwich: Jarrold and Sons, 1961), p. 261.

return to England became the first professor of Chinese at Oxford University, a position he held for twenty years.

Paul Varg of Princeton, not particularly sympathetic to missionary work, had this to say:

> Westerners would have known little about China had it not been for the missionaries. Those who would dismiss them with scorn out of a feeling of revulsion for their obscurantist theological views do them an injustice. Anyone seeking to understand the Orient will find in the many articles written by missionaries, for instance those published in journals of the Royal Asiatic Society, excellent scholarship and will likewise benefit by a reading of their books.[5]

Thinking largely of Africa, Professor E. A. Hootan of Harvard said:

> As an anthropologist, I have completely reversed my opinion of missionaries. These men and women have contributed more to our knowledge of the peoples of the world than have the entire ruck of professional travellers and explorers. They may have done more than the anthropologists themselves.[6]

Missionary scholars were not the only ones to increase our knowledge of the world. The ordinary missionary by his letters and his furlough ministry added greatly to our fund of knowledge. Henry L. Stimson, Secretary of State under Franklin Roosevelt, made the following statement:

> Our most general information of China came through the great missionary movement. . . . The breadth and influence of that movement have not always been adequately appreciated by historians. . . . The news of the work of these missionaries coming through their reports and letters reached a large number of our people in almost every quarter of the land. To many of them the progress of this work was one of their keenest interests.[7]

During World War II President Roosevelt sent Wendell Willkie on a fact-finding world tour. On his return he made this report:

> I came home certain of one clear and significant fact: that there exists in the world today a gigantic reservoir of good will towards the American people. Many things have created this enormous reservoir. At the top of the list go the hospitals, schools, and colleges which American missionaries, teachers, and doctors have founded in the far corners of the world.[8]

10. **The missionaries planted the church in nearly every country in the world.** At the beginning of the modern missionary era the church was

---

[5] Paul A. Varg, *Missionaries, Chinese and Diplomats: The American Protestant Missionary Movement in China, 1890-1952* (princeton: Princeton University Press, 1958), pp. 120-121.

[6] *Christian World Facts* (New York: Foreign Missions Conference of North America, 1941), p. 96.

[7] Henry L. Stimson, *The Far Eastern Crisis* (New York, London: Published for the Council on Foreign Relations by Harper & Bros., 1936), pp. 153-154.

[8] Wendell Willkie, *One World* (New York: Simon and Schuster, 1943), p. 158.

a Western institution, confined almost entirely to Europe and America. Today it is the most truly universal institution in the world—thanks to the work of the missionaries.

When the first German Lutheran missionaries, Ziegenbalg and Plüt-schau, went to India in 1705 they took on a humanly impossible assignment. They were followed by the Moravians, who went to the West Indies in 1732 and Greenland in 1733. Beginning with the nineteenth century, first in Britain and later in the United States, the movement eventually came to life in all parts of the world. Within a period of thirty years missions had been founded in the South Sea Islands, Burma, China, Africa, and the Middle East. By the beginning of the twentieth century missionaries were found in every land that would receive them.

Wherever they went they opened hospitals and schools, but their prime purpose was the founding of churches. To this end they devoted all their resources and energy. Their schools, at least in the beginning, were auxiliary enterprises designed to contribute to the building of strong churches with an educated ministry. Everywhere the gospel was preached; the Bible was translated; Christian literature was disseminated; catechists were instructed in the faith; converts were baptized; pastors, evangelists, and Bible women were trained; churches were organized; and the sacraments were administered.

The raw material out of which the churches were built differed widely from place to place. It included the Brahmins of India, the literati of China, the samurai of Japan, the Hottentots and Bushmen of Africa, the Eskimos of Greenland, the aborigines of Australia, the Indians of South America, the headhunters of New Guinea, the cannibals of the South Seas. All walks of life and all classes of men were included in the gospel invitation. Old and young, rich and poor, literate and illiterate, captains and coolies, soldiers and slaves, tribal chiefs and medicine men, fakirs and philosophers, princes and paupers, scholars and scavengers—all found their way into the Christian fold; all became members of the Body of Christ.

Today there are not more than half-a-dozen small, inaccessible countries without an organized Christian church, and even in those countries there are individual Christians who are shining as lights in a dark place. After two thousand years the Church of Jesus Christ has become truly universal and is fast approaching the day when in deed and in truth it will include in its membership "every tribe and tongue and people and nation" (Rev. 5:9, RSV).

And so it goes. To most of the world the missionary remains something of an enigma even to this day. Is it possible to strike a balance on such a controversial figure? Kenneth Scott Latourette, former Professor of Missions and History at Yale University, has probably come closer to the truth than anyone else:

The missionaries were the one group of foreigners whose major endeavor was to make the impact of the West upon the Middle Kingdom of benefit to the Chinese. Bigoted and narrow they frequently were, occasionally superstitious, and sometimes domineering and serenely convinced of the superiority of Western culture and of their own particular form of Christianity. When all that can be said in criticism of the missionaries has been said, however, and it is not a little, the fact remains that nearly always at considerable and very often at great sacrifice they came to China, and in unsanitary and uncongenial surroundings, usually with insufficient stipends, often at the cost of their own lives or the lives that were dearer to them than their own, labored indefatigably for an alien people who did not want them or their message. Whatever may be the final judgment on the major premises, the methods, and the results of the missionary enterprise, the fact cannot be gainsaid that for sheer altruism and heroic faith here is one of the bright pages in the history of the race.[9]

---

[9] Kenneth Scott Latourette, *A History of Christian Missions in China* (New York: The Macmillan Company, 1929), pp. 824-825.

XV

Missions in Prospect

On one occasion during a particularly difficult period Hudson Taylor was asked what he thought about the future. He replied: "The future is as bright as the promises of God." That is still true. Jesus Christ is not only the Head of the church, He is also the Lord of history. He is working all things after the counsel of His own will. He is in possession of all the facts. He has both the will and the power to achieve His sovereign purpose for both the church and the world.

Some timid souls are afraid that we are about to witness the demise of the missionary enterprise, but such is not the case. The Lord of the harvest has promised to be with His missionary servants to the end of the age (Matt. 28:20). Dictators come and go; kingdoms rise and fall; civilizations wax and wane; but the world mission of the church will continue to the end of the age in spite of the vicissitudes of human history. Problems will doubtless increase, difficulties will abound, costs will soar, but the mission will go on. The mandate will never be rescinded nor will the mission be aborted; in God's time the earth will be filled with the knowledge of the glory of the Lord as the waters cover the sea (Hab. 2:14).

Developing Trends

We are living in a fast-moving age. The world has seen more change in the last thirty years than in the previous thirty centuries. Every country and every culture has been involved. Changes are coming so thick and fast that there is talk of "future shock." These changes have affected the political, social, economic, and religious climate of our time to an amazing extent. No one can predict with any degree of certainty where it is all going to end. Not only are the world and society changing, church and mission are changing, too. We Christians do well to stay abreast of the changing situation.

1. **The popularity of the short-terms-abroad program.** In former times when missionaries signed on the dotted line they committed themselves to a lifetime of service under a particular mission. If for any reason they dropped out along the way they were regarded as "casualties." This situation is rapidly changing.

Short terms abroad is hardly a new concept. Mainline missions have always had a small number of specialists, mostly teachers, who served overseas for a short term of four or five years; but it is only in recent years that the idea has captured the imagination of our youth. The influence of the Peace Corps in the 1960s has doubtless been an important factor in their thinking.

Today there are some 53,000 Protestant missionaries from the USA and Canada. Of these 19 percent are short-termers, compared with only 10 percent seven years ago. Obviously this is a rapidly developing trend with exciting possibilities.

The greatest advantages accrue not to the mission board or the national church but to the short-termer himself. Four important advantages of the short-term program are: (1) It enables him to better understand the aims and goals of the missionary. (2) It provides an enriching exposure to a different culture. (3) It acquaints him with the enormous difficulties faced by a Christian church—often an isolated, sometimes a persecuted, minority—in a non-Christian environment. (4) It helps him to ascertain the will of God for his life. The vast majority—over 95 percent—come back with a deep appreciation for missionaries, both their life and their work.

However, there are problems. No one believes that a short-term missionary is as effective as a career missionary. Certainly the national churches on the receiving end prefer career missionaries. Moreover, how many short-termers can a mission absorb without jeopardizing continuity and stability?

2. **The proliferation of non-professional missionaries.** These are sometimes called "tent-makers." They are not connected with any religious organization. They usually go out under secular auspices and support themselves by plying a trade or following a profession. All this they do for the prime purpose of giving a Christian witness to people who otherwise would have no opportunity to hear the gospel.

The number of non-professional missionaries at the present time is rather small, but as more and more countries tighten up on immigration regulations there will be an increasing demand for them in the days ahead. Most of them serve in countries closed to the Christian missionary. All Communist countries and many Muslim countries fall within this category.

The Peace Corps is not the best place for this kind of missionary, since its volunteers are expected to refrain from any activities that could be construed as "proselytizing." The teaching profession offers the best opportunities. Government service and multinational corporations. are also possible avenues of approach. Students from the West are welcome in any university in the world, and college professors are still needed in some parts of the Third World.

Here again there are problems. Most countries today require expatriates to obtain a work permit. With unemployment running high job opportunities are not as plentiful as they used to be. Governments in many parts of the Third World require that top positions be filled, if at all possible, by nationals. In spite of the problems, however, this is a fruitful form of Christian witness and one that should be pursued with vision and vigor in the future.

3. **A growing emphasis on social action as an integral part of the missionary mandate.** Social service on the part of missionaries is not new. We have always operated schools, hospitals, and other humanitarian institutions; but they have been regarded as auxiliary enterprises, not really an integral part of the gospel mandate. Evangelicals today are adopting a holistic approach to missions. There is more and more talk about "the whole gospel for the whole man." John Stott confesses that between Berlin (1966) and Lausanne (1974) his understanding of mission underwent a change.[1] Evangelism is the proclamation of the evangel—the Good News. Mission is a broader term which denotes what God sent His people into the world to do.[2] Mission is now defined as evangelism plus social action.

Orlando Costas, in his book *The Church and Its Mission,* makes the same point. "The question is no longer what is the church's 'primary' task, but what is her *total* task. The issue today is not whether or not people are being converted to Christ but whether this is happening as part of a total process."[3]

Both of these men are staunch evangelicals who believe that man's supreme need is to be saved from the penalty and power of sin, but they make a distinction between evangelism and mission. Evangelism, important though it is, is only one part of mission; social action is the other part. Both are an integral part of the missionary mandate as spelled out by Christ in John 20:21: "As my Father hath sent Me, even so send I you" (KJV).

4. **The demand for autonomy.** Most of the "daughter" churches in the Third World have reached maturity. Some of them are already in the third generation. Having come of age they naturally desire to be in charge

---

[1] John R. W. Stott, *The Christian Mission in the Modern World* (Downers Grove, IL: Inter-Varsity Press, 1974), p. 23.

[2] Ibid, p. 82.

[3] Orlando Costas, *The Church and Its Mission: A Shattering Critique from the Third World* (Wheaton, IL: Tyndale House Publishers, 1974), p. 11.

of their own affairs. The unholy alliance between the Christian mission and Western imperialism has been severed; but the stigma lives on, and the national churches find themselves on the horns of a dilemma: How can they be truly Christian and truly indigenous at the same time?

They feel that as long as the missionary remains with them they will not be able to achieve full independence. Some of them are calling for a five-year moratorium on men and money from the Western churches. Free from outside control, they hope to attain authentic selfhood, without which they can never realize their full potential as indigenous institutions.

To date, the call for moratorium has come almost exclusively from the mainline denominations. It has not yet become an issue with the younger, more conservative groups. This, however, should not lead us to believe that all is well with church-mission relations. Unless evangelical mission leaders see the handwriting on the wall and begin immediately to do something about the situation, they may find themselves in real trouble in the not-too-distant future. It is a foregone conclusion that all national churches will sooner or later want moratorium unless their autonomy is recognized and missionaries are prepared to serve with and under church leadership. Missionaries who are willing to fill the servant role will always find a welcome.

5. **The need for better-educated missionaries.** In the past the national churches were happy to receive missionaries with a meager education; they were better trained than most national pastors. Besides, they represented something for nothing; consequently the churches were glad to have them. But that day is gone. Today church leaders are more interested in quality than quantity.

Qualifications for missionary service have risen considerably in the last twenty or thirty years, but we still have a long way to go. Many mission boards still accept candidates having only the minimum requirement of one year of biblical studies. Others require a seminary education but say nothing about *professional* training in cross-cultural communications; missionary anthropology; history, philosophy, and theology of missions; and the non-Christian religions—to say nothing of crucial issues or area studies. It is an act of consummate folly for anyone to proceed to the mission field without professional as well as theological training. Yet the practice continues year after year. The time has come to call a halt to this unsatisfactory procedure. Candidate secretaries should begin a campaign to educate the supporting constituencies, especially prospective missionaries, along these lines. We should do our very best to send out fully qualified missionaries. Anything less is unfair to the national churches and dishonoring to the Lord.

6. **The practice of dialogue.** Prior to World War II missionaries were content to engage in monologue. In recent years there has been a good deal of talk in ecumenical circles about "dialogue with men of other faiths," including the Communists. Conservative evangelicals have shied away from

this approach, one reason being the element of risk involved. Dialogue as defined by J. D. Davies in *Dialogue with the World* calls for an openness that leaves the outcome in doubt. The Buddhist may become a Christian, or the Christian may become a Buddhist, or both may end up agnostics! Also, according to this view, dialogue can be genuine only if both parties refrain from any attempt to convert the other.

In spite of the difficulties involved, dialogue is an appropriate form of communicating the Christian gospel to a non-Christian world. It was used by Jesus and Paul in their time, and there is no reason to believe that it cannot be an effective vehicle for the propagation of the gospel in our day.

True dialogue, as John Stott informs us, should be characterized by four things: authenticity, humility, integrity, and sensitivity.[4] If the Christian really believes that in the gospel of Christ he possesses *the* truth about God, man, sin, and salvation, he should have no problem with dialogue. He can afford to listen with patience and profit, knowing that all truth comes ultimately from God. In the process he may come to a better understanding of the other person's point of view and thus be in a better position to lead him to Christ.

7. **The presence of Hindus, Buddhists, and Muslims in the Western World.** At one time one had to cross the ocean to preach the gospel to the "heathen." Now they have arrived in the West, and those who come are business and professional men, engineers, scientists, professors, and politicians.

At the present time there are at least 300,000 foreign nationals studying and doing research in the universities of the USA. Many of the interns in our hospitals are from India, Korea, Thailand, and other Asian countries. Indeed, they are so numerous that if they were recalled the hospitals would be crippled for lack of qualified personnel. In all our large cities there are sizable communities of expatriates from all of the major countries of the world.

In addition millions of tourists visit the United States every year, many of whom come from the non-Christian countries of Asia and Africa. Lake Louise, one of Canada's most beautiful summer resorts, was reported in the summer of 1977 to be a vacation place for many Japanese tourists.

Millions of Muslims are on the move from North Africa, Pakistan, and the Middle East to various parts of Europe, where they are now estimated to number 25 million. There are 2 million Muslims in France, 1.4 million in Germany. In 1973 the Belgian government accepted Islam as one of the official religions to be taught in the school system. Austria did the same in 1976.

These non-Christians, removed from their cultural habitat and no longer under the restraints of friends and family, are much more open to the gospel than they ever were in their home countries.

---

4 Stott, *Christian Mission,* pp. 71-73.

Increasing Difficulties

From the beginning the missionary enterprise has been beset by difficulties of one kind or another. There is no reason to believe that the future will be different from the past. In every decade we have been told that missions are at the crossroads. Missions are indeed at the crossroads. That is where they began. That is where they belong. We should not ignore the difficulties, nor should we be unduly disturbed by them.

1. **The high cost of missionary support.** When the author built a house in China in the 1930s it cost about $15 per room in American currency. Today $15 wouldn't pay for the windows. A galloping inflation abroad and a double devaluation of the American dollar have played havoc with the purchasing power of the American missionary. The British missionary is in even worse straits. The cost of living in Tokyo is the highest in the world—43 percent above that of the USA. In Tehran a modest apartment rents for anywhere from $600 to $1,000 a month. A missionary family going to Europe requires almost $30,000 for outfit, travel, tuition, and support for the first year! It costs less to support a pastor at home than a missionary in Europe.

The American public is disgusted with the high cost of living; in city after city irate citizens are refusing to vote for increased taxes for school buildings and programs—witness Proposition 13 in California in 1978! Will the time come when the American church will refuse to foot the bill for missionary work? Already church members are asking for a closer look at mission finances. Many mainline denominations have reduced their staffs and slashed their budgets in an effort to remain solvent. According to the latest edition of the *Mission Handbook,* North American churches in 1979 gave $1.15 billion to foreign missions, which works out at an average of only $14 per member. That is hardly a backbreaking proposition.

2. **The rise and spread of nationalism.** Colonialism, the strongest force in the nineteenth century, has given way to nationalism, the strongest force in the twentieth century. Now that the colonial system is dead the newly independent countries are wielding considerable influence both in and out of the United Nations. Under the colonial system a Western missionary could come and go as he pleased with a minimum amount of red tape. Today the situation is quite different.

Every sovereign state has the right to exclude or expel anyone deemed undesirable. Communist countries have closed their doors to the Christian missionary. Half a dozen Muslim countries have done the same. Other countries, acting in national self-interest, have passed laws banning or restricting missionary activities. Not only visas, but residence and work permits are required. Sometimes they are granted; at other times they are either withheld or interminably delayed to the utter frustration of the missionary.

Indonesia, always considered friendly to Christian missions, is showing signs of tightening up its immigration laws. The Overseas Missionary Fellowship, with a large commitment in that country, in the last three years has not been granted one visa for church-planting missionaries. Similar difficulties and delays have been experienced from time to time in Nigeria, Malaysia, Guyana, Peru, India, and other countries. In the nineteenth century the missionary's great asset was courage; today it is patience.

3. **Political instability and the demise of democracy.** The United Nations began in 1945 with 51 charter members. Now the membership has reached 157 and it is still climbing. Most of the new members are ex-colonies that have achieved independence since 1960. It was assumed that the demise of the colonial system would bring a full measure of freedom to the oppressed peoples of the Third World, but it has not worked out that way. They started out well; democracy was tried but found wanting. One by one duly elected governments were overthrown; political parties were banned; constitutions were scrapped, and dictatorships were established.

Independence, which was supposed to solve all their problems, turned out to be a mirage, and the long-suffering people were worse off than before. The white *sahibs* were replaced by black and brown *sahibs*. Worse still, economic stagnation and political instability continue to plague the dictatorships. In some parts of the world governments rise and fall almost overnight. The American missionary, with his tradition of an open society with multiparty politics and freedom of speech, press, and assembly, finds life and work under a dictatorship very irksome.

Mass murders have occurred in Sudan, Ethiopia, Chad, Uganda, Cambodia, and Burundi. The situation in other African countries remains highly explosive. Two Christian radio stations have been taken over by government action—Radio Voice of the Gospel in Ethiopia and Radio Cordac in Burundi.

4. **Social unrest and the demand for change.** The world is divided into two groups: the "have" nations and the "have-not" nations. The "have" nations for obvious reasons are quite content with the status quo. The "have-not" nations, for equally obvious reasons, are determined to bring about change. They are in a state of ferment—intellectual, political, economic, and social—which slowly but surely is rising to the point where it will boil over in what Adlai Stevenson called a "revolution of rising expectations."

They prefer peaceful revolution, but if peaceful revolution proves impossible, then violent revolution becomes inevitable. Many of the countries in Latin America, though politically independent for over 150 years, are seething with social unrest. In the summer of 1977 nearly fifty Roman Catholic missionaries in Guatemala were threatened with death because of their efforts to secure social justice for the poverty-stricken people of that country. Guerrilla fighters in Thailand and Zimbabwe have kidnapped and killed missionaries in an effort to embarrass the powers that be. In all such countries missionary work is both difficult and dangerous.

5. **The resurgence of the non-Christian religions.** Fifty years ago missionaries on furlough spoke hopefully of the breakup of the great ethnic religions of Asia. No one talks that way today.

In India Hinduism is making a valiant attempt to win back the hundreds of thousands of converts (former untouchables) lost to Christianity. Some of the more militant Hindus are demanding the expulsion of all missionaries. The Hare Krishna Movement, Transcendental Meditation, and Eastern Mysticism, all from India, are now invading the West and sweeping thousands of American youth off their feet.

Combining prayer and politics, Soka Gakkai in Japan has won millions of converts since 1950. More recently it has spread to the West, where it is making converts in significant numbers. Its leader, Mr. Ikeda, has declared: "Soka Gakkai is not only the hope of Japan, but the hope of the world as well."

Buddhism, known through the centuries for its emphasis on mendicity and meditation, has suddenly become both missionary and militant. In Vietnam Buddhist monks helped to topple more than one Saigon regime during the turbulent sixties. Buddhist scriptures are being translated into the major languages of Europe, and Buddhist missionaries are to be found in all parts of the Western world. Adopting the missionary methods of the West they are now propagating their faith with great determination.

6. **The economic and political clout of the Arab countries.** Islam has never been friendly to Christianity. Several Muslim countries have refused to permit Christian missionaries on their soil. Others have in recent years expelled the few missionaries who were there. Where missionaries have been tolerated it was largely because of the fringe benefits they conferred in the form of schools and hospitals.

Now that Arab states have billions of petro-dollars to invest in the modernization of their society they have no need for the fringe benefits; consequently pressure is now being brought to bear on Christian missions to force them to withdraw. In 1976 delegates from 44 countries meeting in Karachi for the first International Seerat Congress adopted a resolution, proposed by the Islamic World Congress, which called on all Muslim states to take measures to quietly remove all Christian missionaries from their territory.

Saudi Arabia, the richest of all the Arab countries, is using its fabulous oil revenues to fund Muslim missions in Africa and other parts of the world. Libya is doing the same. In 1976 the Islam Mission in Taiwan, supported by Saudi Arabia, reported making 40,000 converts.

Plans are under way to construct a powerful international radio station in Mecca. To be known as "The Voice of Islam," the station will attempt to counter evangelical broadcasts in Africa. Approximately twenty-five Islamic broadcasting organizations are taking part in the venture.

With three hundred mosques and one million adherents, Islam is now the second largest religion in Great Britain. The "World of Islam Festival," designed to acquaint the British people with the glories of Islam, was prominently featured by the British Broadcasting Corporation in a special three-hour Easter Sunday broadcast in 1976.

7. **The appeal and threat of Communism.** Though Communism is not as openly brazen and aggressive as it was during the heyday of the Cold War, it is by no means a spent force, as recent events in Africa indicate. In spite of all the high-sounding phrases associated with *détente,* neither the USSR nor Communist China has given the slightest indication that it has given up its ultimate goal of world revolution. For the present it suits both the Soviet Union and Communist China to curry favor with the USA, but the *rapprochement* between the two systems is only a convenient expedient.

On the other hand it would be foolish to deny that Communism has a strong appeal for the downtrodden, economically oppressed peoples of the Third World. They are living under corrupt regimes that have little or no concern for the welfare of the people. Coups and countercoups leave them precisely where they were. The Communists are the only ones who know how to appeal to the land-hungry peoples of the non-Western world. In Latin America even Christian theologians are talking about the inevitability of a Marxist revolution.

But wherever the Communists come to power democracy withers and dies; sooner or later the missionaries are expelled and the church brought under control. The latest example is Vietnam, where over fifty pastors of the Evangelical Church were in prison in 1977. There is evidence of increased persecution of Christians in Eastern Europe. Let there be no doubt about it; Communism, for all its good points, is still the implacable foe of religion. Its leaders, like Voltaire, will never be satisfied until the last king has been hanged by the entrails of the last priest.

Encouraging Signs

In spite of the many difficulties besetting the missionary enterprise, the picture is by no means dark. There are many things that make us wonder and weep. There are an equal number of things that make us sing for joy. We should not allow ourselves to be discouraged by the problems, nor should we be unduly elated by the victories. We must learn to take the bitter with the sweet and rejoice in the battles fought and the victories won. Certainly there is no cause for dismay. We are living in exciting times and our best days are ahead.

1. **Spiritual renewal in the home churches.** Water cannot rise any higher than its source, nor can the mission overseas be any stronger than the supporting church at home. A sick church can never save a dying world. Only a strong, virile, spiritually alive church can successfully engage in missions at home or abroad. Throughout history, revival at home and missions abroad have always gone together.

The Holy Spirit's work is twofold—regeneration and renewal. Regeneration is that act of the Holy Spirit by which spiritual life is imparted to the soul. Renewal is that act of the Holy Spirit by which He continues to nourish the life imparted at the time of regeneration. Without regeneration the sinner remains dead in trespasses and sins. Without renewal the church languishes in moral and spiritual weakness, unable to accomplish her mission in the world.

We can be devoutly thankful for the gracious way in which the Holy Spirit is at work in our day renewing the health of the church—especially here in the United States. In the sixties the institutional church was fighting with her back to the wall. Preachers, teachers, and even theologians were writing her obituary. In ten short years the religious climate has changed drastically. Church attendance, seminary enrollment, and Christian giving are all on the increase.

As a result missionary interest is being revived. Enrollment in the Bible colleges continues to increase at an annual rate of 5 or 6 percent. The spiritual tone in the Christian liberal arts colleges is reported to be the best in many years. Every year thousands of college students spend their summer vacation in missionary work overseas. Once again a missionary career is a live option with our young people.

2. **An increasing awareness of world problems.** It has often been said that one half of the world does not know how the other half lives. Fortunately that attitude is changing. More and more Christians, especially college and seminary students, are genuinely concerned about the massive problems of the Third World—poverty, hunger, malnutrition, illiteracy, and disease, to say nothing of oppression, exploitation, and the absence of human rights in general.

There is a growing awareness that it is not enough to be loyal Christians; we must be *world* Christians, with a world view that embraces the entire human race with all its economic, social, political, and spiritual needs. Stan Mooneyham's *What Do You Say to a Hungry World?* and James Scherer's *Global Living Here and Now* are but two of the many recent books calling on American Christians to take seriously the social implications of the gospel. John Stott has reminded us that the Great Commission—preach the gospel and make disciples of all nations—should never be divorced from the Great Commandment—practice love toward all our neighbors.

A Presbyterian church in Wichita, Kansas, had plans to erect a new $525,000 building when news came of the earthquake in Guatemala in

1976 which demolished hundreds of church buildings. After an on-the-spot investigation by the church elders, the congregation enthusiastically endorsed a plan to build a more modest edifice costing only $180,000. This permitted them to borrow $120,000 from a local bank to send to Guatemala, where it was used to rebuild twenty-six churches and twenty-eight parsonages! Inspired by the example of the Wichita church, another congregation modified its building plans and sent $60,000 to Guatemala. And a church in India, hearing about these projects, raised $1,200 for Guatemala relief.

3. **An increasing interest in evangelism.** At home and abroad there is an unprecedented interest in evangelism. Billy Graham, more than any other person, is responsible for this phenomenon. Largely through his influence evangelism has become respectable even in liberal circles. Mainline denominations, which ten years ago had lost all interest in evangelism, are once again devoting men and money to this worthy cause. The Berlin Congress on Evangelism in 1966 spawned dozens of national and regional congresses on the same theme. Evangelism-in-Depth, launched by the Latin America Mission in 1960, has in recent years been exported to Asia and Africa. George W. Peters returned from an investigative trip overseas, saying: "The peoples of the world are more willing to hear the gospel than we are to preach it. This is indeed the day of salvation."

Never before in history have the non-Christian peoples of the world been so open to the claims of Christ. Millions in all walks of life are showing an unprecedented interest in the Christian faith. Animists in Africa, Hindus in India, Buddhists in Southeast Asia, and even Muslims in the Middle East are reading Christian literature, listening to gospel broadcasts, and enrolling in Bible correspondence courses in record numbers. Everywhere the Holy Spirit is at work, creating a genuine hunger for the Bread of Life. And this quest for spiritual reality is not confined to the poverty-stricken masses whose interest in religion might be suspect. It includes teachers, students, government officials, and successful business and professional people whose hearts have been touched by the Holy Spirit.

4. **An increasing interest in church growth.** For this increasing interest in church growth we are indebted to Donald McGavran, the father of the church growth movement. First at the Institute of Church Growth in Eugene, Oregon, and later at Fuller Theological Seminary he developed and propounded his theory of church growth with great courage, confidence and cogency. Today it is without doubt the most dynamic of all church movements anywhere in the world. In the early years its studies and principles were confined mostly to the mission field. Today they are being applied on the home front with gratifying results.

Church growth workshops have been held in some forty countries. Resource personnel have been unable to respond to the many calls that have come from all parts of the world. Vergil Gerber's book *God's*

Way to Keep the Church Going and Growing is now available in over fifty languages, with more on the way. Journals devoted exclusively to church growth are being published in the USA, Canada, India, and elsewhere. Hundreds of books on church growth, many of them monographs, have been published in the last twenty-five years. Missionaries and church leaders in all parts of the world are discussing the problems and possibilities of church growth. This is true even in Muslim countries.

5. **Guided tours of the mission fields.** With jet travel it is now possible for pastors and church members to visit the mission field and thereby get a firsthand glimpse of missionaries and national church leaders at work. It is one thing to sit at home and read a book about missionary work; it is quite another to visit the mission field in person and see for oneself the exciting developments that are taking place.

Such guided tours have in the past been organized by travel agents, but in recent years a growing number of mission boards have taken it upon themselves to sponsor such tours of their various fields. The tours are fairly expensive, and one wonders if the money would not go farther if devoted to some worthy project beyond the financial ability of the hard-pressed national churches and their pastors. The fact remains that these tours provide American church members with a very valuable education that could not be procured in any other way; in all likelihood the money would not be available for other projects. People who have participated in such tours invariably return with a heightened awareness of, and a profound appreciation for, the contribution missionaries are making to the extension of the kingdom of God in other lands. Not a few of them increase their giving to missions; others have included mission societies in their wills. Perhaps the greatest benefit of all is that they can pray more intelligently, and therefore more effectively, for the missionaries they have been supporting through the years.

6. **Missiology as a respectable academic discipline.** Kenneth Scott Latourette, for many years professor of missions at Yale University, confessed that he had a difficult time trying to persuade his fellow academicians that Christian missions is a genuine academic discipline on a par with other disciplines in the humanities. We still have some way to go, but the situation has vastly improved in the last decade. Bible colleges have always emphasized missions, and some of them, like Moody, Columbia, and Prairie, have trained thousands of missionary candidates; but in recent years many theological seminaries have also introduced mission courses or enriched their offerings. Some have developed a complete department, awarding an M.A. in mission and evangelism. A few, such as Fuller and Trinity, have a school of world mission offering the Doctor of Missiology degree.

The cause of Christian missions was greatly enhanced in academic circles by the founding in 1973 of the American Society of Missiology. Its official organ, *Missiology: An International Review,* both in format and content would be a credit to any professional society.

Thirty years ago a book on missions, other than a biography, was something of an event. Today books on all aspects of the Christian world mission are coming off the press in such numbers that it is almost impossible to buy, much less to read, them all.

Unprecedented Opportunities

As indicated in the preceding section, the Christian mission is faced with difficulties and problems unknown in the past. At the same time there are marvelous opportunities which should not be overlooked.

After his five-day crusade in Korea in 1973, attended by 4.5 million people, Billy Graham said: "I seriously doubt if my ministry can ever be the same again." He went on to say that the center of gravity in the Christian world may be shifting from the West to the East. Dr. Myron Augsburger after a recent world tour said that he is convinced that the Third World is the cutting edge of the Christian church today. Missionaries on furlough are using two adjectives to describe the exciting situation in many parts of the world: *fabulous* and *fantastic.* One thing is clear: God is doing a new work in our day and we ought to get with Him if we want a piece of the action.

1. **Open hearts on the part of the people.** To be successful the missionary needs two things: open doors and open hearts. In the nineteenth century he found open doors in all parts of the colonial world, but when he got there he encountered closed hearts. It is increasingly difficult to get into some countries, but once we are in there is no end to the possibilities for Christian work and witness.

Most of the ill will, mistrust, and animosity in the world today has been generated by government action. It is they who make laws, break treaties, and declare war. Trade barriers, immigration quotas, and other obstacles designed to keep peoples apart are established by the politicians. Left to themselves people usually manage to get along quite well with other people.

In spite of the much discussed "Missionary Go Home" syndrome, missionaries, with few exceptions, are still needed and wanted. When they returned to Zaire after the Simba uprising in 1964 they were welcomed with open arms. The Christians danced in the streets, waved flags, sang hymns, and hugged and kissed the missionaries. Even local government officials went out of their way to greet them.

Now that the colonial system is dead there is a new openness of mind, a spirit of inquiry, a willingness to examine the claims of Christ, particularly on the part of the educated classes. Christianity no longer bears the stigma of being associated with Western imperialism, and national Christians cannot be accused of being "the running dogs of the foreigner." Consequently the peoples of the Third World—Christians and non-Christians alike—are now free to fraternize with the missionaries on an equal basis without encountering criticism from the community. Now that China has once again turned her face to the West, it is interesting to note that the Chinese people, after thirty years of unrelenting anti-American propaganda, are manifesting a surprising friendliness to Western tourists now flocking to China in unprecedented numbers.

2. **Teaching religious knowledge in the public schools.** Very few countries in the Third World have anything like the argument we Americans have over the separation of church and state. Religion, being an integral part of culture, is regarded as a fit subject in the school curriculum. Consequently, religious knowledge is a required course in the elementary and high schools. The fact that many of these societies are pluralistic poses no problem. Islam is taught to the children from Muslim families and Christianity to those from a Christian background.

Formerly the missions had to own and operate their own schools in order to teach Christianity. Now the governments assume full responsibility for the schools and pay the missionaries to teach Christianity as a required course. The teacher is free to select his own textbook; so of course the Bible is used as source material. In this way the missionaries have a made-to-order situation—a captive audience in a structured program and the government paying the bill! Such opportunities are not available in the United States. One missionary in Nigeria wrote: "I am doing more direct missionary work now than I have done in my sixteen years in Nigeria." Another missionary reports thirty-seven Bible classes a week in the government schools in Kano and more opportunities for personal witness than he can handle. In two countries, Indonesia and South Africa, missionaries were hired to write the curricula for the entire course on Christianity, from elementary school through high school. One could hardly imagine a more strategic ministry.

3. **The translation and distribution of the Scriptures.** Never has the demand for the Word of God been as great as it is today. Although the Bible, in whole or in part, has been translated into over 1,740 languages and dialects, the work of translation continues on all six continents. As a result of Vatican II the Roman Catholic Church for the first time in history is now cooperating in the translation and distribution of the Scriptures.

The United Bible Societies is now engaged in over 800 projects, most of them involving revision of existing translations in an effort to make the Scriptures available to modern man in a language he can readily understand. Wycliffe Bible Translators, working exclusively in Bible translation, hopes to have some portion of the Word of God available to every tribe by the close of the century. Other organizations engaged exclusively in the distribution of the Scriptures include the Pocket Testament League, Gideons International, World Home Bible League, and Bibles for the World, Incorporated. In 1981 world distribution by the United Bible Societies totaled more than 440 million Scriptures.

Here at home, where we have the English Bible in a dozen modern versions, we are apt to take the Holy Scriptures for granted. Not so in the Third World. When the New Testament in the Bassa language of Liberia went on sale for the first time the people danced in the streets. Three hundred copies were sold in the first fifteen minutes! So great was the crush that they had to lock the iron burglar grill across the doorway to prevent a riot. June Hobley, the missionary who translated the Bassa New Testament, was hugged and greeted by the buyers.

4. **Worldwide radio broadcasts.** In addition to the sixty-five mission-owned and operated radio stations, thousands of commercial stations are being used for the propagation of the gospel. In some countries Christian churches and missions have been requested to furnish religious programs for airing over government stations free of charge.

The exciting thing about missionary radio is that it can penetrate countries closed to professional missionaries. Also, illiterate persons, who cannot benefit from Christian literature, can hear and understand the gospel coming to them in audible form. Millions of transistor radios, made in Japan and found in all parts of the world, enable even poor peasants to keep in touch with world events, including the Good News of the gospel.

5. **Open doors in the student world.** In times past students in the Third World were in the vanguard of the independence movements, in which role they opposed everything foreign, including Christianity. In China in the 1920s they attacked missionaries, destroyed churches, and even burned down their own mission schools. Today they are in a much different mood. In Europe, which is burned-over ground, the students, many of them professing Marxists, consider it beneath their dignity to discuss religion; but everywhere in the Third World students are quiet, courteous, inquisitive, and keenly interested in the presentation of the gospel. More and more of them are becoming disillusioned with their own religions and are willing to examine seriously the claims of Christianity. On a recent visit to Bangladesh, Dr. Lionel Gurney found himself on a river boat with several hundred students, most of them Muslims, who plied him with questions regarding the Christian faith from mid-morning until late afternoon. Not one derogatory remark was made during the entire dialogue.

The International Fellowship of Evangelical Students, with headquarters in London, now has full-time workers in over sixty countries. The General Secretary, Chua Wee Hian, writes, "We are working toward the time when hundreds of graduates will cross national and cultural frontiers in obedience to the Lord's missionary mandate to 'go into all the world and make disciples of all nations.' "[5]

---

[5] IFES Newsletter, October 1973.

World mission: Facts and figures

World population: 4.5 billion. Annual increase of 1.9 percent. In 1960 Christians were 33 percent of the world's population. In 1970 the ratio dropped to 30 percent. In 1980 it was 26 percent.

Christian population: Estimated to be 1.2 billion; divided as follows: Roman Catholics 750 million, Protestants 350 million, Orthodox 100 million.

Protestant missions: Total force: 85,000 (career and short term); divided as follows: North America, 53,000; Europe, 13,000; Australia and New Zealand, 3,500; Third World, 15,500.

Catholic missions: Total force: 138,000. 6,400 from USA. The majority is from Canada, Spain, France, Italy.

American missions: Mainline denominations are retrenching:

	1971	1979
American Baptist Convention	290	200
United Presbyterian Church, USA	810	359
Southern Presbyterian Church, US	391	259
United Methodist Church (including EUB)	1,175	938
Protestant Episcopalian Church	138	69
United Church of Christ	356	160
Total number of missionaries	3,160	1,985
		37 percent loss

Some denominations have increased their overseas commitments: Southern Baptist Convention has almost 3,200 missionaries and plans to reach 5,000 by A.D. 2000. Wycliffe Bible Translators has 4,200 workers. New Tribes Mission has 1,600.

Missionary associations in the USA: There are four associations: Division of Overseas Ministries (NCC), Interdenominational Foreign Mission Association, Evangelical Foreign Missions Association, and Fellowship of Missions.

Association	Missions	Workers	Total income	Per missionary
DOM	43	4,800	$ 146 million	$30,400
IFMA	49	6,575	98 million	14,700
EFMA	72	9,800	285 million	29,000
FOM	2	2,300	?	?
Unaffiliated	?	32,300	620 million	16,400
Total	166	55,775	1,149 million	21,500

Short-term-abroad program: There has been a phenomenal increase in the last decade. In 1973 only 126 missions employed short-termers. By 1979 the number increased to 256. Short-termers in DOM: 28 percent; EFMA: 16 percent; IFMA: 10 percent. Overall average from North America: 19 percent; from the United Kingdom: 12 percent. 25 percent of the short-termers become career missionaries. Some missions employ *only* short-termers: Youth with a Mission, Teen Missions, Operation Mobilization, etc.

Statistics: North American–Based Missions – 1979

Missions with 1,000 workers	4
Missions with 500–1,000 workers	16
Missions with fewer than 100	589
Total missions	714
New missions since 1975	47

Fifty percent of all personnel are in fifteen agencies.
Sending missions: 470. Supporting missions: 244.
Women outnumber men fifty-five to forty-five. Single women outnumber single men four to one. Forty percent of all married women do not engage in missionary work.

Number of retired workers:	3,546
Number of candidates for overseas service:	3,119
Number of missionaries on furlough at any one time:	20 percent

Countries receiving the most missionaries:

Brazil	1,995	India	1,433
Japan	1,855	Indonesia	1,363
Philippines	1,775	Kenya	1,307
Mexico	1,611	Colombia	1,043

Geographical distribution of missionaries:

Asia	30%
Latin America	33%
Africa	22%
Europe	10%
Oceania	4%

Number of Mormon missionaries in 75 countries:	30,300
Number of Jehovah's Witnesses:	100

Agencies with the largest number of missionaries:

Wycliffe Bible Translators	4,200
Southern Baptists	3,200
New Tribes Mission	1,600
Assemblies of God	1,200
C&MA	1,000
TEAM	1,000
Seventh-day Adventists	1,000
United Methodists	938
Campus Crusade for Christ International	3,000

Mission income as a percentage of total church income:

1960 —	5.3	1975 —	12.0
1965 —	7.5	1979 —	13.5
1970 —	10.5		

The above statistics have been taken from the *Mission Handbook: North American Protestant Ministries Overseas, 1980.*

Statistics: United Kingdom–based missions – 1980

4,200 UK missionaries from over 200 agencies are serving in 136 countries. If associated members and retired workers were included the figure would be 5,900.

Over the last decade UK missionaries have declined at the rate of 2.4 percent per year.

Short-term service is not nearly as popular in the UK as in the USA. In 1976 short-termers accounted for 5 percent of the total force. By 1980 the percentage rose to 12 percent—compared with 19 percent in the USA.

A fairly large number of the 200 agencies reported are branches of North American–based organizations: Campus Crusade, Navigators, Africa Inland Mission, Sudan Interior Mission, Operation Mobilization.

The Evangelical Missionary Alliance (1958) is the counterpart of the Interdenominational Foreign Mission Association in the USA. It has some seventy-five members, including some Bible schools.

Societies with the largest number of missionaries:

United Society for the Propagation of the Gospel	369
Church Missionary Society	369
Overseas Missionary Fellowship	279
Worldwide Evangelization Crusade	238
Salvation Army	213
Baptist Missionary Society	191
Bible and Medical Missionary Fellowship	156
Wycliffe Bible Translators	154
Methodist Church (Overseas Division)	149
Church of Scotland (Overseas Council)	146

Countries receiving the largest number of missionaries:

India	387	Zaire	158
Nigeria	233	Pakistan	129
Kenya	226	Thailand	123
South Africa	206	Nepal	118
Brazil	205	Papua New Guinea	110

A surprising number of UK missionaries are working in Europe. Of a total of 1,023, 607 are located in the UK itself.

Retired personnel: The number is very high—1,432, or just over 40 percent of the total missionary force. There has been an increase of 60 percent in the last eight years.

The above statistics have been taken from the *UK Christian Handbook, 1981.*

Overall view of the modern missionary movement

After 275 years the movement is still going strong, with more missionaries in more countries than at any time in the history of the church. By contrast, the Peace Corps, barely twenty years old, is definitely on the wane and probably will not outlast the decade.

New interest in evangelism and missions. It began with the Berlin Congress in 1966, followed by Lausanne in 1974. These spawned congresses in all parts of the world. The Urbana Missionary Convention in December 1981 attracted 14,000 college students, half of whom signed the pledge. Even the mainline denominations and the Catholic Church are showing an interest in evangelism.

Increasing interest in church growth. The church owes a debt of gratitude to Donald McGavran, the father and founder of the church-growth movement which has now spread to all six continents. Even in the Muslim world they are talking about "church growth"! Scores of workshops have been held in all parts of the world and hundreds of books and articles on church growth have been published in the last twenty years.

New interest in "hidden peoples." Ralph Winter, general director of the U.S. Center for World Mission, has located 16,750 unreached groups that are said to be beyond the reach of any existing church or mission. These peoples have first claim when it comes to evangelism. Already the idea is catching on and many evangelical missions and churches are rearranging their priorities and gearing up for a major thrust in pioneer evangelism. The watchword of the movement is, "A church for every people by the year 2000."

Universal hunger for spiritual reality. Millions of people in all walks of life are showing an unprecedented interest in the Christian faith. Animists in Africa, Hindus in India, Buddhists in Southeast Asia, and even Muslims in the Middle East are reading Christian literature, listening to gospel broadcasts, and enrolling in Bible correspondence courses in record numbers. Everywhere the Holy Spirit is at work, creating a genuine hunger for the Bread of Life.

The situation in the third world. Myron Augsburger, returning from his world tour, stated that "the cutting edge of the Christian church today is in the Third World." Billy Graham after his 1973 crusade in Korea remarked, "It may be that the center of spiritual gravity is shifting from the West to the East." The time may come when the churches in the West will be receiving missionaries from the churches in the East.

Missionary outreach of the "younger churches." From the beginning of the modern missionary movement it has been assumed that the evangelization of the world is the "white man's burden." That notion is fast fading. Reliable estimates now place the number of Third World missionaries at 15,250, and the number is growing each year. Most of the countries of Asia now have some kind of missionary association whose purpose is to promote home and foreign missions among evangelical churches.

In the U.S. In recent years some of the mainline denominations—particularly the United Presbyterians and the United Methodists—have witnessed a sharp decline in membership. On the other hand, the smaller, more conservative denominations have shown consistent growth. Parachurch organizations, especially Campus Crusade for Christ, have been increasingly active and very effective. The "electronic church" has tens of millions of listeners and supporters. Christian day schools are expanding rapidly and threaten to supplant the tax-supported school system by the year 2000. Enrollment in the Bible schools continues to climb. Bible-study groups are on the increase in all parts of the country. The New Testament published by the American Bible Society, *Good News for Modern Man,* has sold over sixty million copies in fifteen years, and Ken Taylor's *Living Bible* has sold over twenty-five million copies.

In Europe. From one point of view Europe is the "darkest" continent of all. Once a so-called Christian continent, today it is a burnt-over area. Humanism, rationalism, materialism, and Communism are all enemies of the Christian faith. The two great Protestant communions are the Anglicans in England and the Lutherans in Germany and Scandinavia, both largely devoid of spiritual life. Indeed, the most virile churches in Europe are behind the Iron Curtain. Once a strong staging area for world missions, Europe is today a mission field.

In the Communist world. Today 1.5 billion persons live under some form of Communism. All suffer some degree of persecution. Missionaries are excluded from these countries. In the USSR there are 40 million Russian Orthodox Christians and 5 million evangelicals. In Latvia and Estonia there are 3 to 4 million Roman Catholics. In addition there are some 40 million Muslims. In China the visible church was destroyed during the Cultural Revolution. In recent years a measure of religious freedom has been restored. Some 250 Protestant churches are now open. Several million believers continue to worship in the "house" churches. It is doubtful that missionaries will be permitted to return.

In the Muslim world. There are 750 million Muslims in some 44 Muslim countries of the world. Some countries are closed to missionaries: Saudi Arabia, Syria, Iraq, Iran, Afghanistan, Libya, Algeria, and Mauritania. Converts are rare except in Indonesia. There are signs that some Muslim countries are getting ready to terminate missionary work. At the same time, there is a new and strange interest in the evangelization of the Muslim world. There is a movement to contextualize the missionary approach to Islam, especially in Bangladesh.

In Asia. With almost 3 billion souls, Asia continues to present the Christian church with its greatest challenge. It is the home of the great ethnic religions of the world, which to date have proven unusually resistant to the claims of Christ. After 275 years of Protestant missionary endeavor slightly less than 3 percent of the population is Christian. The Roman Catholics made their greatest gains in the Philippines, where they now claim some 80 percent of the population. The Protestants have done best in Korea where almost 20 percent of the population are Protestant church members. One Presbyterian church in Seoul has 40,000 members; Central Church of the Assemblies of God (also in Seoul) has 200,000 members! Alas, there are more non-Christians in India and China than there are Christians in the entire world.

In Africa. It is here that Christian missions have been most successful. We have made more converts here than in all the rest of the world together. One reason has been the absence of the great ethnic religions–Buddhism, Hinduism, and Islam—which traditionally have proven most resistant to the gospel. Africa is the homeland of animism; and animists, once they are educated, want to be identified with a higher form of religion, and one which has a worldwide fellowship. Hence Christianity has made a strong appeal to the soul of Africa. Islam is also active in this part of the world, and is making headway, but not nearly as fast as Christianity. It is estimated that 20,000 persons in Black Africa embrace Christianity every day. Some prefer Roman Catholicism; others join the Protestant churches. The influx is so great that it is impossible to give each convert adequate training. Hence one great danger in the African church is Christopaganism. One unique aspect of Christian missions is the opportunity to teach religious knowledge in the tax-supported school system in many countries of Anglophone Africa.

In Latin America. Here the Protestant churches are growing at an annual rate of 10 percent. This of course is largely at the expense of the Catholic Church. The greatest growth is among the Pentecostal churches. In Brazil it is estimated that 3,000 new congregations appear every year. Only 15,000 of the 75,000 pastors have had any formal theological training. Hence Theological Education by Extension, which began in Guatemala in the early 1960s, has been widely employed with great effect. The winds of change are blowing through the RC Church. Persecution of the evangelicals has ceased. Bible reading is encouraged. Maryknoll missionaries and church leaders, including not a few bishops, are actively espousing a "theology of liberation" as the only hope of improving the lot of the oppressed peasants and workers.

Bible translation. Year after year the translation of the Holy Scriptures continues to be an important phase of missionary work. As of December 31, 1981, the Scriptures had been translated into 1,739 languages and dialects of the world. The whole Bible is now available in 277 languages; the New Testament in another 518 languages; and at least one book of the Bible is available in a further 944 languages. This means that 90 percent of the world's population now has the entire Bible in the vernacular. Another 5 percent has the New Testament. Another 3 percent has at least one book. This leaves only 2 percent without any portion of the Word of God; and Wycliffe Bible Translators is focusing attention on that neglected segment of the human race.

Significant Dates in Mission History

YEAR	EVENT
29	Pentecost and the birth of the church.
36	Conversion of Paul.
39	Peter preaches to the Gentiles.
49	First church council in Jerusalem.
52	Apostle Thomas takes gospel to India.(?)
62	Paul arrives in Rome.
64	Beginning of Nero's persecution.
67	Martyrdom of Peter and Paul.
70	Destruction of Jerusalem.
180	Pantaenus preaches in India.
206	Conversion of Abgar IX of Edessa.
313	Conversion of Constantine.
313	Edict of Milan legalizes Christianity.
328	Frumentius takes the gospel to Ethiopia.
360	Martin of Tours begins missionary work.
430	Vandals overrun North Africa.
432	Patrick begins conversion of Ireland.
496	Conversion of Clovis, King of the Franks.
563	Columba takes the gospel to Scotland.
596	Gregory the Great sends Augustine to England.
597	Baptism of King Ethelbert of Kent.
627	Baptism of King Edwin of Northumbria.
631	Conversion of the East Angles.
635	Nestorian mission arrives in China.
637	Lombards become Christians.
685	Wilfrid completes conversion of England.

YEAR	EVENT
716	Boniface begins long missionary career.
723	Felling of the Oak of Thor.
826	King Harald of Denmark is baptized.
827	Ansgar evangelizes Denmark.
831	Ansgar begins work in Sweden.
862	Cyril and Methodius sent to Moravia.
864	Conversion of Prince Boris of Bulgaria.
954	Baptism of Princess Olga of Russia.
987	Baptism of Prince Vladimir of Russia.
1000	Leif the Lucky evangelizes Greenland.
1219	Franciscan friars sent to North Africa.
1295	John of Montecorvino reaches Peking.
1368	Christianity abolished by Ming Dynasty.
1493	Demarcation bull announced by Pope Alexander VI.
1493	R.C. missionaries arrive in the New World.
1498	R.C. missionaries accompany Vasco da Gama to India.
1517	Martin Luther proclaims ninety-five theses.
1534	Arrival of Cartier with missionaries in Canada.
1540	Society of Jesus begins missionary work.
1542	Francis Xavier begins missionary career.
1555	Calvin sends Huguenots to Brazil.
1564	Augustinians arrive in Philippines.
1583	Matteo Ricci arrives in China.
1593	Franciscans arrive in Japan.
1606	Robert de Nobili arrives in Madura.
1614	Anti-Christian edicts issued in Japan.
1622	Pope Gregory XV establishes Sacred Congregation for the Propagation of the Faith.
1649	Society for the Propagation of the Gospel in New England founded.
1664	Von Weltz issues call for missions.
1698	Society for Promoting Christian Knowledge founded.
1701	Society for the Propagation of the Gospel in Foreign Parts established.
1705	Danish-Halle Mission founded.
1722	Zinzendorf establishes *Herrnhut*.

YEAR	EVENT
1732	Moravians send out first missionary.
1736	Anti-Christian edicts in China.
1747	Jonathan Edwards appeals for prayer for world missions.
1759	Jesuits expelled from Brazil.
1773	Society of Jesus suppressed.
1793	William Carey sails for India.
1795	London Missionary Society founded.
1797	Netherlands Missionary Society organized.
1799	Church Missionary Society founded.
1799	Religious Tract Society organized.
1804	British and Foreign Bible Society founded.
1807	Robert Morrison arrives in China.
1810	American Board of Commissioners for Foreign Missions formed.
1812	First American missionaries sail for India.
1814	Restoration of Society of Jesus.
1815	Basel Missionary Society organized.
1816	American Bible Society founded.
1817	Robert Moffat arrives in Africa.
1819	London Secretaries' Association formed.
1822	Paris Evangelical Missionary Society formed.
1825	American Tract Society formed.
1826	American Home Missionary Society established.
1828	Rhenish Missionary Association formed.
1840	David Livingstone arrives in Africa.
1842	Treaty of Nanking opens China.
1846	Evangelical Alliance (London) formed.
1852	Bible and Medical Missionary Fellowship formed.
1854	London Missionary Conference.
1854	New York Missionary Conference.
1859	Protestant missionaries arrive in Japan.
1860	Liverpool Missionary Conference.
1860	Women's Union Missionary Society organized.
1861	National Bible Society of Scotland founded.
1865	China Inland Mission founded.
1867	Scripture Union established.

YEAR	EVENT
1880	Inter-Seminary Missionary Alliance formed.
1884	Protestant missionaries arrive in Korea.
1886	Student Volunteer Movement launched.
1888	Scripture Gift Mission founded.
1888	Centenary Missionary Conference, London.
1893	Foreign Missions Conference of North America organized.
1900	Boxer Rebellion disrupts mission work in China.
1900	New York Missionary Conference.
1905	National Missionary Society of India formed.
1910	Edinburgh Missionary Conference.
1912	*International Review of Missions* begins publication.
1912	Conference of British Missionary Societies formed.
1917	Interdenominational Foreign Mission Association formed.
1921	Norwegian Mission Council formed.
1921	International Missionary Council formed.
1927	Near East Christian Council established.
1928	Jerusalem Conference of IMC.
1930	Laymen's Foreign Mission Inquiry visits Asia.
1931	Radio Station HCJB (Ecuador) goes on the air.
1936	Student Foreign Missions Fellowship formed.
1938	Madras Conference of IMC.
1942	British Council of Churches formed.
1945	Evangelical Foreign Missions Association formed.
1946	First Inter-Varsity missionary convention.
1946	United Bible Societies formed.
1946	Church World Service founded.
1947	Lutheran World Federation organized.
1947	International Fellowship of Evangelical Students founded.
1947	Whitby Conference of IMC.
1948	World Council of Churches formed.
1951	World Evangelical Fellowship organized.
1951	Campus Crusade for Christ founded.
1951	Evacuation of China begins.
1952	Willingen Conference of IMC.
1957	Theological Education Fund established.

YEAR	EVENT
1958	Ghana Conference of IMC.
1958	Evangelical Missionary Alliance formed in Britain.
1959	Inaugural Assembly of Asia Christian Conference.
1960	Theological Education by Extension gets under way.
1960	Evangelism-in-Depth begins in Nicaragua.
1961	IMC merges with WCC.
1963	DWME Meeting in Mexico City.
1964	*Evangelical Missions Quarterly* begins publication.
1966	Association of Evangelicals of Africa and Madagascar formed.
1966	Missionaries expelled from Burma.
1966	Red Guards destroy church in China.
1966	Pacific Conference of Churches organized.
1966	Berlin Congress on Evangelism.
1968	Asia-South Pacific Congress on Evangelism in Singapore.
1970	All-Philippine Congress on Evangelization.
1970	Chinese Congress on Evangelism in Taiwan.
1971	Japan Overseas Missions Association formed.
1973	American Society of Missiology founded.
1973	DWME Meeting in Bangkok.
1973	All-Asia Student Missionary Convention in Philippines.
1973	All-Asia Mission Consultation in Seoul.
1974	International Congress on World Evangelization in Lausanne.
1974	Japan Congress on Evangelism.
1974	Campus Crusade for Christ Expo in Korea.
1975	East-West Center for Mission Research and Development established in Seoul.
1975	Missionaries evacuate Indo-China.
1975	Asia Missions Association formed.
1976	Chinese Congress on World Evangelization in Hong Kong.
1976	Islamic World Congress calls for withdrawal of missionaries.
1977	All-India Congress on Mission and Evangelization.
1977	India Missions Association organized.
1978	North American Conference for Muslim Evangelization.
1979	First churches reopen in China.
1980	Philippine Congress on Discipling a Nation.
1980	DWME Conference in Melbourne.

YEAR	EVENT
1980	LCWE Conference in Pattaya.
1981	Second Chinese Congress on World Evangelization in Singapore.
1981	*World Christian Encyclopedia* published.
1982	Consultation on the Relationship between Evangelism and Social Responsibility in Grand Rapids.
1982	Triennial Convention of Asia Missions Association in Seoul.
1982	Third World Theologians Consultation in Seoul.

Select Bibliography

Anderson, Gerald H., ed. *Christ and Crisis in South East Asia.* New York: Friendship Press, 1968.

Aprem, Mar. *Nestorian Missions.* Trichur, Kerala: Mar Narsai Press, 1976.

Arpee, Leon. *A Century of Armenian Protestantism 1846-1946.* New York: Armenian Missionary Association, 1946.

Baeta, C. G., ed. *Christianity in Tropical Africa.* London: Oxford University Press, 1968.

Barrett, David B. *World Christian Encyclopedia.* New York: Oxford University Press, 1981.

———, et al. *Kenya Churches Yearbook. The Development of Kenyan Christianity 1498-1973.* Kisumu, Kenya: Evangel Publishing House, 1973.

Bates, M. Searle, and Pauck, W. *Prospects of Christianity Throughout the World.* New York: Scribners, 1964.

Beaver, R. Pierce. *American Protestant Women in World Mission: A History of the First Feminist Movement in North America.* Grand Rapids, Wm. B. Eerdmans, 1980.

———. *Ecumenical Beginnings in Protestant World Mission.* New York: Nelson, 1962.

———, ed. *The Gospel and Frontier Peoples.* South Pasadena, CA: William Carey Library, 1973.

Beetham, T. A. *Christianity and the New Africa.* London: Pall Mall Press, 1967.

Berkhoffer, Robert F. *Salvation and the Savage. An Analysis of Protestant Missions and the American Indian Response 1787-1862.* New York: Athenaeum Press, 1972.

Bernard, Miguel A. *The Christianization of the Philippines: Problems and Perspectives.* Manila: Filipiniana Book Guild, 1972.

Bliss, David. *Student Mission Power: Student Volunteer Movement.* South Pasadena, CA: William Carey Library, 1979.

Braithwaite, Joan. *Handbook of Churches in the Caribbean.* Bridgetown, Barbados: Christian Action for Development in the Caribbean, 1973.

Bryant, David. *In the Gap: What It Means to Be a World Christian.* Downers Grove, IL: InterVarsity Press, 1979.

Chaney, Charles L. *The Birth of Missions in America.* South Pasadena, CA: William Carey Library, 1976.

Cho, David J. *New Forces in Missions.* Seoul, Korea: East-West Center for Mission Research and Development, 1976.

Clark, Allen D. *History of the Church in Korea.* Seoul: Christian Literature Society, 1971.

Coggins, Wade T., and Frizen, Edwin L., eds. *Christ and Caesar in Christian Missions.* South Pasadena, CA: William Carey Library, 1979.

Cooley, Frank L. *Indonesia: Church and Society.* New York: Friendship Press, 1968.

Cooley, John K. *Baal, Christ, and Mohammed: Religion and Revolution in North Africa.* New York: Holt, Rinehart and Winston, 1965.

Coxwell, H. Wakelin, and Grubb, Kenneth, eds. *World Christian Handbook, 1968.* Nashville: Abingdon Press, 1968.

Dachs, Anthony J., ed. *Christianity South of the Zambezi.* Gwelo, Rhodesia: Mambo Press, 1973.

Davidson, Allan K. *Missionary Propaganda—Its Early Development and Influence with Respect to the British Missionary Movement and India.* Dunedin: Presbyterian Historical Society of New Zealand, 1974.

Davies, Horton, and Shepherd, R. H. W. *South Africa Missions 1800-1950.* London: Nelson, 1954.

Dayton, Edward R., ed. *Mission Handbook: North American Protestant Ministries Overseas.* Monrovia, CA: Missions Advanced Research and Communication Center, 1976.

Detzler, Wayne A. *The Changing Church in Europe.* Grand Rapids: Zondervan, 1979.

Douglas, Donald E., ed. *Evangelical Perspectives on China.* Farmington, MI: Evangelical China Committee, 1976.

Douglas, J. D., ed. *Let the Earth Hear His Voice.* Minneapolis: World Wide Publications, 1975.

Drummond, Richard H. *A History of Christianity in Japan.* Grand Rapids: Wm. B. Eerdmans, 1970.

Du Plessis, J. A. *A History of Christian Missions in South Africa.* New York: Longmans, Green and Co., 1911.

Edman, V. Raymond. *The Light in Dark Ages.* Wheaton, IL: Van Kampen, 1949.

Engstrom, Ted W. *What in the World Is God Doing: The New Face of Missions.* Waco, TX: Word Books, 1978.

Evans, Robert B. *Let Europe Hear.* Chicago: Moody Press, 1964.

Fairbank, John K., ed. *The Missionary Enterprise in China and America.* Cambridge: Harvard University Press, 1974.

Falk, Peter. *The Growth of the Church in Africa.* Grand Rapids: Zondervan, 1979.

Gibbon, Edward. *The Triumph of Christendom in the Roman Empire.* New York: Harper and Row, 1958.

Gibbs, Mildred E. *The Anglican Church in India 1600-1970.* Delhi: Indian Society for Promoting Christian Knowledge, 1972.

Goddard, Burdon L., ed. *The Encyclopedia of Modern Christian Missions: The Agencies.* Camden, NJ: Nelson, 1967.

Gowing, Peter G. *Islands Under the Cross: The Story of the Church in the Philippines.* Manila: National Council of Churches in the Philippines, 1967.

Grabill, Joseph L. *Protestant Diplomacy and the Near East: Missionary Influence on American Policy, 1810-1927.* Minneapolis: University of Minnesota Press, 1970.

Groves, C. P. *The Planting of Christianity in Africa 1840-1954.* 4 vols. London: Lutterworth, 1948-1958.

Harnack, Adolf. *The Mission and Expansion of Christianity in the First Three Centuries.* 2 vols. New York: Putnam, 1908.

Harr, Wilbur C., ed. *Frontiers of the Christian World Mission Since 1938.* New York: Harper & Row, 1962.

Hastings, Adrian. *A History of African Christianity, 1950–1975.* Cambridge: Cambridge University Press, 1979.

———. *Church and Mission in Modern Africa.* Bronx, NY: Fordham University Press, 1970.

Hedlund, Roger E. *World Christianity: South Asia.* Monrovia, CA: Missions Advanced Research and Communication Center, 1979.

Hogg, William R. *Ecumenical Foundations: A History of the International Missionary Council and Its Nineteenth Century Background.* New York: Harper and Row, 1952.

Hoke, Donald E. *The Church in Asia.* Chicago: Moody Press, 1975.

Horner, Norman A. *Rediscovering Christianity Where It Began. A Survey of Contemporary Churches in the Middle East and Ethiopia.* Beirut: Near East Council of Churches, 1974.

Howard, David M., ed. *Declare His Glory Among the Nations.* Downers Grove, IL: InterVarsity Press, 1977.

Hutton, J. E. *A History of Moravian Missions.* London: Moravian Publication Office, 1923.

Jennes, Joseph. *A History of the Catholic Church in Japan from Its Beginnings to the Early Meiji Era (1549-1873).* Tokyo: Orients Institute for Religious Research, 1973.

Johnstone, Patrick J. *World Handbook for the World Christian.* South Pasadena, CA: William Carey Library, 1976.

Kandall, Elliott. *The End of an Era: Africa and the Missionary.* London: SPCK, 1978.

Kane, J. Herbert. *The Christian World Mission: Today and Tomorrow.* Grand Rapids: Baker Book House, 1981.

_____. *A Global View of Christian Missions.* Grand Rapids: Baker Book House, 1971.

Lacy, Creighton. *The Word Carrying Giant: The Growth of the American Bible Society (1816-1966).* South Pasadena, CA: William Carey Library, 1977.

Latourette, Kenneth Scott. *Christianity Through the Ages.* New York: Harper & Row, 1965.

_____. *A History of Christian Missions in China.* New York: Macmillan, 1929.

_____. *A History of the Expansion of Christianity.* 7 vols. New York: Harper & Brothers, 1937-1945.

Lehman, E. Arno. *It Began at Tranquebar.* Madras: Christian Literature Society, 1956.

Liao, David C.E., ed. *World Christianity: Eastern Asia.* Monrovia, CA: Missions Advanced Research and Communication Center, 1979.

McCracken, John. *Politics and Christianity in Malawi 1875-1940. The Impact of the Livingstonia Mission in the Northern Province.* Cambridge: Cambridge University Press, 1977.

McCurry, Don M., ed. *World Christianity: Middle East.* Monrovia, CA: Missions Advanced Research and Communication Center, 1979.

Manikam, Rajah B., and Thomas, Winburn T. *The Church in Southeast Asia.* New York: Friendship Press, 1956.

Markovitz, Marvin D. *Cross and Sword. The Political Role of Christian Missions in the Belgian Congo, 1908-1960.* Stanford, CA: Hoover Institution Press, 1973.

Mathews, Basil J. *Forward Through the Ages.* New York: Friendship Press, 1951.

Mellis, Charles J. *Committed Communities: Fresh Streams for World Missions.* South Pasadena, CA: William Carey Library, 1976.

Moore, John A. *Baptist Witness in Catholic Europe.* Rome: Baptist Publishing House, 1973.

Moorhouse, Geoffrey. *The Missionaries.* Philadelphia: Lippincott, 1973.

Moraes, George Mark. *A History of Christianity in India: From Early Times to St. Francis Xavier, A.D. 52-1542.* Bombay: Manaktalas, 1964.

Mufuka, Kenneth Nyamayaro. *Missions and Politics in Malawi.* Kingston, Ontario: Limestone Press, 1977.

Neill, Stephen. *Call to Mission.* Philadelphia: Fortress Press, 1971.

_____. *Colonialism and Christian Missions.* New York: McGraw-Hill, 1966.

_____. *A History of Christian Missions.* New York: McGraw-Hill, 1964.

_____. *The Story of the Christian Church in India and Pakistan.* Grand Rapids: Wm. B. Eerdmans, 1970.

_____; Anderson, Gerald H; and Goodwin, John, eds. *Concise Dictionary of the Christian World Mission.* London: Lutterworth, 1970.

Nelson, Martin L. *The How and Why of Third World Missions.* South Pasadena, CA: William Carey Library, 1976.

_____, ed. *Readings in Third World Missions.* South Pasadena, CA: William Carey Library, 1976.

Noshy, Ibrahim. *The Coptic Church: Christianity in Egypt.* Washington, DC: Ruth Sloan Associates, 1955.

Oliver, Roland A. *The Missionary Factor in East Africa.* New York: Humanities, 1968.

Orr, J. Edwin. *Evangelical Awakenings in Africa.* Minneapolis: Bethany Fellow-ship, 1975.

―――. *Evangelical Awakenings in Eastern Asia.* Minneapolis: Bethany Fellow-ship, 1975.

―――. *Evangelical Awakenings in Southern Asia.* Minneapolis: Bethany Fellow-ship, 1975.

―――. *Evangelical Awakenings in the South Seas.* Minneapolis: Bethany Fellow-ship, 1976.

Patterson, George N. *Christianity in Communist China.* Waco, TX: Word Books, 1969.

Payne, Ernest A. *The Growth of the World Church.* London: Edinburgh House, 1955.

Pro Mundi Vita. *The Church in Central America and Panama.* Pro Mundi Vita, 46, 1973.

Ranger, T. O., and Weller, John, eds. *Themes in the Christian History of Central Africa.* London: Heinemann, 1975.

Read, William R., and Ineson, Frank A. *Brazil 1980. The Protestant Handbook.* Monrovia, CA: Missions Advanced Research and Communication Center, 1973.

Richter, Julius. *A History of Protestant Missions in the Near East.* New York: Revell, 1910.

Sales, Jane M. *The Planting of the Church in South Africa.* Grand Rapids: Wm. B. Eerdmans, 1971.

Schmitt, Karl M., ed. *The Roman Catholic Church in Modern Latin America.* New York: Knopf, 1972.

Shenk, Wilbert R. *Mission Focus: Current Issues.* Scottdale, PA: Herald Press, 1980.

Stewart, John. *Nestorian Missionary Enterprise: The Story of a Church on Fire.* Edinburgh, Scotland: Clark, 1928.

Sundkler, Bengt. *The World of Mission.* Grand Rapids: Wm. B. Eerdmans, 1965.

Taber, Charles R. *The Church in Africa.* South Pasadena, CA: William Carey Library, 1978.

Temu, A. J. *British Protestant Missions.* New York: Longmann, 1973.

Thiessen, John C. *A Survey of World Missions.* Chicago: Moody Press, 1961.

Trimingham, J. Spencer. *The Christian Church and Islam in West Africa.* London: SCM Press, 1955.

Vander Werff, Lyle L. *Christian Mission to Muslims: The Record: Anglican and Reformed Approaches in India and the Near East, 1800–1938.* South Pasadena, CA: William Carey Library, 1977.

Van Ess, Dorothy F. *History of the Arabian Mission 1926-1957.* New York: Board for the Christian World Mission of the Reformed Church in America, 1958.

Varg, Paul A. *Missionaries, Chinese and Diplomats: The American Protestant Missionary Movement in China 1890-1952.* Princeton, NJ: Princeton University Press, 1958.

Verkuyl, Johannes. *Contemporary Missiology.* Grand Rapids: Wm. B. Eerdmans, 1978.

Vought, Dale G. *Protestants in Modern Spain.* South Pasadena, CA: William Carey Library, 1973.

Wagner, C. Peter. *Look Out! The Pentecostals are Coming.* Carol Stream, IL: Creation House, 1973.

Wakatama, Pius. *Independence for the Third World Church: An African's Perspective on Missionary Work.* Downers Grove, IL: InterVarsity Press, 1976.

Wallstrom, Timothy C. *The Creation of a Student Movement to Evangelize the World.* South Pasadena, CA: William Carey International University, 1980.

Warneck, Gustaf. *History of Protestant Missions.* New York: Revell, 1904.

Warren, Max. *The Missionary Movement from Britain in Modern History.* London: SCM Press, 1965.

―――. *Social History and Christian Mission.* London: SCM Press, 1967.

Wells, Kenneth E. *History of Protestant Work in Thailand 1828-1958.* Bangkok: Church of Christ in Thailand, 1958.

Wilson, J. Christy, Jr. *Today's Tentmakers/Self-Support: An Alternative Model for Worldwide Witness.* Wheaton, IL: Tyndale Publishing House, 1978.

Wilson, Samuel, ed. *Mission Handbook: North American Protestant Ministries Overseas.* 12th ed. Monrovia, CA: Missions Advanced Research and Communication Center, 1980.

Winter, Ralph D. *The Twenty-Five Unbelievable Years 1945-1969.* South Pasadena, CA: William Carey Library, 1970.

————, and Hawthorne, Steven C., eds. *Perspectives on the World Christian Movement: A Reader.* South Pasadena, CA: William Carey Library, 1981.

Wong, Peter, ed. *Missions from the Third World: A World Survey of Non-Western Missions in Asia, Africa, and Latin America.* Singapore: Church Growth Centre, 1973.

Index